Create, Innovate, and Serve

Create, Innovate, and Serve

A RADICAL APPROACH TO CHILDREN'S AND YOUTH PROGRAMMING

Edited by Kathleen Campana and J. Elizabeth Mills

Foreword by Susan Hildreth

ALA
Neal-Schuman

CHICAGO :: 2019

© 2019 by the American Library Association

Extensive effort has gone into ensuring the reliability of the information in this book; however, the publisher makes no warranty, express or implied, with respect to the material contained herein.

ISBNs
978-0-8389-1720-6 (paper)
978-0-8389-1797-8 (PDF)
978-0-8389-1796-1 (ePub)
978-0-8389-1798-5 (Kindle)

Library of Congress Cataloging-in-Publication Data
Names: Campana, Kathleen, editor. | Mills, J. Elizabeth, editor.
Title: Create, innovate, and serve : a radical approach to children's and youth programming / edited by Kathleen Campana and J. Elizabeth Mills ; foreword by Susan Hildreth.
Description: Chicago : ALA Neal-Schuman, An imprint of the American Library Association, 2019. | Includes bibliographical references and index.
Identifiers: LCCN 2018037982| ISBN 9780838917206 (paper : alk. paper) | ISBN 9780838917961 (epub) | ISBN 9780838917978 (pdf) | ISBN 9780838917985 (kindle)
Subjects: LCSH: Children's libraries—Activity programs. | Children's libraries—Activity programs—United States—Case studies. | Young adults' libraries—Activity programs. | Young adults' libraries—Activity programs—United States—Case studies.
Classification: LCC Z718.3 .C74 2018 | DDC 027.62/5—dc23 LC record available at https://lccn.loc.gov/2018037982

Cover design by Alejandra Diaz. Images © Adobe Stock.
Book design and composition by Karen Sheets de Gracia in the Cardea and Acumin Pro typefaces.

♾ This paper meets the requirements of ANSI/NISO Z39.48–1992 (Permanence of Paper).

Printed in the United States of America
23 22 21 20 19   5 4 3 2 1

CONTENTS

Part II **Program Profiles** 93

THE LIBRARY AS COMMUNITY ANCHOR

An Opening Perspective

Susan Hildreth

T he public library has fulfilled many different roles during its existence. These roles have been informed by the needs of the community the library serves. The current concept of library as "community anchor" stems from the 2010 National Broadband Plan that identified libraries, schools, and hospitals as critical providers of broadband access. The important role that libraries play in providing access to public computing has been well-documented, and the inclusion of libraries with schools and hospitals as on-ramps to the information superhighway has lifted libraries from their previous "nice to have" status to "need to have"—they are essential for healthy communities. Yet the public library's role as community anchor reaches far beyond supplying high-speed broadband to creating a platform that facilitates people acting individually and in groups in support of knowledge and community.

The role of the public library as community anchor has been clearly articulated in recent library literature. In *Creating a Nation of Learners: Strategic Plan 2012-2016*, the Institute of Museum and Library Services (IMLS 2014a) identifies libraries as strong community anchors that enhance civic engagement, economic vitality, and lifelong learning. Healthy communities require institutions that strengthen civic life, respond to community needs, and provide opportunities for community members to learn together through common experiences and shared interests. Libraries advance solutions to their communities' most difficult problems by providing safe places for the community to gather, centers for community vitality, a connecting point to community services, and a venue for lifelong learning. Library services and programs are designed to encourage the participation and dialogue that are crucial to create a sense of place and to strengthen the link between individuals and their communities.

In the Aspen Institute's report, "Rising to the Challenge: Re-Envisioning Public Libraries" (Garner 2014), the successful twenty-first-century library is described as an entity with three critical components—people, place, and platform. Although the library as community anchor is integral to both the place and platform components, with the platform clearly aligned with the library's virtual space, the library as place anchors it most firmly in the community. The iconic physical presence of the library represents a key gathering point for access to knowledge, learning, and the spirit of the community. As noted in the Aspen Institute Report, libraries as community anchors provide many services that are unique and valued by their users and political advocates:

- Establish personal connections that help define community needs and interests.
- Provide an anchor for economic development and neighborhood revitalization.
- Strengthen community identity in ways that yield significant return on investment, including drawing people together for diverse purposes.
- Provide a safe and trusted location for community services, such as health clinics, emergency response centers, small business incubators, workforce development centers, and immigrant resource centers.

To be successful in fulfilling the community anchor role, libraries must explore, understand, and value the priorities of their communities. Aligning library services with community goals, one of the most critical strategies for success (Garner 2014), is essential to effectively serve communities and gain the support of policy-makers. Librarians no longer can provide collections or services that they personally believe are "best" for the community. All programs, collections, and services must be driven by the priorities of the community. Even if those priorities may not to be directly related to the traditional mission of the library, it is the critical role of the twenty-first-century librarian to determine how existing or new resources can be organized and promoted to support the key priorities of the community.

By embracing its role in civic engagement, the library can identify those critical community priorities that are crucial to serve as a successful community anchor. The library is uniquely positioned to serve as the community convener that identifies local challenges and brings together participants to address those challenges. The library is a trusted institution with easy access to information that can discuss community issues. It can provide a physical space and a safe environment for dialogue on potentially contentious issues. This is a role that libraries must take on purposefully because it will require library staff to become skilled in facilitating challenging conversations. In an era when civil dialogue is fast disappearing, it is critical that libraries move into the civic-engagement space. More than any other institution, libraries have the potential to succeed in this special niche.

Successfully fulfilling the community anchor role and adopting civic engagement as a strategic library initiative are critical components for a twenty-first century library to be essential in its community. One of the most widely respected and well-known library activities is serving the young people of the community. Successful youth development is a significant component of healthy communities, and libraries are key community assets in achieving that goal. It is critical that the library is recognized as an essential member of the community's educational ecosystem. The library must have a place at the community's planning table when determining how impactful services for youth will be developed and delivered. The role of the library as community anchor and partner provides a great opportunity to enhance success in youth-development initiatives.

A recent example of libraries leveraging their assets with other community organizations to provide engaging youth services is the successful collaboration of libraries, museums, and early childhood systems in working collectively to provide integrated services to early learners. Led by IMLS and the BUILD Initiative, an organization that provides support for state-level early learning policy-makers, leaders in early childhood systems worked together with their library and museum colleagues in five pilot states to better understand their missions and to complement and leverage the resources and assets of these unique institutions. Museums and libraries are too often on the periphery of state- and local-level conversations about early childhood systems. By creating intentional relationships and working together more closely, libraries, museums, and the early childhood community can offer children and families a wide range of formal and informal learning opportunities. The product of this important work is *BUILDing Supportive Communities with Libraries, Museums and Early Childhood Systems: A Toolkit for Collaborative Efforts to Improve Outcomes for Young Children and Their Families* (2016), a useful tool for librarians interested in working effectively with early childhood providers in their communities.

IMLS and the John D. and Catherine T. MacArthur Foundation collaborated to provide opportunities to transform the lives of teens in libraries and museums. Based on the key role of the library as a trusted space in the community, learning labs have been developed as "innovative spaces that prepare youth to meet the challenges of a complex global economy and gain the skills they need to succeed in a rapidly changing world, while allowing them to follow their passions and to inspire one another" (IMLS 2014b). The focus on personal interests and passions of youth is the foundational organizing principle for these spaces. With access to peers, supportive and knowledgeable mentors, and a combination of digital media and traditional tools, teens can develop skills that lead to successful careers in the digital world. Although the initial funding supported the development of twenty-four learning labs, many more have been created since grant funding ended in 2013. *Learning Labs in Libraries and Museums: Transformative Spaces for Teens* (2014b) documents best practices in developing and supporting these transformative spaces.

Successful youth development cannot be achieved without family support and engagement. Libraries play a unique role in family engagement—they serve as the safe spaces and the community anchors where parents or caregivers can participate in learning experiences with their children and receive the guidance and support they need to serve as their children's first teachers. The knowledge, attitudes, values, and behaviors that enable children to be motivated, enthusiastic, and successful learners are critical for families to understand and provide for their children. In 2015, the Public Library Association made a commitment to foster family engagement in libraries through its initiative, "Libraries for the 21st Century: It's a Family Thing," with funding from the David and Lucille Packard Foundation. Two significant documents are products of this investment. *Public Libraries: A Vital Space for Family Engagement,* published in 2016, is a call to action for libraries to make family engagement an integral part of their services (Lopez, Caspe, and McWilliams 2016). *Ideabook: Libraries for Families*, published in 2016, presents a research-based framework to guide and broaden family engagement in libraries, along with examples of many successful programs already in place (Weiss et al. 2016).

To continue evolving and innovating in how they serve children, youth, and families, libraries need new viewpoints and insights. Library school students represent the next generation of thinkers and shapers in the ever-changing landscape of public librarianship. They are developing their own ideas about how libraries and communities will fit together in the future and how they will shape each other. *Create, Innovate, and Serve: A Radical Approach to Children's and Youth Programming* offers a research-based conversation, balancing both academic and practitioner voices, that invites MLIS students, new and seasoned librarians, and LIS scholars alike to reflect, reimagine, and rejuvenate children's and youth services in today's public libraries. This book includes broad, critical discussions of diversity, the importance of play and story, the role of outcome-based program planning, and outreach services that find their grounding in real-life library profiles, complete with vivid details of what librarianship looks like all around the country in libraries big and small, in communities rural and urban. Delineated by age, part II's focus on developmental stages and sociocultural learning, as well as relevant library-related research, enables readers to gain a deep understanding of the complexities of planning and delivering programs and services for children and youth, and offers inspiration in the form of examples of successful, creative, and community-focused programs and services that promote a love of reading, learning, and being part of our world. In the twenty-first century, libraries have truly become community anchors that provide a platform for individual and community creation, learning, and growth. The library is a safe and trusted space for all community members, and particularly for our children and families. Libraries make a significant contribution to the health and development of our children—and successful, engaged children lead to strong communities. I am excited to see where the essays in this book will take our field and help us envision what is just over the horizon for public libraries and the communities they serve.

REFERENCES

BUILD Initiative in Partnership with the Institute of Museum and Library Services. 2016. *BUILDing Supportive Communities with Libraries, Museums, and Early Childhood Systems: A Toolkit for Collaborative Efforts to Improve Outcomes for Young Children and Their Families.* http://buildinitiative.org/WhatsNew/ViewArticle/tabid/96/ArticleId/693/BUILDing-Supportive-Communities-with-Libraries-Museums-and-Early-Childhood-Systems.aspx.

Garner, A. K. 2014. *Rising to the Challenge: Re-Envisioning Public Libraries.* A report of the Aspen Institute Dialogue on Public Libraries. Washington, DC: Aspen Institute. www.libraryvision.org/.

Institute of Museum and Library Services. 2014a. *Creating a Nation of Learners: Strategic Plan 2012–2016.* https://www.imls.gov/about-us/strategic-plan.

———. 2014b. *Learning Labs in Libraries and Museums: Transformative Spaces for Teens.* Washington, DC.: Association of Science-Technology Centers and Urban Libraries Council. https://www.imls.gov/sites/default/files/publications/documents/learninglabsreport_0.pdf.

Lopez, M. E., M. Caspe, and L. McWilliams. 2016. *Public Libraries: A Vital Space for Family Engagement.* Cambridge, MA: Harvard Family Research Project. www.hfrp.org/publications-resources/browse-our-publications/public-libraries-a-vital-space-for-family-engagement.

Weiss, H. B., M. Caspe, M. E. Lopez, and L. McWilliams. 2016. *Ideabook: Libraries for Families.* Cambridge, MA: Harvard Family Research Project. https://www.packard.org/wp-content/uploads/2017/05/IdeaBook.pdf.

INTRODUCTION

Welcome to *Create, Innovate, and Serve: A Radical Approach to Children's and Youth Programming*. We are so happy you're here. We'll begin with a bit about the background behind the idea for this book and explain how we've set up the content to support you in your journey to the field of children's and youth librarianship.

First, a bit of background. In the spring of 2015, we taught a brand-new MLIS course at the University of Washington Information School entitled Libraries as Learning Labs in a Digital Age, designed by the late esteemed Eliza T. Dresang. As we developed the curriculum for this course, we looked around for a textbook that covered programming for ages from birth to age eighteen, one that brought together the voices of both academics and practitioners who were passionate about and vested in programs and services for children, youth, and families to share in the discourse about how best to reach and support families and children in their learning. We also wanted a book that would emphasize the importance of diversity, learning through play, outreach, and community in every aspect of what children's librarians do every day. However, we could not find one.

So, as we taught the course, we listened to what our students were looking for, how they digested the information they learned and shared with one another, and how they used the course information in their future jobs. And then we decided to create the book we were looking for, with the help of an esteemed cohort of academics and practitioners who were kind enough to share their expertise with you, our reader.

We used the framework of Radical Change, created by Eliza T. Dresang, as the structure for our course and for this book. Dresang defined *radical* as "a departure from the usual or traditional . . . extremely different from commonly existing views" (Dresang 1999, 4). Radical Change identifies the ways in which digital-age children are connecting and creating in this new world as exemplary of this departure from tradition, representing a new world for educators and librarians. In her framework, Dresang identifies the digital-age principles of connectivity, interactivity, and access, along with three types of radical change: changing forms and formats, changing perspectives, and changing boundaries, based on the belief that children are capable of making connections and that children's literature and media are evolving to reflect these tenets. Her theory has been applied to explain the information-seeking behavior of youth (Dresang and Koh 2009), and we have since adapted it to describe today's children's and youth programming as librarians focus on how to enable and support youth in their learning trajectories (Mills et al. 2015). Programming that focuses on providing children and youth with opportunities to push boundaries, to create new forms and formats, and to change the perspectives of their peers and their communities all embody the spirit and framework of Radical Change.

This book is intended to give a broad overview of this radical landscape for public libraries in which librarians are creating innovative, interactive, participatory programming for children and youth by examining seven critical domains that occur across programming as a whole in part I and by taking an in-depth look at the different types of programs that are offered to children and youth that exemplify one or more of these domains in part II.

Library services to children and youth are undergoing a major shift in which an emphasis is now being placed on serving children and youth populations by creating interactive, innovative, participatory, and often production-centered, programming. The chapters in this book have been contributed by leaders in the field—both researchers and practitioners—to provide in-depth information about:

1. Critical domains stretching across programming as a whole, and how to recognize and incorporate these trends in all types of programs, and
2. Types of programs, with critical information on how to create and deliver them.

Perspectives from practice and research provide a holistic examination of library programming for children and youth from birth to age eighteen, with an emphasis on an inclusive approach to programming while incorporating research-based theories and frameworks to demonstrate how they inform and influence recent trends and time-tested practices. As the emphasis on creating interactive, innovative, participatory, and often production-centered programming in the public library grows, we hope this book will support ongoing instruction on library programming for children and youth in the new landscape of library services.

Our title is meant to capture three ways in which librarians are acting radically in how they design, deliver, and assess programs and services for children and youth. Librarians are creating new versions of traditional programs through sensory storytimes, coding clubs, media labs, and more, thus celebrating the radical nature of digital-age youth. Librarians are innovating by trying unusual, unexpected, and timely themes and program structures that speak to the social, political, and cultural events of the time. Finally, librarians are constantly seeking to serve their communities by using community need assessments and teen advisory boards, as well as various research methods, such as observations, surveys, and informal interviews, with families and youth to inform, create, and refine their programs to fit their communities' needs and support families in their learning trajectories.

HOW TO READ THIS BOOK

Eliza T. Dresang would encourage you to read radically and synergistically, skipping around, reading what fits with what you need to know in the moment, and not necessarily reading in a linear fashion. We encourage you to do this, but should you wish to read this book from front to back we'll provide some brief information about each of the parts to help you orient yourself. Be sure to read the introductions to each part to gain further advice and suggestions for reading the chapters therein, regarding structure and content.

Part I provides short, yet deep, dives into the seven critical domains: Diversity, Storytelling, Play and Production, Media Mentorship, Assessment, Outreach and Partnerships, and Advocacy, to give you a foundation and grounding in the relevant topics, frameworks, and research that inform these domains. We see these as crucial to developing the kind of programs and services that meet the needs of digital-age youth and enable them to produce and consume high-quality content in today's world.

Part II takes these domains and embeds them into program profiles for children and youth. Each program profile includes background information about the library, the genesis of the program, the target community, the outcomes and goals of the program, and future plans. These profiles are meant to provide enough information to enable you to adapt and refine them to meet the needs of the library and community you serve, or will serve, in your current or future work. We purposefully chose libraries from across the United States to provide a wide variety of perspectives and program profiles. We hope you become inspired and learn new ways of serving children, youth, and families through these programs and services. Part II is not meant to be exhaustive, but rather to give you a head start, by sharing resources, references, and information that will get you creating, innovating, and ready to serve your community.

The foreword by Susan Hildreth sets the tone for this book, placing communities at the center of all that children's and youth librarians do every day to serve families and children in their community. We encourage you to return to the foreword at various points when reading this book to remind yourself of the importance of putting community needs at the heart of radical children's and youth program design and delivery.

REFERENCES

Dresang, E. T., and K. Koh. 2009. "Radical Change Theory, Youth Information Behavior, and School Libraries." *Library Trends* 58 (1): 26-50.

Mills, J. E., A. Y. Goldsmith, K. Campana, B. J. Patin, and S. A. Evans. 2015. "Putting Youth First: The Radical Eliza T. Dresang." *Journal of Research on Libraries and Young Adults* 5. http://bit.ly/1MxvPqM.

ACKNOWLEDGMENTS

We would like to thank all of our contributors for their time, expertise, and patience with us in the development of this contributed volume. We knew when we conceived the idea for this book that we could not write this alone; rather we were certain that the strength of this book lay in the community it represents—the librarians and scholars whose work exemplifies creativity, innovation, and service to their larger communities. We are so grateful for their generosity.

We would also like to thank our board members for their close, careful readings of our chapters. Any remaining misspeaks or sweeping generalizations are ours and ours alone.

We thank the editorial, production, and marketing staff at ALA Editions and Neal Schuman, especially Rachel Chance and Jamie Santoro—thank you for believing in this ambitious project and helping to make it happen.

Finally, we thank all the librarians out there who do this work every day, who strive to provide diverse, playful, and educational programs for children of all ages in an effort not only to contribute to lifelong learning and success but also to further situate libraries as community anchors that embody the values and heart of the families and children you serve. Although we could not include every librarian and every story, we hope that you will see yourselves reflected in this book and be inspired to continue your important work.

PART I

Foundations and Transformations

Before you dive into part I, we wanted to provide some background and context to the changes in library services for children and youth. As libraries have transitioned into informal learning environments that actively support learning inside and outside of their walls, we have seen changes in their programs and services. Children's and youth services and programming have become so much more than just connecting children and youth with books. Programs for children and youth work to encourage learning across multiple domains of learning and development, while also supporting twenty-first-century learning and providing opportunities to empower children and youth to connect and engage with the world around them. To accomplish all of this, librarians are using their creativity to innovate in order to reach, serve, and have an impact on their communities. Libraries are changing and evolving, especially in the eyes of the communities they serve.

Adopting the label *informal learning environment* has allowed libraries to expand beyond their core, traditional literacy services. However, it has also brought some changes related to learning. As informal learning environments, libraries are often lumped in with museums, zoos, and aquariums. Informal learning environments are gaining attention. They can be incredibly powerful because children and youth will spend a relatively small portion of their childhood and adolescence in formal learning environments. The remaining portion of their time will be spent in these informal learning environments.

As a result, it is important to consider the learning that occurs in these spaces. This learning has been referred to as informal learning, out-of-school learning or free-choice learning. What occurs in informal learning spaces can be very different than most of the learning that occurs in formal school spaces. The Institute of Museum and Library Services has described it as life-long, life-wide and life-deep, which is important when considering programming for children and teens because the library has an ability to make an impact early on and establish the base that supports a child's lifelong learning.

Some of the learning that is occurring may be related to topics that are also covered in formal learning environments; however, the learning process and the learning outcomes may look very different across the two environments. In informal learning spaces, the learning is typically:

- Learner-motivated
- Learner-centered
- Open-ended, ongoing, and ubiquitous

- Individual and social
- Hands-on

The learning that occurs in library programs often carries several of these characteristics of learning in informal spaces. *Learner-motivated* and *learner-centered* refer to how, in informal learning environments, learners get to choose whether to engage in the program or topic and how to tailor the learning experience to their interests and needs. This can be seen in library programs because they are always structured so that youth can choose whether or not to participate; often library programs, or at least a part of a program, can be tailored to the youth's interests. The learning that is supported in library programs is often open-ended, ongoing, and ubiquitous, in that learners can engage with a topic in many different ways, as long as they like, and across multiple environments. Library programs are frequently hands-on and offer social opportunities for youth to interact and learn from and with their peers or with adults. The programs in libraries that encourage these aspects of learning for youth may take the form of traditional programs, such as storytime or book clubs—but with an intentional focus on learning or a new twist—or they may be a radically innovative new type of program.

Library programs look completely different in libraries throughout the United States as they work to meet the needs of their unique communities, which you will see in part II, but we have found that there are many commonalities across library programming as a whole. The critical domains presented in part I represent some of these commonalities that can and should be present across library programs for children and youth of all ages. Although there are many critical domains for library programming, it would be impossible to present them all in this book. Therefore, we have identified seven that are important when entering the world of children's and youth programming

Before you dive into part I, we will quickly present each critical domain, its corresponding chapter, and its importance for library programs.

DIVERSITY

Chapter 1, When *All* Really Means *All*: Creating Library Programs for Children and Teens That Embrace All Types of Diversity, by Jamie Naidoo

Our world has become incredibly diverse, but many of our library programs have not changed to reflect the actual demographics of our communities. Because libraries are community organizations, we need to shift our programming focus so that it is inclusive of *all* our communities. In his chapter, Naidoo provides an overview of this issue, along with strategies and tips for working to ensure your programming is inclusive, open, and welcoming to all members and groups in your community.

THE IMPORTANCE OF STORY

Chapter 2, The Power of a Story: Telling to Transform the World, by Annette Y. Goldsmith and Michelle H. Martin

While stories and storytelling are often included in programming for young children, they sometimes taper off in programming for older children and teens. Because stories are important for all ages, it is important for librarians to keep a focus on stories, especially oral stories, in a variety of programs targeted at all ages. Goldsmith and Martin review the subject and offer information for getting started with the craft of oral storytelling.

PLAY AND PRODUCTION-CENTERED PROGRAMS

Chapter 3, Playing to Learn, Learning to Play: A Play and Making Framework for Libraries, by Sarah Ward and Sarah A. Evans

In the past few years, the importance of play and production (creating things) for children and youth has become more prominent. The acts of play and production are important for the learning and development of children and youth, but many schools cannot and do not provide enough opportunities for play or production. Because schools are not meeting this need, many informal learning environments have begun to provide opportunities for play and production through the programs they offer for children and youth. In their chapter, Ward and Evans provide background and a framework for approaching play- and production-centered programs for children and youth.

MEDIA MENTORSHIP

Chapter 4, Librarians as Media Mentors: Building Media Literacy with Programming, Advisory, and Access, by Amy Koester and Claudia Haines

Technology is becoming more ubiquitous in the lives of families. However, there are a wide assortment of devices and resources from which to choose that can be used with and by children and teens. Because of this, many families are overwhelmed and looking for guidance when it comes to technology for their children and teens. You can help by acting as a media mentor. The Association for Library Service to Children (ALSC) has identified this as an important role for children's and youth librarians. In their chapter, Koester and Haines provide background and guidance for understanding more about media mentorship and how to fulfill this role.

OUTCOME-BASED PLANNING AND EVALUATION

Chapter 5, The Five-Step Outcome-Based Planning and Evaluation Model for Children's and Young Adult Program Assessment, by Melissa Gross

In the past, libraries have tracked their programs and services using basic numbers or outputs, such as program attendance or circulation statistics. However, as library funding continues to decrease, libraries are feeling pressured to demonstrate more than just outputs. They want to demonstrate their value and the impact that they have in their communities. Because of this, many libraries are looking at how to demonstrate the outcomes of their programs and services. In her chapter, Gross presents a process for incorporating outcomes into the planning and assessment process for your programs, which should help you in the future with understanding the value and impact of your programs.

OUTREACH AND PARTNERSHIPS

Chapter 6, Taking the Library to Unexpected Places: Outreach and Partnerships in Youth Services, by Beth Crist

As libraries begin to place a stronger emphasis on serving *all* their communities, especially those who most need the support, outreach is quickly becoming a core library service. Outreach allows you to take your programs outside of your library and use them to reach and serve those who cannot or do not come into the library. Because you are working out in the community in your outreach programs, partnerships with other community organizations become essential for being effective and successful in this work. In her chapter, Crist provides an overview along with strategies and tips for getting started with outreach and partnerships.

ADVOCACY

Chapter 7, The Ever-Changing Library: Advocating for Impact, Value, and Purpose, by Judy T. Nelson

Advocacy has become a crucial part of any librarian's job. Although you might be a bit overwhelmed by the thought of advocacy, Nelson uses her chapter to help portray advocacy as an approachable and important task. Through her chapter you should begin to understand that not all advocacy efforts have to be at the government level. In fact, children's and youth librarians can expect to become an advocate on many levels. You will need to advocate for your families, your programs, your department, and your library. Nelson provides some tips and insight for how to approach advocacy on a variety of levels.

■ ■ ■

As you read each of these chapters, we hope that you will begin to see why these critical domains are crucial for library programs for youth. Ideally, they will provide you with ways to approach your programming and help you design programs that offer rich learning experiences that embody the characteristics of learning in informal learning spaces.

HOW TO READ PART I

We have ordered the chapters in part I intentionally so that they build on each other. We began with Diversity to emphasize how crucial it is to design and deliver programming that is inclusive and seeks to serve marginalized communities. We then moved on to Storytelling and Play and Production, because these are effective methods for delivering programming that is simultaneously informal and meaningful for children and youth. Media Mentorship follows next, because it is an important aspect of librarianship that has recently acquired its timely moniker and yet is grounded in the work children's and youth librarians have been doing for more than a century—evaluating, recommending, and sharing high-quality media with children and families. We then transition to Outcome-Based Planning and Evaluation, followed by Outreach and Partnerships, which we see as building blocks for high-quality programs that are sustainable and community-focused. Last but not least, Advocacy provides suggestions about how to go to bat for the programs you develop, for the communities you seek to serve, and for the work you do every day in creating innovative programs. You are welcome to read these chapters in the order that most makes sense for you. Because every chapter stands on its own, you are welcome to pick and choose the chapters that you want to read and come back to the others later. However you choose to read, we hope that these chapters will help to inform and guide your practice as you work to create innovative programs that reach and serve the children and youth in your community.

CHAPTER 1

When *All* Really Means *All*

Creating Library Programs for Children and Teens That Embrace All Types of Diversity

Jamie Naidoo

> Culture is not a costume that one wears on certain days. . . . [A child's] cultural heritage is their unique identity, which constantly seeks self-expression.
>
> (Gonzalez 2000)

INTRODUCTION

Now more than ever it is critical that librarians incorporate diversity into their daily library programs for children and teens and create inclusive spaces where patrons from all cultural backgrounds feel welcomed. The term *diversity* can have numerous definitions that include and exclude various culturally diverse populations depending on personal views or the context in which diversity is being described. When discussing diversity in library programming, it is recommended that you be as expansive as possible. Race, ethnicity, ancestry, physical and mental ability, family composition, gender expression, sexual orientation, citizenship status, language fluency, domicile, socioeconomic status, religious preference, and age are just a few of the many ways that diversity is expressed within a community served by the library. All these cultural characteristics should be considered when planning library programs. To be impactful, however, diversity cannot be viewed as an add-on component to programming or something that is addressed only during specific programs or times of the year, for example, Black History Month, Developmental Disabilities Month, LGBTQ+ Pride Month, and so forth. Relegating celebrations of diversity to specific months only emphasizes the cultural divides within our current society. To create an environment where everyone feels included in everyday programs, it is critical for library staff to use print and digital materials that represent diverse family structures, daily experiences, and cultures in everyday programs.

We live and work in an increasingly diverse society, yet we have become increasingly hostile toward certain groups of people. Anti-*other* sentiment fosters incivility and intimidating environments that threaten the lives of people within our communities, not to mention the values and principles of librarianship. It is critical that librarians provide safe havens for all children and families from all cultural backgrounds. Even if the patrons that visit your library appear to be ethnically or racially homogeneous, they are still diverse in terms of learning and physical ability, religious preference, gender identity, sexual orientation, domicile, linguistic ability, and many other cultural characteristics. Often youth librarians and other library staff working with youth erroneously believe that they must match their programs to their populations. For instance, if they have a large Latinx population, they may presume that those children and teens will only want to read about characters representing their cultural group. The idea of introducing books about Filipino traditions or Eastern European culture seems almost absurd.

Books are windows into the larger world around us. Rudine Sims Bishop is credited with first making the analogy of books as windows into the lives of other cultures or mirrors that reflect a reader's own cultural experiences (Bishop 1997). Without a doubt, all children and teens need opportunities to see their own cultures represented in the books they read and the digital media with which they interact. Equally important is the ability to learn about other cultures and reveal similarities in daily experiences and perspectives. Sometimes librarians state that their communities are predominantly White and thus their library collections and programs do not need to include representations of racial or ethnic diversity. Children and teens are formulating their understanding of the world around them and need opportunities to encounter the "other" to develop an appreciation for life experiences different than their own to broaden their worldviews. Children's book publisher Barefoot Books provides a useful list of prompting questions that library staff can use to help children make intercultural or cross-cultural connections between their lives and those of characters from a different culture. These questions begin by asking children to think about their own cultural identities (languages spoken, family traditions, etc.) and then asking them to discern how their lives are similar to those of diverse book characters (Weider 2016). An exercise such as this provides a forum for children to think more globally and can be also be adapted for use with teens.

Diversity in library programming allows children, teens, families, and youth librarians to develop *cultural competence,* the appreciation of their own culture as well as the cultures of other people. It is vitally important to offer library programming that promotes cultural competence and develops the ability to see that we are all the "same, same but different." In theory, a separate chapter on diversity in a book on youth programming should not be needed. Attention toward the needs of diverse children, teens, and families should motivate all the library programs, services, and collections we offer. Unfortunately, we have yet to reach this ideal as a profession.

This chapter provides an overview of considerations for planning programs for diverse populations, ideas for programmatic themes, suggestions for displays and marketing, and recommendations of professional resources that can assist librarians as they incorporate diversity into routine programming for children and teens.

PLANNING CONSIDERATIONS

Librarians who have little to no experience planning cultural programs may be hesitant to start. Some are worried that they do not know enough about a particular population to plan culturally sensitive programs, whereas others may cite poorly attended programs, community demographics, negative attitudes from administrators and coworkers, or limited budgets. Nonetheless, providing programs that celebrate diversity and promote cultural competence can be extremely motivating and rewarding. They can also be the most fulfilling of all programs offered by a library system.

For any program to be successful, librarians should plan in advance, secure funding, and develop evaluation strategies. Programs celebrating diversity should be aligned with the mission, vision, and value statements of a library and be incorporated into regular library programming rather than considered exclusive or special events. Using this approach, funding for recurring diversity programs can be drawn from regular line items in the library's or youth department's budget. In addition, by including diverse material in regular programming, all families are included in routine programs and their experiences are normalized. For special events, specific funding can be sought. Below are a few examples of specialized grants for youth librarians planning programs that celebrate cultural diversity.

- The Autism Welcome Here: Library Programs, Services, and More Grant. Given by Libraries and Autism: We're Connected and funded by Barbara Klipper, this grant offers public libraries up to $5,000 to develop targeted programs or services for youth with autism and their families. http://librariesandautism.org/grant.
- Center for the Study of Multicultural Children's Literature El Día de Los Niño's/El Día de Los Libros (Children's Day/Book Day) Grant. Awarded by the Center for the Study of Multicultural Children's Literature in Inglewood, California, this grant provides winning libraries with $500 in multicultural books if they develop a diversity program for the Día that has a focus on African American culture. https://www.csmcl.org/about1-c14s1.
- Ezra Jack Keats Mini-grants for Public Libraries and Public Schools. Awarded by the Ezra Jack Keats Foundation, these grants provide $500 for programs that foster creativity, collaboration, and community building with a specific focus on diversity. www.ezra-jack-keats.org/section/ezra-jack-keats-mini-grant-program-for-public-libraries-public-schools/.
- The Light the Way Grant Awarded by the Association for Library Service to Children and sponsored by Candlewick Press, this $3,000 grant supports an exemplary library outreach program for underserved children. According to the grant website, "Special population children may include those who have learning or physical differences, those who speak English as a second language, those who are in a non-traditional school environment, those who live in foster care settings, those who are in the juvenile justice system, those who live in gay and lesbian families, those who have teen parents, and those who need accommodation service to meet their needs" (ALSC 2017).
- The Estela and Raul Mora Award. Awarded by First Book and sponsored by Latina children's author and poet Pat Mora and her siblings, this award provides books to an exemplary program that celebrates Día: Children's Day, Book Day. Winners receive a $1,000 First Book Marketplace credit. Two honor awards of $500 in First Book Marketplace credits are also given. www.patmora.com/mora-award/.
- Talk Story: Sharing Stories, Sharing Culture Grants Awarded by The American Indian Library Association and the Asian/Pacific American Librarians Association and funded by Toyota Financial Services, these $750 grants support programs that introduce the Talk Story program into

the library to celebrate and explore Asian Pacific American and American Indian/Alaska Native cultures. http://talkstorytogether.org/grants.

During the planning of diversity-related programs, librarians will also want to connect with the local community to develop an advisory board and identify potential partnerships. An advisory board will include diverse members from the community to allow for community buy-in and to ensure cultural sensitivity of program materials and activities. When advisory boards help plan a program, they are more invested in its success and more likely to promote the program within their communities. They can be useful to youth librarians trying to identify books and digital materials that are respectful, culturally authentic, and, if applicable, linguistically relevant. Advisory boards can also assist in selecting activities, crafts, and refreshments that help prevent librarians from perpetuating stereotypes or reinforcing microaggressions, which are subtle, often unintended, discriminations against members from specific cultural groups. However, it is important to remember that one person from a particular group cannot speak for their entire culture. Rather, they can provide information from their own perspective.

When implementing programs, it is imperative that youth librarians avoid the Five F's—Food, Festival, Folklore, Fashion, and Famous People—approach as the avenue for infusing diversity into programmatic content. This practice, which has been a very common way to explore diversity in library programming, generally emphasizes stereotypes about a culture and provides the ideal opportunities for fostering microaggressions. It also serves to exoticize those that represent a culture different from the normative mainstream. Although this method is not completely objectionable, it cannot be the only way to include diversity into programming. For instance, reading folktales from a culture can provide some information about culture beliefs and mores. However, only sharing folktales with youth provides a distorted, dated view of a culture.

Librarians should also not assume they are the experts on a particular culture outside their own or engage in cultural appropriation activities, such as having children make feathered headbands to dress up as Native Americans or wearing a Geisha costume when reading a book about Japanese culture. These practices create divisions between cultures rather than promoting understanding and cultural competence. A particularly useful resource to spark discussions on this topic are the "We're a Culture, not a Costume" posters created by Ohio University's Students Teaching about Racism in Society (https://www.ohio.edu/orgs/stars/Home.html). Similarly, librarians may be partial to using classic children's titles such as *Tikki Tikki Tembo* by Arlene Mosel or newer favorites such as *Skippyjon Jones* by Judy Schachner to introduce children to a new culture or allow them to experiment with the language of another culture. Using these books with children, no matter how much a librarian may like them, is not appropriate as they perpetuate racism and cultural misunderstandings, as noted by Grace Lin and Beverly Slapin in their blog posts on the topic (Lin 2017; Slapin 2013).

Additional planning considerations for diversity programming include the following:

- Do you know your local community demographics? Have you conducted a needs assessment and environmental scan to determine the informational, recreational, and cultural needs of children, teens, and families? A *needs assessment* is a research strategy employed by librarians to survey their local library communities to better understand what they want from the library and if those needs are currently being met. An *environmental scan* is a practice that allows librarians to examine their local community government, businesses, schools, and so on, to determine strengths, weaknesses, opportunities, and threats in the surrounding environment and the influence they have upon library services. An excellent source for learning how to conduct a needs assessment and environmental scan in relation to serving diverse populations is Sondra Cuban's *Serving New Immigrant Communities in the Library* (2007).

- Have you identified community organizations that also serve particular cultural populations in your community? Have you approached them for potential partnerships?
- Have you sought input from the target populations to determine how best to celebrate a particular cultural event and to identify any potential community conflicts in program times? If you do not speak the language of a particular cultural group, an option would be to make connections with bilingual educators, influential community leaders, or parents (to name a few sources) who can assist you with working with the target population, to translate and provide legitimacy to the work you are doing. A useful resource that demonstrates this with a Latinx or Spanish-speaking population is the second chapter of Jamie Campbell Naidoo and Katie Scherrer's *Once Upon a Cuento: Bilingual Storytimes in English and Spanish* (2016).
- Does your physical library, collection, and staff foster an inclusive environment that is a supportive, safe place for diverse populations? Have you taken the time to conduct training to help yourself and other staff members identify personal biases and covert stereotypes that you have toward specific cultural groups? Do you have a plan on how best to overcome these biases? A particularly useful resource to help library staff explore this area of enquiry is the Culturally Responsive Library Walk (http://bridgetolit.web.unc.edu/?page_id=842) developed by Sandra Hughes-Hassell and Amanda Hitson.
- When thinking about inclusive practices while hosting and planning library programs for children and teens, do library staff take into account how specific populations are inherently included and excluded? For instance, the Deaf community is routinely excluded from community events that do not provide American Sign Language interpreters. Similarly, offering Christmas-themed programs in December disenfranchises families that are not Christians, as does planning library programs on key holidays of other religious or cultural groups. Another example is exclusively using materials with heterosexual families and characters in programming, which reinforces institutionalized and societal heteronormative behaviors and practices. Finally, although library staff may ensure that the library is ADA-compliant, there still may be barriers that must be addressed, such as the use of adaptive technology and strategies that make programs inclusive of patrons with specific learning needs.

While this is not an exhaustive list of planning considerations, the information provides a foundation for beginning the exciting journey of planning inclusive and diverse programs. What else should a librarian know? The following interview with Johanna Ulloa Girón, Outreach Department Manager for the Poudre River Public Library system in Fort Collins,

Colorado, will give readers a perspective from frontline library staff. Johanna and her team's outreach efforts to diverse populations are a shining example of how to engage in diversity programming.

Diversity Programming in Action with Johanna Ulloa Girón

Johanna Ulloa Girón is the Outreach Department Manager for the Poudre River Public Library District in Fort Collins, Colorado. She is a passionate librarian working at both the local and national levels to help librarians effectively conduct outreach to diverse communities. Johanna and her team of outreach librarians offer numerous types of programs to diverse library patrons throughout the Fort Collins area. Following is an interview sharing some of Johanna's work in diversity programming.

Jamie: You have a background in social work. How did you transition into librarianship? How did you get started doing outreach in your current library?

Johanna: I have loved books since as long as I can remember. I am from Bogota, Colombia, and in my country there is still a myth that libraries and reading belong to the elite, to academia. My family was very poor and no one graduated from a higher education program.

Growing up, we endured and survived the drug war and Pablo Escobar's rise to power. Those were scary times—a terror I can't possibly describe. Contrary to our economic status, my grandfather was a reader, and he became my first library. He kept his books in a closed box under his bed—the books were that precious to him! During a terrifying time with bombs going off in the city, books kept me psychologically alive. Unfortunately, libraries were never a destination for us or even a factor in our lives. When I was a child, libraries were sterile, academic places where books were not accessible for all. Then my father began to work in a bookstore and my life changed forever. My love of letters was sealed. Fast forward many years and I became a psychologist, came to the US and became a social worker.

For many years I worked as a therapist in different scenarios and with different people: with families, with child victims of sexual abuse or domestic violence, at a residential facility for children, and as a child protection case worker. And in all those instances, therapists and health care providers would have conversations around provision of services for families and individuals that were heavily created and delivered at a tertiary level of care, meaning that services were more accessible once something, usually a traumatic event, had already happened and caused incredible damage. I loved social work and providing services at the tertiary level, but I found myself pondering what it would be like to be a social worker, a clinician designing programs and services at a primary level. And then, almost serendipitously, the opening for outreach manager at the library opened up. The job description stated that a *librarian degree* was required. I remember thinking that I will never be contacted but still submitted my resume. To my surprise, they did!

The decision to move from social work to librarianship was hard at the time. It meant I would have to give up many parts of the profession I love. Fortunately, the similarity between the mission, values, and professional statements from the National Association of Social Work and the American Library Association made the decision easier. ALA has core values that speak the same language as the values of social work, specifically around service, diversity, and social responsibility. Furthermore, the policies of ALA (combating prejudice, stereotyping, and discrimination) spoke directly to the fiber of social justice and my own journey as an immigrant.

I have been the manager for outreach services for four years and I do not regret that decision. Now I get to design, evaluate, and deliver programs and services in the community with input from diverse community members. I get to work with an amazing team of talented individuals whose work on social justice, diversity, and equity is accomplished through literacy and at a primary level. We have embedded our programs and services in the community, providing opportunities to co-create programs where we are catalysts for growth and change. Best of all, I get to work at a library where beautiful and important books surround my daily experiences.

Jamie: *What are some of the diverse populations that you serve in your library district?*

Johanna: We serve marginalized, diverse communities that, for various reasons, cannot access the services of the library at our branches. We focus on low-income brackets of our community, providing services to homebound populations, Latinx communities, LGBTQAI+ individuals, immigrants, and people transitioning back into the community from jail, as well as individuals in shelters, residential care facilities, senior living centers, and mobile home parks. We are intentionally at the table of many community groups working on policy, evaluating services, and providing community services.

Our outreach department interprets the library experience for many individuals, from immigrants who think the library is not for them to people in the community who have no concept of the myriad high-quality services the library provides. We like to think we are decolonizing reading and the library experience. It is an intentional paradigm shift rooted in ALA policies. In fact, we have aligned our mission to facilitate our outreach efforts: *The Poudre River Public Library District Outreach Department strives to create and implement library programs that are inclusive and culturally responsive to traditionally marginalized populations.*

Using a social justice framework, we aligned all our programs and services to the ALA Office for Diversity, Literacy and Outreach Services Office's mission (http://www .ala.org/offices/diversity). We create and support all-inclusive spaces and programs that serve and represent the people in our District.

Jamie: *What is the biggest challenge in offering diversity programming?*

Johanna: Immigrants, minorities, people of color, and marginalized communities have many things in common. One of them is that we have created our identities, our vision of self and community in the shadow of colonization. Even our history has been rewritten and reshaped. We work under the parameters established by oppressors, and we even react to their oppression in prescribed ways. Divesting oneself of that historic DNA takes a high amount of mental and emotional energy. It takes questioning, many times over, the decisions you make, the reactions you experienced, and the actions you take. It is a journey that has no end.

As a result, the biggest challenge is to design programming that you know does not and cannot represent and serve all cultures, but to do it with enough curiosity and humility that intentionally includes the *other*. It is very important to acknowledge that you will make mistakes.

Another challenge is planning diversity programing that is fun and respectful. This takes more time and requires considerable work *behind the scenes* to get things right.

Jamie: Do you have any words of advice for librarians just starting outreach to diverse populations via children's programming?

Johanna: You have to be relevant. Become a data geek of your community, understand the role of your library district within larger society, and see your community as an entity where the library can do amazing things. To be successful, you cannot stay in the library; you must be in the community.

Your word is valuable and represents your library. If you tell the community you will do something, provide something, help at something, then do it. Word of mouth is a powerful thing and you do not want the community to think that the library is not responsive or responsible.

Think big and do not let your coworkers and others dictate your programs, services, and collections using the motto, "That's not how things are done." Libraries and cultural organizations are going through a growing phase where incredible things can happen. It is important to be informed. Read and study the ALA policies—the answers to so many conundrums librarians encounter are answered there.

Jamie: What are some of your favorite diversity projects, programs, or collaborations?

Johanna: I loved our first Día celebration. We decided to honor Frida Kahlo and invited the community to do it with us. We hosted a fashion show where community members dressed their kids as Frida or Diego Rivera. We had music, dancers, and a painter who actually finished their creation on stage. Professional models also dressed up as Diego and Frida and we had one of the models in a wheelchair on stage, since Frida spent much of her time on a wheelchair. We read *Frida* by Yuyi Morales and the night was incredible! Univision came and covered the event. We had over 350 participants and many of them expressed surprise, adding that they never expected their library would host programs like this one. It was a night that will stay with me for a long time. We made literacy alive, fun, accessible, and unexpected—all in one program!

I also think our Pelicano program is successful. We have kids in elementary schools here in the United States paired with pen pals in Nicaragua and Mexico. They exchange letters and participate in video conferencing. They learn about other cultures and establish a bond with someone who has a different life in a different country.

Ludy Rueda, the outreach librarian, coordinates the World Language Storytimes for our district. In partnership with the Colorado State University Foreign Languages Department, we provide storytimes in Mandarin, French, Arabic, American Sign Language, and Russian. I could share many stories about this program, but I think the biggest surprise was the unintended outcome of community building. At the end of storytimes, parents stay to exchange numbers and talk about their migrant stories. Even non-immigrant families, who bring their children to the program to learn a new language, will linger to socialize with the other families. What a wonderful community-building exercise!

PROGRAMMATIC THEMES AND IDEAS

When deciding on themes or topics for programs inclusive of diverse populations, librarians have many options. Numerous established model programs currently exist that can provide a springboard for youth librarians interested in developing culturally diverse programs for children and teens. Many of these programs offer bibliographies of recommended books as well as suggestions for developmentally appropriate, culturally sensitive activities that honor a specific cultural group. In addition, most of these programs are developed by individuals who are either cultural insiders or who have extensive knowledge of the culture group.

The Collaborative Summer Library Program (CSLP), which many public libraries use as a source for their themes, booklists, and materials for annual summer reading programs, frequently employs themes that lend themselves to creating programs that promote cultural competence. In 2011, the children's theme was "One World, Many Stories." The 2017 theme was "Build a Better World." Both programmatic themes empower youth librarians to utilize print and digital materials to promote cross-cultural understanding and intercultural explorations. A quick search on Pinterest as well as the CSLP program manuals can provide a wealth of resources to begin planning sessions.

Another particularly useful resource for helping youth librarians choose thematic content and understand the nuances in planning programs with diverse content is the classic book *Beyond Heroes and Holidays: A Practical Guide to K–12 Anti-Racist, Multicultural Education and Staff Development* (Lee, Menkart, and Okazawa-Rey 2008). This book provides examples of both successful and unsuccessful diversity-related programs and provides opportunities for librarians and educators to evaluate their own beliefs and biases. Themes are suggested in areas such as science, technology, math, and the arts.

Collectively, the resources discussed above can help youth librarians as they select diversity-related content for their programs. In the following section, we will discuss how to promote these themes and topics in sensitive ways.

DISPLAYS AND MARKETING

Creating physical library spaces and environments that are inclusive to all diverse populations is extremely important for librarians promoting cultural competence through

■ Recommended **Diversity Program Resources**

- **Bridging Cultures: Muslim Journeys** by National Endowment for the Humanities in collaboration with the American Library Association's Public Program Office. http://bridgingcultures.neh.gov/muslimjourneys/.

- **¡Colorín Colorado!** by Reading Rockets. http://www.colorincolorado.org/.

- **Dai Xiang Chuan: Bridging Generations, a Bag at a Time** by the Chinese American Librarians Association. http://daidai.cala-web.org/.

- **Día: El día de los niños/El día de los libros (Day of the Child/Day of the Book)** by the Association for Library Service to Children, Pat Mora, and REFORMA. http://dia.ala.org/.

- **Embracing Diversity: Sharing Our Songs and Rhymes** by Burnaby Public Library (Canada). http://bpl.bc.ca/kids/embracing-diversity/program-ideas.

- **International Children's Book Day** by the International Board on Books for Young People (IBBY). http://www.ibby.org/1494.0.html.

- **Libraries and Autism: We're Connected** by Library Connections. http://librariesandautism.org/index.htm.

- **Noche de Cuentos** by REFORMA (The National Association to Promote Library and Information Services to Latinos and the Spanish Speaking). http://nochedecuentos.org/.

- **Perspectives for a Diverse America** by Teaching Tolerance. http://perspectives.tolerance.org/.

- **Programming Librarian** by the American Library Association. http://www.programminglibrarian.org/.

- **Reading Is Grand! Celebrating Grand-Families @ Your Library** by the Black Caucus of the American Library Association. http://bcalareadingisgrand.weebly.com/.

- **Sister Libraries Program** by Libraries for Children and Young Adults Section of the International Federation of Library Associations and Institutions (IFLA). http://sisterlibraries.wordpress.com/ and http://www.ifla.org/node/1746.

- **Talk Story: Sharing Stories, Sharing Culture** by American Indian Library Association and the Asian/Pacific American Librarians Association. http://talkstorytogether.org/.

- **We Stories: Raising Big-Hearted Kids** by the We Stories nonprofit organization in St. Louis. http://www.westories.org/.

- **Welcoming Schools** by the Human Rights Campaign Foundation. http://www.welcomingschools.org/resources/lesson-plans/.

programming. Patrons need opportunities to encounter book displays, marketing materials, signage, and decor that depict diverse cultural perspectives, are accessible according to the Americans with Disabilities Act (ADA) guidelines, and represent the multiple languages spoken by patrons within the community. Marketing materials and decor should be free of cultural stereotypes and seek to represent all types of diversity. It is essential when selecting graphics and clipart to avoid cutesy images that, although seemingly diverse, perpetuate misinformation about a culture. For instance, it is common to see library bulletin boards or programming calendars and fliers that include images of children of the world that depict them in traditional garb from different countries. Often these children are holding hands and encircling a globe. The problem with such images is that they do not foster cross-cultural understanding or unity. Rather, because of the traditional costumes, which rarely represent how children in other countries actually dress, these images create a sense of otherness among children and perpetuate outdated notions of diversity and internationalism.

Fortunately, high-quality posters and images are available that accurately represent culturally diverse populations. In early 2017, librarian Rebecca McCorkindale worked with other librarians to create a series of graphics that emphasize the role of libraries in serving all library patrons. These colorful, attractive graphics, accessible on the Hafuboti Blog (https://hafuboti.com/2017/02/02/libraries-are-for-everyone/), in over forty languages—including sign language—are freely available for library and educational use and provide a wonderful opportunity for youth librarians to demonstrate their commitment to serving their diverse communities. Displaying these images on a library's website, program calendars, signage, and other visual materials can send a clear message of the library's inclusiveness. The Rainbow Families Council, a volunteer community organization in Victoria, Australia, also provides free posters and attractive information sheets that represent family diversity (www.rainbowfamilies.org.au/resources/whos-in-your-family/). These can be used in library displays as a way to be inclusive of lesbian, gay, bisexual, transgender, and queer or questioning (LGBTQ) families.

Another consideration when creating marketing materials and displays is language. If a program is targeted toward a bilingual population, then both English and the language of the population should be used on fliers and posters. Librarians should make a concerted effort to ensure the accuracy of translations. An advisory board member from the target population, local foreign-language club, university foreign-language department, or a native speaker can assist in acquiring proper translations. If a librarian does not know where to turn, then they might consider contacting one of the Ethnic Affiliates of the American Library Association (discussed in the list of resources at the end of this chapter). As tempting as it may be, librarians should not rely on tools such as Google Translate to create marketing materials that will be distributed within the community.

The importance of community buy-in for diversity programs cannot be emphasized enough. When youth librarians are looking for venues to market their program, it is critical to know the gatekeepers of a particular cultural community. They are often community leaders, well-established educators, or trusted caregivers. If a youth librarian can gain the trust of a community's gatekeeper, then they will have a better idea of where to advertise programs and how to get children, teens, and families from the cultural community to attend the library's programs. When a gatekeeper respects the librarian and endorses the services and activities the library is planning for a particular cultural group, they can help connect the librarian to other influential people within the community, assist with program marketing, and suggest specialized advertising venues that will reach large segments of the population.

A final consideration when creating displays and marketing materials relates to sensitivity. Not every cultural group will be comfortable having displays and targeted programming. Some groups may be fearful to attend a program or interact with a display about their culture. For instance, not every member of the LGBTQ community is open about their identity. If a youth librarian were to plan a Rainbow Family Storytime or Queer Teen Book Club, then LGBTQ youth and their families might not attend for fear of revealing themselves to the larger community. They may also not go to a LGBTQ display and select reading material. Similarly, a storytime for Autistic children and their caregivers might not be well-attended because of the sense of otherness fostered by having a separate program. Marketing materials that bill the program as being for Autistic children and families may actually deter patrons from attending. Some librarians have found it useful to focus on inclusive programming and displays rather than targeted programming and specialized displays. This makes it easier to incorporate diversity into regularly scheduled events and avoid marginalizing specific populations.

RECOMMENDED RESOURCES

We have discussed how to plan programs, select culturally sensitive themes, and considerations for displays and marketing. To further assist youth librarians, a list of recommended resources is provided at the end of the chapter that will be beneficial when learning about specific strategies for outreach to specialized populations. The list includes online and print resources that focus on library services to specific cultural groups or critical conversations surrounding diversity in children's and young adult materials. Please note this is not an exhaustive list. There are many new, high-quality resources appearing on a regular basis. Also note that some resources, for example, the white paper entitled "Importance of Diversity in Library Programs and Material Collections for Children" (Naidoo 2014), provide extensive bibliographies and suggestions to other professional tools for critically thinking about diversity.

CONCLUDING THOUGHTS AND FUTURE WORK

Children from diverse cultural backgrounds deserve access to well-stocked libraries staffed by culturally competent librarians. From selecting high-quality, culturally authentic materials to planning dynamic, inclusive programs that promote cultural understanding, children's librarians can be engaged in activities that model best practices and create safe spaces for *all* patrons. Although this chapter has provided many points to consider when planning and implementing diversity programming, this is a topic that is constantly changing with shifts in our larger sociopolitical environments. Although many examples of cultural programs have been suggested, current information is always needed on how to encourage specific diverse populations to attend library programs and how to motivate all librarians to see the importance of incorporating diversity into regular programming. Training programs that can assist youth librarians in developing cultural competence are in high demand, but there are not enough trainers available. Hopefully this chapter will encourage and engage readers to continue the conversation and become diversity advocates who rise up to meet these needs. Are you ready to accept the challenge?

REFERENCES

Association for Library Service to Children. 2017. ALSC/Candlewick Press. "Light the Way" Grant. www.ala.org/alsc/awardsgrants/profawards/candlewicklighttheway.

Bishop, R. S. 1997. "Selecting Literature for a Multicultural Curriculum." In *Using Multiethnic Literature in the K–8 Classroom,* edited by Violet Harris, 1–20. Norwood, MA: Christopher-Gordon Publishers.

Cuban, S. 2007. *Serving New Immigrant Communities in the Library.* Westport, CT: Libraries Unlimited.

Gonzalez, L. 2000. "Developing Culturally Integrated Children's Programs." In *Library Services to Youth of Hispanic Heritage,* edited by Barbara Immroth and Kathleen de la Peña McCook, 19–24. Jefferson, NC: McFarland and Company.

Lee, E., D. Menkart, and M. Okazawa-Rey. 2008. *Beyond Heroes and Holidays: A Practical Guide to K–12 Anti-Racist, Multicultural Education and Staff Development.* 4th edition. Washington, DC: Teaching for Change.

Lin, G. 2017. *GraceLinBlog,* "The Problem with Celebrating Tikki Tikki Tembo," posted May 3, 2017, www.gracelinblog.com/2017/05/the-problem-with-celebrating-tikki_22.html.

Naidoo, J. C. 2014. "Importance of Diversity in Library Programs and Material Collections for Children." Association for Library Services to Children. http://www.ala.org/alsc/publications-resources/white-papers/importance-diversity.

Naidoo, J. C., and K. Scherrer. 2016. "Beginning Outreach to Latino and Spanish-Speaking Communities," in *Once Upon a Cuento: Bilingual Storytimes in English and Spanish,* by Jamie Campbell Naidoo and Katie Scherrer, 11–24. Chicago: ALA Editions.

Slapin, B. 2013. "Skippyjon Jones: Transforming a Racist Stereotype into an Industry," *De Colores* (blog), posted April 6, 2013. http://decoloresreviews.blogspot.com/2013/04/skippyjon-jones-and-big-bones.html.

Weider, S. P. 2016. *How to Facilitate Important Conversations with Kids Using Diverse and Inclusive Books.* Barefoot Books Discussion Guide for The Barefoot Book of Children. https://www.barefootbooks.com/files/9914/7585/8565/BFB_BFBofChildren_DiscussionGuide_MyStoryActivity_0816_Wieder.pdf.

SUGGESTED PROFESSIONAL RESOURCES

ONLINE

American Indians in Children's Literature. Blog by librarian, scholar, and researcher Debbie Reese that critically examines the representation of indigenous characters in youth literature. http://americanindiansinchildrensliterature.blogspot.com.

Creating More Inclusive Libraries **webstreams.** Produced by the Lincoln Trail Library System via an IMLS grant, these highly recommended training videos featuring diversity trainer Susan O'Halloran provide opportunities for librarians to think about their cultural biases and how that influences the library services they offer to diverse populations. Note that there are several webstreams; 1A, 1 B, 1C, 1D, 2A, 2B, 2C, 2D, 3A, 3B, and 3C all on the right side of the screen. http://lincolntrail.typepad.com/ltls_quick_connections/2011/06/cmil-session-1a.html.

"The Danger of a Single Story." TED Talk by author Chimamanda Ngozi Adichie, 2009. Describes the importance for books and other media to accurately depict our culturally pluralistic society. http://www.ted.com/talks/chimamanda_adichie_the_danger_of_a_single_story.html.

Disability in Kid Lit. Critical blog dedicated to examining the representation of characters with disabilities in children's middle grade novels as well as young adult literature. http://disabilityinkidlit.com/.

De Colores. Critical review blog of Latinx and some Spanish-language children's and young adult books. Provides in-depth reviews as well as critical commentary. http://decoloresreviews.blogspot.com/.

"Importance of Diversity in Library Programs and Material Collections for Children." White paper published by the Association for Library Service to Children (ALSC) that describes why youth librarians should provide diversity in the services, programs, and collections they offer. http://www.ala.org/alsc/sites/ala.org.alsc/files/content/ALSCwhitepaper_importance%20of%20diversity _with%20graphics_FINAL.pdf.

Latinxs in Kid Lit: Exploring the World of Latinx YA, MG, and Children's Literature. Critical blog that provides suggestions and commentary related to examining how Latinx cultures are depicted in children's and YA books. https://latinosinkidlit.com/.

Let's Talk About Race in Storytime. YouTube webinar by Jessica Anne Bratt that explores how to approach the topic of race with young children in the library. https://www.youtube.com/watch?v=BT2ImUZRw-g.

Library Service to Special Population Children and their Caregivers. Developed by ALSC, this toolkit provides suggestions on how to help *all* children and families feel welcome at the library. http://www.ala.org/alsc/sites/ala.org.alsc/files/content/professional-tools/lsspcc-toolkit-2015.pdf.

Mirrors Windows Doors: Celebrating Diversity in a Whole World of Children's and YA Literature. UK-based resource blog that includes thoughtful articles about cultural diversity in youth literature, interviews with diverse authors and illustrators, and rich information about connecting children and teens with culturally diverse books around the world. http://mirrorswindowsdoors.org/wp/.

"Multicultural Library Manifesto." Developed by International Federation of Library Associations and Institutions (IFLA) and United Nations Educational, Scientific, and Cultural Organization (UNESCO), this resource provides helpful information for librarians interested in serving diverse populations. http://www.ifla.org/files/assets/library-services-to-multicultural-populations/publications/multicultural_library_manifesto-en.pdf.

Open Book. Blog hosted by the children's book publisher Lee and Low Books, which provides snapshots on diversity in children's and adult media as well as critical commentary on diversity publishing. http://blog.leeandlow.com.

Reading While White. Critical blog by White children's librarians that examines cultural diversity in children's and YA literature and how White culture influences interactions with diverse books. http://readingwhilewhite.blogspot.com.

Rich in Color. Blog dedicated to promoting young adult literature with diverse characters or written by authors of color. http://richincolor.com.

Social Justice Books (A Teaching for Change Project). Provides recommendations of children's and YA books divided by categories such as Arabs and Arab Americans, Early Childhood Anti-Bias, Disabilities, and so on. https://socialjusticebooks.org/booklists/.

We Need Diverse Books Campaign. Grassroots effort started in April 2014 to address the lack of diversity in children's and YA publishing. http://weneeddiversebooks.org/.

"The Windows and Mirrors of Your Child's Bookshelf." TED Talk by author/illustrator Grace Lin, 2016. Describes why it is important for children's books to reflect the diversity of our world. http://www.gracelinblog.com/2016/03/my-tedx-talk-some-of-my-thoughts-and.html.

The World Through Picture Books: Librarians' Favourite Books from Their Country. Booklist produced by the IFLA Libraries for Children and Young Adults Section, IFLA Literacy and Reading Section, and IBBY. Includes recommended children's books from thirty-six counties that can be used to promote diversity in programming. http://www.ifla.org/files/assets/hq/publications/professional-report/135.pdf.

BOOKS

Cooke, Nicole. 2017. *Information Services to Diverse Populations: Developing Culturally Competent Library Professionals.* Santa Barbara, CA: Libraries Unlimited.

Farmer, Lesley. 2013. *Library Services for Youth with Autism Spectrum Disorders.* Chicago: ALA Editions.

Feinberg, Sandra, Barbara Jordan, Kathleen Deerr, and Michelle Langa. 2013. *Including Families of Children with Special Needs: A How-to-Do-It Manual for Librarians,* rev. ed. Revised by Carrie Banks. Chicago: ALA/Neal-Schuman.

Harrod, Kerol, and Carol Smallwood, eds. 2014. *Library Youth Outreach: 26 Ways to Connect with Children, Young Adults and Their Families.* Jefferson, NC: McFarland.

Hughes-Hassell, Sandra, Pauletta Brown Bracy, and Casey H. Rawson, eds. 2016. *Libraries, Literacy, and African American Youth: Research and Practice.* Santa Barbara, CA: Libraries Unlimited.

Klipper, Barbara. 2014. *Programming for Children and Teens with Autism Spectrum Disorder.* Chicago: ALA Editions.

Larson, Jeanette. 2011. *El día de los niños/El día de los libros: Building a Culture of Literacy in Your Community through Día.* Chicago: ALA Editions.

Montiel-Overall, Patricia, Annabelle Villaescusa Nuñez, and Verónica Reyes-Escudero. 2015. *Latinos in Libraries, Museums, and Archives: Cultural Competence in Action! An Asset-Based Approach.* Lanham, MD: Rowman and Littlefield Publishers.

Naidoo, Jamie Campbell. 2012. *Rainbow Family Collections: Selecting and Using Children's Books with Lesbian, Gay, Bisexual, Transgender, and Queer Content.* Santa Barbara, CA: Libraries Unlimited.

———. 2014. *Diversity Programming for Digital Youth: Promoting Cultural Competence in the Children's Library.* Santa Barbara, CA: Libraries Unlimited.

Naidoo, Jamie, and Katie Scherrer. 2016. *Once Upon a Cuento: Bilingual Storytimes in English and Spanish.* Chicago: ALA Editions.

Smallwood, Carol, and Kim Becnel, eds. 2013. *Library Services for Multicultural Patrons: Strategies to Encourage Library Use.* Jefferson, NC: McFarland.

ARTICLES

Cottrell, M. 2016. "Storytime for the Spectrum: Libraries Add Services for Children with Autism." *American Libraries Online,* March 1. https://americanlibraries magazine.org/2016/03/01/sensory-storytime-spectrum-libraries-add-services -for-children-with-autism/.

Montiel Overall, Patricia. 2009. "Cultural Competence: A Conceptual Framework for Library and Information Science Professionals." *Library Quarterly* 79 (2): 174– 204.

Prendergast, Tess. 2016. "Seeking Early Literacy for All: An Investigation of Children's Librarians and Parents of Young Children with Disabilities' Experiences at the Public Library." *Library Trends* 65 (1): 65-91.

Ríos-Balderama. Sandra. 2000. "This Trend Called Diversity." *Library Trends* 49 (1): 194-214.

ORGANIZATIONS

Numerous nonprofit library and literacy organizations, such as the Ethnic Caucuses/ Affiliates of the American Library Association (ALA), also provide a wealth of information that can help youth librarians learn more about diversity. These organizations promote high-quality library services and programs that are reflective of and respectful to the people they represent. Youth librarians can utilize resources from the following organizations to get a jump start on planning diverse programs:

The American Indian Library Association is a nonprofit organization dedicated to serving the library and information needs of American Indian. http://reforma.org/.

The Asian/Pacific American Librarians Association (APALA) is a nonprofit organization committed to supporting librarians who serve Asian Pacific Americans. www.apalaweb.org/.

The Association for Specialized and Cooperative Library Agencies (ASCLA) is a nonprofit organization that helps librarians plan programs and services for specialized populations. Its website includes information about serving the needs of individuals with varying physical and mental abilities. www.ala.org/ascla/.

The Association of Jewish Libraries (AJL) is a nonprofit organization that promotes informational and cultural literacy about Jewish culture. http://jewishlibraries.org/.

The Association of Tribal Archives, Libraries, and Museums (ATALM) is an international nonprofit organization providing culturally relevant programming and services for Native Nations worldwide. www.atalm.org/.

The Black Caucus of the American Library Association (BCALA) is a nonprofit organization devoted to providing high-quality library and information services to African Americans. www.bcala.org/.

The Chinese American Librarians Association (CALA) is a nonprofit organization whose main purpose is to serve the informational and library needs of Chinese Americans. www.cala-web.org/.

The Colorado Association of Libraries Special Populations and Issues Interest Group, a part of the Colorado Association of Libraries, is dedicated to providing librarians with resources to better serve diverse and underserved populations. http://calspecial pops.cvlsites.org/.

The Ethnic and Multicultural Information Exchange Round Table (EMIERT) of ALA is a nonprofit organization dedicated to assisting librarians serving various diverse populations including African American, Armenian, and Jewish patrons. www.ala.org/emiert/.

The Gay, Lesbian, Bisexual, and Transgender Round Table (GLBTRT) of ALA is a nonprofit organization serving the literacy and information needs of the GLBT library community, families, and other individuals. www.ala.org/glbtrt/glbtrt.

The International Board on Books for Young People (IBBY) is an international nonprofit with chapters around the world dedicated to promoting intercultural understanding and diversity through global children's and young adult literature. http://ibby.org/.

The National Library Service for the Blind and Physically Handicapped (NLS/BPH) is a free library program operated through the Library of Congress that offers resources for libraries serving patrons with different abilities. www.loc.gov/nls/.

REFORMA (The National Association to Promote Library and Information Services to Latinos and the Spanish Speaking) is a nonprofit organization dedicated to assisting libraries with planning services and programs to Latinx. http://reforma.org/.

CHAPTER 2

The Power of a Story

Telling to Transform the World

Annette Y. Goldsmith and Michelle H. Martin

INTRODUCTION

When Michelle was about seven years old, she heard an African American South Carolina storyteller, Tommy Scott Young, tell a tale of three magic dogs named Barney McCabe, Doodly Doo, and Sue Boy. In the story, two children have three magic dogs, but they also have three grains of magic corn. "And when you use a grain of magic corn, somethin' good gonna happen, and everything's gonna be all right." Like Hansel and Gretel, Jack and Mary go for a walk in the forest, but unlike them, Mary cleverly leaves her glass of milk on the mantel at home for their mother, telling her, "If that glass of milk turns blood-red, you'll know we've used up all our grains of corn, and you need to let the dogs go so that they can help us." As a 1970s storyteller, Young had a huge afro, deep dimples, a smile Michelle couldn't forget, and he could spin a yarn capable of keeping youngsters (and old folks) spellbound and breathless. However, despite Michelle's adoration of Tommy Scott Young and his stories, in time she forgot the Barney McCabe story . . . or so she thought.

Fast forward about fifteen years. Immediately after graduating from The College of William & Mary, Michelle moved to the Sierra Nevada in California to work at a residential outdoor-education school in Springville, California, that serves the sixth-grade students of the Tulare County School District. The children come up to SCICON (The Clemmie Gill School of Science and Conservation) for a week-long environmental education experience with their teachers and students from area high schools who serve as counselors. As one of twelve interns, Michelle taught science lessons outdoors and supervised the counselors in the residential villages. To learn more stories for evening programs, Michelle bought some cassette tapes (it was the late eighties, after all) of storytellers, and lo and behold, one featured the story of Barney McCabe. But this storyteller, a White teller, played the musical interludes on the guitar and sang all the songs to a tune that just did not sound right to Michelle. Tommy Scott Young's tunes came back to her from the days of sitting on the floor, listening to him at her all-African American neighborhood elementary school. And from then on, whenever Michelle tells that story, she tells it the way she first heard it. *That* is the power of story!

STORYTELLING DEFINED AND DESCRIBED

Stories are everywhere, and everyone tells them in one form or other. The trick is to be able to engage and pull others into the story you are telling. The National Storytelling Network defines storytelling as "the interactive art of using words and actions to reveal the elements and images of a story while encouraging the listener's imagination" (National Storytelling Network n.d.). In short, the story is told live, without the text in hand, to an audience, as opposed to reading a story aloud from a book. The story is a shared experience created in the space between the teller and the audience: the teller communicates the story, and listeners recreate it in their imagination. Today library storytimes tend to rely more on text (reading aloud) but will sometimes still include oral stories accompanied by visuals, such as props or flannelboards. We think it's important to see more storytelling in storytime and other library programs—and perhaps by the end of this chapter, you will agree!

Though storytelling has always been an integral part of human life, the research on it has emerged only recently. The early youth services librarians intuitively understood the importance of storytelling to their work, but they had no research to support this notion. Scientist and storyteller Kendall Haven has filled this gap with *Story Proof*, a compendium of storytelling research, some of it his own, in which he emphasizes three key takeaways from neurological research:

1. The human brain "is predisposed to think in story terms";
2. "Cells that fire together, wire together"; and
3. Story exposure in childhood results in adults who are "irrevocably hard-wired to think in story terms (Haven 2007).

If you've ever felt "lost in a story," you're not alone. According to Fran Stallings (1998), many listeners go into a "storylistening trance," a state akin to light hypnosis. Based on his findings from interviews with twenty-two listeners at eight storytelling events, Brian W. Sturm (2000) determined six characteristics of the storylistening trance:

- A sense of realism
- Lack of awareness of one's surroundings
- Engaged receptive channels
- A lack or loss of control of the experience
- A "placeness"
- A sense of time distortion (Sturm 2000)

When you see that transfixed look on children's faces, there's a good chance they are experiencing a storylistening trance.

That storytelling, as Greene and Del Negro (2010) attest, "has been called the oldest and the newest of the arts," suggests its continuing relevance for library programs. Indeed, storytelling can be a crucial piece of all library programs for children and youth, and intergenerational programs, too. It can be adapted for all ages, is interactive, honors community, bridges diversity gaps, requires little or no equipment, and works even when the power goes out!

LITERACY BENEFITS OF STORYTELLING

African American librarian and storyteller Augusta Baker made clear connections between the value of storytelling and the librarian's role in the promotion of literacy. In 1964, Baker published a second edition of "Once Upon a Time," a sixteen-page booklet prepared by Baker, Spencer Shaw, Kathleen Sheehan, and Ida G. Silk from the Children's and YA Services Section of the New York Library Association, to offer helpful advice to librarians who provide story hours to children of all ages. In the introductory paragraphs, the authors explain that: "experimentation with methods and materials, other than those mentioned in the following section, 'The Story Hour,' should be considered but we must never forget our stock in trade—books" (Baker et al. 1964). For Baker, exposing children to books was the point of story hour. In Baker's 1990 interview, she argued that despite the opinion of some that storytelling is a lost or dying art: "libraries will never let it die" (Chepesiuk 1990).

"Storytellers," she said, "are not actors. There are no Broadway talent scouts out in the audience. Just children. *The purpose of storytelling is to motivate children to read.* A storyteller wants a child to remember the story and [the] book from which it came. We hope that this will encourage the child to go to the library" (Chepesiuk 1990. Emphasis added). Therefore, in considering the clear line that Baker drew from storytelling to books and back again, it's always a good idea when telling stories in a library setting to have a cart of books, ready and waiting, for children to peruse and check out. And if some of your stories point them to particular books, that may positively reinforce the connections between storytelling, books, and reading. And if you later hear the children singing or repeating bits of your stories that stuck with them as they leave with a pile of books in their arms, you know that they too are experiencing the power of story.

More recently, Denise Agosto (2016) designed a study to test the assumed literacy benefits of storytelling. She told stories to twenty second-graders in a suburban Title 1 school—the first time these children had heard live storytelling. She then analyzed the thank-you cards that they wrote and drew for her, along with their verbal descriptions of the cards they had made. Her findings identify four literacy benefits that storytelling can provide: visualization, cognitive engagement, critical thinking, and story sequencing ability. Though a small, preliminary study, it does provide some evidence of the importance of storytelling in school and public libraries. Her data suggest that the following post-storytelling extension activities can enhance the literacy benefits of storytelling:

- Follow-up questions
- Personal connection building
- Reenactments
- Retellings
- Connections to books
- Connections to other stories
- Response drawings
- Response writing

And as Agosto (2016) points out, children may well associate the joy of storytelling with their library time.

The recognition that children learn through story is the impetus behind Talk Story: Sharing Story, Sharing Culture (http://talkstorytogether.org/), a grant-based program sponsored by the American Indian Library Association (AILA) and the Asian/Pacific American

Librarians Association (APALA) to encourage community building through storytelling in libraries. We *are* our stories, and sharing them in a positive way speaks once more to the power of story!

CHOOSING YOUR STORY

Augusta Baker believed that the tale chooses the teller; the teller doesn't choose the tale. Baker sometimes shared this advice with budding tellers who felt frustrated about a story that just wouldn't come out right: "Perhaps that story did not choose you." You must find the stories that are meant for you, or, better still, let them find you (Feehan 1996). So look for a story that you really care about and wish to share. If you have a genuine connection with the story, you will not mind practicing it over and over and adapting it for different audiences. Your enjoyment of the story will be contagious. You may also discover new possibilities and personal meaning as you continue to explore the story.

Here's an example: Annette tells a very short story she learned from Alice Kane called "A Second Language" (1997). Miss Kane (as the staff called her) was a retired Toronto Public Library children's librarian and storyteller who was born in Ireland. She had the most beautiful, haunting lilt to her voice, and no one could tell the Irish epics like she could. Every year, the Christmas meeting of Toronto Public Library children's staff would feature librarians who, having just completed the staff in-service storytelling training, would tell stories to their colleagues. These novices faced an imposing front row of retired librarian storytellers, including Miss Kane.

Annette's version of the story is close to the published version. It goes like this: One day a mother mouse was out with her children, enjoying the day. Suddenly a cat appeared in the road in front of them. The children, terrified, rushed behind their mother's skirts. The brave mother mouse faced that cat and in her loudest voice cried out, "BOW WOW!" The cat, startled, turned tail and ran. The children emerged, and the mother mouse said to them, "Let that be a lesson to you, my dears. Never underestimate the value of a second language!"

Annette loves this story because it maintains her connection with Miss Kane, who passed away in 2003. Also, because Annette majored in French Literature, she appreciates

■ Selected Storytelling Picture Books

Cooney, Barbara. 1985. *Miss Rumphius.* Illustrated by the author. London: Puffin.

Gilani-Williams, Fawzia. 2010 *Nabeel's New Pants: An Eid Tale*. Illustrated by Proiti Roy. Singapore: Marshall Cavendish.

McGovern, Ann. 1992. *Too Much Noise.* Illustrated by Simms Taback. Boston: Houghton Mifflin Harcourt BFYR.

Rosen, Michael. 2014. *We're Going on a Bear Hunt.* Illustrated by Helen Oxenbury. Somerville, MA: Candlewick.

■ Selected Storytelling Collections

Geras, Adèle. 2003. *My Grandmother's Stories: A Collection of Jewish Folk Tales.*
Illustrated by Anita Lobel. New York: Knopf BFYR.

MacDonald, Margaret Read. 2005. *Twenty Tellable Tales: Audience Participation
Folktales for the Beginning Storyteller.* Illustrated by Roxane Murphy. Chicago:
ALA Editions.

Raff, Steffani. 2015. *The Ravenous Gown and 14 More Tales about Real Beauty.* Sanger,
CA: Familius.

Shannon, George. 2000. *Stories to Solve: Folktales from Around the World.* Illustrated
by Peter Sís. New York: Greenwillow.

Wolkstein, Diane. 1997. *The Magic Orange Tree and Other Haitian Folktales.* Illustrated
by Elsa Henriquez. New York: Schocken.

Yee, Paul. 2011. *Tales from Gold Mountain: Stories of the Chinese in the New World.*
Illustrated by Simon Ng. Toronto: Groundwood.

the value of a second language and cross-cultural connections. So imagine her surprise—and pleasure—when she attended a Miami storytelling event where she heard that same story … with Cuban characters! It was a folktale that had traveled well.

In *The Family of Stories: An Anthology of Children's Literature* (1986), Anita Moss and Jon C. Stott discuss theories related to how stories travel and why so many stories in disparate locales have the same elements. Whether you believe that tales migrate across the world from single places of origin (*monogenesis*) or that humans create similar stories because we share some basic human characteristics (*polygenesis*), or some combination of the two theories, it's useful to know that many scholars have thought deeply about this phenomenon—especially with reference to folktales.

WORKING WITH FOLKTALES

Librarians who wish to tell stories should look first to folk and fairy tales (also called traditional tales), those stories "circulated by word of mouth among the common people, especially a tale characteristically anonymous and timeless" (Haven and Ducey 2007). When an author's name is associated with a folktale—think of the Brothers Grimm—it is usually as a collector or re-teller. Modern fairy tales with a named author, such as Hans Christian Andersen or Oscar Wilde, are often conflated with traditional stories because they both use the "once upon a time" language of story. If you tell a modern fairy tale, you should credit the author.

Librarians can mine a vast treasure trove of folk literature for material. Though many online folktale portals exist (see Recommended Resources), poring through the folktale section of the library may be more fun. Along with picture-book versions of folk and fairy tales, you will often find out-of-print older collections with riveting stories that, when buried in a thick book with few pictures, children and teens will rarely read on their own. When weeding, keep these folktale collections!

Remember to balance your artistic freedom to tell a story with cultural sensitivity to the material. In a brief but important article called "What Is Authentic?" Eliza T. Dresang reflects on what makes multicultural literature authentic. Working from a dictionary definition, she describes three levels of authenticity:

1. Based on fact (cultural accuracy)
2. Reproducing essential features of an original (cultural accuracy)
3. True to the creator's own cultural personality, spirit, or character (cultural immersion).

Cultural accuracy is important, but cultural immersion—which can come from insider status or serious research—is the gold standard (Dresang 1997).

Some research will be necessary to understand the cultural context of your story. For Native American stories, Debbie Reese's blog, *American Indians in Children's Literature* is an authoritative resource (n.d.). A librarian and academic tribally enrolled in the Nambe Pueblo nation, Reese recommends culturally appropriate texts and provides many examples of books with Native American content that have been misinterpreted by well-meaning non-tribal writers and re-tellers.

Some stories are simply not yours to tell. Some you can tell with permission. Native Americans tell some stories only in certain seasons. Those who tell stories from particular tribes must know the protocol for which stories to tell and when. Consult the Storytell LISTSERV (see Recommended Resources) to learn about acceptable storytelling practices for a teller outside of the culture.

Once you've taken cultural sensitivity into consideration, the rule of thumb is that you do not need permission to tell stories as a librarian in a school or public library setting. Since telling stories promotes literacy in general and your collection in particular, it is considered educational use. If, however, you tell stories as a paid performer, you must ask permission of the author (if there is one) because you are using that person's intellectual property. Even if you are not telling for profit, if you tell or adapt the work of a living author, you might let that person know as a courtesy. Most authors are happy to see their stories shared in this way—and if they're not, you shouldn't use their material.

LEARNING YOUR STORY

It may seem counterintuitive, but the best way to learn a story is to *not* memorize it—except for the beginning, the end, and any important words and phrases (e.g., a refrain). Write out the "bones" (highlights) of the story to help you remember how it goes. Some people can learn a story by watching a movie of it play out in their mind's eye. Others benefit from the visual reminder of a storyboard (sequential thumbnail sketches of the action). Only if it's a literary story—the work of an identifiable author—should you memorize to help you stay

Challenges and Rewards of Storytelling

For those who would tell, consider these challenges:

- Becoming intimately familiar with a story for telling takes time. Tell to the mirror, to the dog, in the car, at bedtime, and so on.
- Telling a story can be intimidating. To be successful, you want to capture the attention of the audience and keep it. On the other hand, every telling session is unique; sometimes the storylistening trance happens, and sometimes it doesn't.
- The environment can easily interfere—noise, weather, a competing attraction, etc.
- Props to aid in the telling can be valuable with young children, but props can also distract.
- A story that runs too long can fail as spectacularly as a story that the teller hasn't learned well enough to tell publicly yet.
- Reading aloud from a book tends to be much easier; telling is a craft that must be practiced and honed.

And conversely, telling comes with its own rewards:

- A practiced, well-told tale creates a shared experience between the teller and the listeners that has few parallels—similar, perhaps, to what musicians feel when they play for a spellbound audience.
- Becoming a storyteller connects the teller with a tradition that goes back to the beginning of humanity. Even if the tale is contemporary, the craft enables us to take part in an art form that goes back and back and back—one that in large part distinguishes humans from other life forms.
- You will be carrying on an important library tradition, following in the footsteps of distinguished librarian storytellers such as Marie Shedlock, Ruth Sawyer, Frances Clarke Sayers, Alice Kane, Rita Cox, Spencer Shaw, and Augusta Baker.

Program Planning Tips for Tellers

- Tailor the style of telling, content, and length of the story (or stories) to your audience.
- Know your material well enough to be able to adapt it if you draw an audience that is quite different from the one you expected.
- If your audience is not used to listening to stories, you may want to briefly explain what storytelling is ("I'm going to tell you the story without the book while you see the pictures in your imagination") and what kind of behavior is required ("Look at me and listen to the story. Please save your questions until the end.").
- If it's a participatory story, you may wish to teach your audience their part and cue them for joining in before you begin.
- You may wish to rearrange the room's setup to suit your needs.
- With an audience of young children, you might want to sit to avoid towering over them, or even sit on the floor with them to be on their level.
- If you are using props, practice with them in the space where you'll be telling.
- Post someone at the door to let people in and out quietly.
- Think about how you might handle mistakes. For example, if you miss something, you can slip it in later. Never stop and correct yourself while you're telling—it will pull your listeners out of the story. Chances are you will be the only one who realizes that you made a mistake.
- Make sure to leave time at the end for discussion but remember that silent reflection is also a legitimate response.

faithful to the language and style of the original. However, it is fine to diverge from the text in small ways from time to time.

When you learn a traditional story, consider yourself a conduit rather than a performer. The story will still be filtered through your personality, and you will make it your own. As storyteller Aubrey Davis (2010) says, "It's not about being a star... [it's about] doing the best thing you can for the listener, and doing the best you can for the story." Annette calls this "serving the story." Augusta Baker was well known (notorious, even) for insisting that tellers avoid dramatics—animated voices, hand waving, jumping around—in their tellings. Any ALA member who learned Baker's storytelling method will confirm that Baker felt that the teller should stay out of the way and let the story itself speak. Though we recommend the storyteller-as-conduit approach, if your natural inclination is to be more dramatic, you should do what works for you—as long as it also serves the story.

STORYTELLING IN ACTION

Mother Goose on the Loose®

Storytelling can be used with the youngest of children. Betsy Diamant-Cohen, creator of Mother Goose on the Loose®, a research-based nursery rhyme program for babies and toddlers, has also applied her "whole child" approach to preschool storytime. One of the hallmarks of the program, described in *Transforming Preschool Storytime* (Diamant-Cohen and Hetrick 2013), is to incorporate different ways of engaging with the same story over six weeks to help develop multiple intelligences. Introduce the story as a read-aloud, tell it as a flannelboard story, narrate the story with the children acting it out, read other retellings, read a "fractured" version, and give children props to use while they retell the story themselves. The children will benefit from the repetition but also from the rich exploration of story (Diamant-Cohen and Hetrick 2013). This example of storytelling for young children can easily employ all five practices from Every Child Ready to Read® @ your library®, Second Edition (ECRR2)—talking, singing, reading, writing, and playing (ECRR2 Resources n.d.).

Read-a-Rama®

Michelle created a program in 2001 as a service-learning project for her students that uses all the ECRR2 Practices and takes an immersive approach to literature-rich day camps for children ages four to eleven. Camp Read-a-Rama® (www.Read-a-Rama.org) uses children's books as the springboard for all other activities, of which storytelling is one component, and encourages children to "live books."[1] A brief description of the 2017 summer camp will illustrate how Camp employs an immersive approach to combating summer slide.

Read-a-Rama® partnered with two local Lutheran churches and an affordable housing complex for formerly homeless families in downtown Seattle to offer camps that would serve children most susceptible to summer learning loss. Thirty-six children attended camp for two weeks in July, and the themes were "Read-a-Rama Rocks" (Geology and Music) and "Read-a-Rama Tell Your Story." Both themes were chosen by the children. Each camp week included theme-appropriate read-alouds or storytelling, songs, movement, field trips, hands-on crafts, writing, and more. Twenty-three guest readers and artists visited camp, including a variety of storytellers. Campers and their families attended a Family Literacy Night, during which the campers performed skits and talked about what they learned and experienced. At the end of camp, every child received six free books and a Family Literacy Backpack loaded with school supplies and a pamphlet to encourage positive family literacy practices at home. This program illustrates how storytelling can be paired with hands-on activities to create an immersive learning experience for children.

DIGITAL STORYTELLING—STORY FIRST, DIGITAL TOOLS SECOND!

Though traditional oral storytelling is as powerful as ever, the ability to tell stories using a variety of media is another important skill for youth in a digital age. The Educational Uses of Digital Storytelling site defines digital storytelling in this way:

As with traditional storytelling, most digital stories focus on a specific topic and contain a particular point of view. However, as the name implies, digital stories usually contain some mixture of computer-based images, text, recorded audio narration, video clips, and music. Digital stories can vary in length, but most of the stories used in education typically last between two and ten minutes ("What is Digital Storytelling" n.d.).

Briefly, a digital story is "a short, first-person video-narrative created by combining recorded voice, still and moving images, and music or other sounds."[2] Digital storytelling can be simple or sophisticated. Since the tools are increasingly easy to use, with a little guidance, even young children can create their own digital stories. In his *Digital Storytelling Cookbook*, Joe Lambert, a pioneering digital storytelling educator, outlines the Seven Elements that a personal digital story needs. It's important for the story to have a point and also present a *point (of view)*. The *dramatic question* at the heart of the story should be clear. The story should have *emotional content*. Sometimes that can come from *the gift of your voice*—hearing you tell your own story. The *power of the soundtrack*—music, sound effects, etc.—also sets the tone. Finally, a strong digital story is characterized by *economy*—less is usually more— and appropriate *pacing* (Lambert 2010).

Making a digital story draws on all the twenty-first-century skills associated with the connected learning framework. Connected learning is interest-powered, production-centered, peer-supported; has shared purpose; and is academically oriented in an openly networked environment (Heick 2014). Digital storytellers choose a story that is important to them and then bring together the media assets they will need to create their video. Collaboration aids this process, and the project focuses on self-expression and communication. As with oral storytelling, creators must give credit to the source of the story. Students must learn at least a little about fair use—what they can and cannot include in their story—and should end the video with a list of credits.

Digital storytelling skills are also valuable for transmedia storytelling. From this description by Henry Jenkins, the theorist who has largely defined the phenomenon, it is clear that transmedia storytelling is an open-ended space full of possibility:

In transmedia, elements of a story are dispersed systematically across multiple media platforms, each making their own unique contribution to the whole. Each medium does what it does best—comics might provide back-story, games might allow you to explore the world, and the television series offers unfolding episodes (Jenkins 2011).

We can easily imagine youth digital storytelling inspired by and connected to a larger, meaningful story world.

SHOWCASE TELLERS . . . AND YOUR LIBRARY

Showcase tellers at your library by connecting with oral storytelling events. Celebrate World Storytelling Day (www.freewebs.com/worldstorytellingday/) on March 20 and Tellabration (www.tellabration.org/), an international celebration of storytelling, on or around the third Saturday in November. Or "grow" your own festival. For example, since 1987, Richland Library in South Carolina has hosted Augusta Baker's Dozen: A Celebration of Stories. Do you have a local storytelling guild willing to partner on such an event? Use the National Storytelling Network's calendar (www.storynet.org/events/calendar.php) to find active storytelling groups in your community.

Work to encourage the children and teens at your library to tell their own stories by hosting programs where they create digital stories. These programs can be built around competitions such as the annual Collaborative Summer Library Program (CSLP) Teen Video Challenge to motivate digital storytellers or simply provide inspiration; the 2017 theme was "Build a Better World" (https://www.cslpreads.org/2017-teen-video-challenge/). After you've worked on creating digital stories with youth, have a digital storytelling festival to share and celebrate!

Once you're feeling comfortable with storytelling, whether oral or digital, consider using it to advocate for youth services in general. As Kate McDowell shows in her work on "well-evidenced stories," applied storytelling is an important skill for librarians to use when partnering with other organizations that work with youth (McDowell 2016). Certainly the American Library Association's Everyday Advocacy initiative recognizes the power of storytelling for this purpose and encourages librarians to share their advocacy stories (www.ala.org/everyday-advocacy/share-your-advocacy-story).

CONCLUSION

Storytelling marries the old and the new: oral storytelling is an age-old practice that can be applied to contemporary circumstances, and digital storytelling capitalizes on twenty-first-century skills while still being grounded in the knowledge of what makes a good story. Whatever the form or format, storytelling supports the programming goals of youth service librarians by engaging, empowering, and enlightening both the audience and the teller.

NOTES

1. Michelle and her co-director Rachelle D. Washington operated Camp Read-a-Rama® out of Clemson University's English Department from 2009 to 2011. When Michelle became the Augusta Baker Chair at University of South Carolina (USC), the program moved with her, operating out of USC for three summers. In 2015, Read-a-Rama® became a 501(c)(3); in 2016, it obtained trademarking.
2. Dresang's definition originally appeared on the StoryCenter site but is no longer available.

REFERENCES

Agosto, D. E. 2016. "Why Storytelling Matters: Unveiling the Literacy Benefits of Storytelling," *Children and Libraries* 14, no. 2 (Summer): 21–26.

Baker, A, S. Shaw, K. Sheehan, and I. G. Silk. 1964. *Once Upon a Time,* 2nd ed., 4. New York: New York Library Association.

Chepesiuk, R. 1990. "South Carolina's Master Storyteller," *Sandlapper: The Magazine of South Carolina* 1 (6): 39.

Davis, A., from a conversation with Annette Goldsmith recorded in Toronto, 2010.

Diamant-Cohen, B., and M. A. Hetrick. 2013. *Transforming Preschool Storytime: A Modern Vision and a Year of Programs.* Chicago: ALA Neal-Schuman.

Dresang, E. T. 1997. "What is Authentic?" Posted to Kay Vandergrift's blog, which is no longer available.

"ECRR2 Resources," n.d. Every Child Ready to Read® @your library®, Public Library Association and Association for Library Services to Children. www.everychildreadytoread.org/ecrr2-resources.

Feehan, P. 1996. *Augusta Baker: Celebrating America's Storyteller.* Columbia, SC: University of South Carolina College of Library and Information Science. Videocassette (VHS), 18 min.

Greene, E., and J. M. Del Negro. 2010. *Storytelling: Art and Technique.* 4th ed., 3. Santa Barbara, CA: Libraries Unlimited.

Haven, K. 2007. *Story Proof: The Science Behind the Startling Power of Story*, 27. Westport, CT: Libraries Unlimited.

Haven, K. F., and M. G. Ducey. 2007. *Crash Course in Storytelling*, 105. Westport, CT: Libraries Unlimited.

Heick, T. 2014. "6 Design Principles of Connected Learning," *TeachThought,* December 19. www.teachthought.com/terry-heick/6-design-principles-connected-learning/.

Kane, A. 1997. "A Second Language," in *Laughs: Funny Stories,* selected by Claire Mackay Plattsburgh, NY and Toronto: Tundra Books, 99.

Jenkins, H. 2011. "Seven Myths about Transmedia Storytelling Debunked," *Fastcompany.com,* April 8.

Lambert, J. *The Digital Storytelling Education Cookbook* (Berkeley, CA: Center for Digital Storytelling, 2010).

McDowell, K. 2016. *A Storytelling Scholar* (blog), posted November 7, 2016. https://storytellingscholar .blogspot.com/2016/11/story-across-organizations.html?m=0.

Moss, A., and J. C. Stott. 1986. *The Family of Stories: An Anthology of Children's Literature.* Fort Worth, TX: Holt, Rinehart and Winston.

National Storytelling Network, n.d. "What is Storytelling?" https://storynet.org/what-is-storytelling/.

Reese, D. n.d. *American Indians in Children's Literature* https://americanindiansinchildrensliterature .blogspot.com/.

Stallings, F. 1988. "The Web of Silence: Storytelling's Power to Hypnotize," *National Storytelling Journal* (Spring/Summer): 6–19.

Sturm, B. W. 2000. "The 'Storylistening' Trance Experience," *Journal of American Folklore* 113, no. 449 (Summer): 289–95, www.jstor.org/stable/542104.

"What is Digital Storytelling?" *Educational Uses of Digital Storytelling,* University of Houston, College of Education. http://digitalstorytelling.coe.uh.edu/page.cfm?id=27.

RECOMMENDED RESOURCES

I. ORAL STORYTELLING

Ashliman, D. L. *Folklore and Mythology Electronic Texts* and *Folklinks: Folk and Fairy-Tale Sites.* www.pitt .edu/~dash/folklinks.html.

Chace, K. *The Story Bug.* http://storybug.net/.

Folk Mic. https://folkmic.weebly.com/.
An ongoing project designed to capture and provide access to folktales and original stories so aspiring tellers can see how it's done. Designed as a capstone by Kian Flynn, Martha Karavitis, and Brian Lindsey when they were Annette's students at the University of Washington iSchool. Help build the repository—take the mic and tell your story!

Forest, H. *Story Arts.* www.storyarts.org. Includes "Stories in a Nutshell," brief folktales to tell.

Freeman, J., and C. F. Bauer. 2015. *The Handbook for Storytellers.* Chicago: ALA Editions.

Hayes. J. https://www.youtube.com/user/joehayesstoryteller/feed.
YouTube channel of 100+ stories, including Spanish and bilingual tales—an amazing resource from a well-known teller.

MacDonald, M. R. 1993. *The Storyteller's Start-Up Book: Finding, Learning, Performing and Using Folktales.* Atlanta, GA: August House.

_____. 2008. *Tell the World: Storytelling Across Language Barriers.* Westport, CT: Libraries Unlimited, 2008.

MacDonald, M. R., and B. W. Sturm. 2001. *The Storyteller's Sourcebook: A Subject, Title, and Motif Index to Folklore Collections for Children, 1983–1999.* Detroit, MI: Gale.

MacDonald, M. R., J. M. Whitman, and N. F. Whitman. 2013. *Teaching with Story: Classroom Connections to Storytelling.* Atlanta: August House.

McWilliams, B. 1998. *Effective Storytelling: A Manual for Beginners.*
www.eldrbarry.net/roos/eest.htm.

National Storytelling Network. An impressive resource! Check out its LISTSERV, Storytell, at www.storynet .org/storytell.html. You can also use the site to search for storytelling events: www.storynet.org/ events/calendar.php. In addition, the NSN publishes *Storytelling Magazine,* which is included with membership. www.storynet.org/.

Pellowski, A. 1995. *The Family Storytelling Handbook.* Atlanta: August House.

Sheppard, T. *Tim Sheppard's Storytelling Resources for Storytellers.* www.timsheppard.co.uk/story/. See especially Storytelling FAQs at www.timsheppard.co.uk/story/faq.html#Introduction, and Storylinks at www.timsheppard.co.uk/story/storylinks.html, an impressive number of wide-ranging, tellable stories.

Storytelling, Self, Society: An Interdisciplinary Journal of Storytelling Studies. www.wsupress.wayne.edu/ journals/detail/storytelling-self-society.

Storytelling World Resource Awards. This link is to the most recent list of awards. Go to http://storytelling world.com/ for the earlier lists. The awards are for stories for telling as well as for background material with potential to be worked up into a story. www.storytellingworld.com/2017/.

"Apps and Sites for Storytelling" *Common Sense Media.* https://www.commonsense.org/education/ top-picks/apps-and-sites-for-storytelling. Common Sense Media is a solid source for current digital storytelling tools.

"Digital Storytelling in the Classroom." 2017. *Creative Educator* (blog). http://creativeeducator.tech4 1earning.com/digital-storytelling. A set of eight articles by various authors about digital storytelling with students.

Levine, A. 2010. *50+ Web 2.0 Ways to Tell a Story.* http://50ways.wikispaces.com/. Levine showcases multiple examples of the same digital story told using different presentation tools and approaches. Still well worth visiting despite some broken links.

Pappas, C. February 28, 2013; updated November 2015. *18 Free Digital Storytelling Tools for Teachers and Students.* https://elearningindustry.com/18-free-digital-storytelling-tools-for-teachers-and-students. This site's commitment to updating content ensures a reasonably current list of digital storytelling tools.

Story Center (formerly the Center for Digital Storytelling) http://storycenter.org/. A very rich resource for facilitated community storytelling. Scroll through the stories on the Story Center YouTube channel to get a sense of what's there: www.youtube.com/user/CenterOfTheStory. See especially the Youth Voices playlist: https://www.youtube.com/playlist?list=PL2zMrq22-Y2t-vKELM2K5jdxzwej54cmF.

CHAPTER 3

Playing to Learn, Learning to Play

A Play and Making Framework for Libraries

Sarah Ward and Sarah A. Evans

INTRODUCTION

Play and the act of making—learning through doing—are important for socio-emotional development, imaginative and creative development, and overall well-being (Piaget 1969; Paley 2004; Whitebread et al. 2009; Myck-Wayne 2010), but what does that have to do with libraries? Play and making are intrinsically related to learning, and more recently libraries have identified themselves as informal learning environments. The importance of learning in informal learning environments is that it "prepares people for lifelong learning. It teaches people that learning is a part of everyday life . . . [It] reinforces learning for its own sake, and reminds us that learning can be both fun and exciting" (Diamond et al. 2009, 13). Play and making are at the heart of creating learning opportunities for children and youth that are both fun and exciting.

Traditionally we have not thought of libraries as spaces where people play or make things. Yet, when we look closer we find that playing and making are happening all the time in our libraries. We often see toddlers building with blocks, a group of elementary students working on a project with Popsicle sticks and glue, and adolescents playing video games. Although these examples are all easily recognizable and valuable forms of play and making, the purpose of this chapter is to reinforce the ideas behind play and making, particularly as they relate to learning in libraries. We propose that beyond these obvious activities, libraries are fundamentally play- and-making-based places and that librarians can actively and intentionally facilitate these activities by thinking creatively about the unique people, resources, and space that libraries embody.

To support the facilitation of play and making programming in libraries, this chapter will explore how libraries already implement play- and making-based practices, why libraries are uniquely positioned to do this work, and ways in which librarians can think differently about their role in creating play and making programming. In addition, we introduce a Play and Making Programming Framework to help librarians design play and making programming by leveraging and thinking critically about their unique resources, people, and spaces. Once you begin working with the ideas presented in this chapter, we hope you will discover the magic of how play and making can help you change your activities into wondrous learning opportunities and simultaneously respond to your community's needs.

WHY ARE PLAY AND MAKING IMPORTANT?

Play and making activities can create memorable experiences by engaging youth mentally, physically, and emotionally and providing them with opportunities to participate in subjects that interest them. Together, play and making encourage creative and imaginative thinking, enhance youth experiences, and support healthy whole-child development.

In the case of programming, play can be understood as a way to engage youth through the imaginative and physical act of play. Play can include videogames, building blocks, taking on characters and roles—any number of activities. It is often understood by adults as "something that children do," yet it contributes to the overall development of youth in the cognitive, social, language, emotional, and physical skill spheres. Over the course of the past few decades, research has increasingly touted the benefits of play and play-based learning (Whitebread et al. 2012). For instance, researchers and practitioners have advocated against cutting recess at schools, arguing that time for play is necessary not only for whole child-development, but also for academic success. Playgrounds have become spaces where designers have created collaborative play opportunities and improved playground structures for fine and gross motor skills. Beyond physical development, play research has particularly promoted play and play-based learning for its ability to help children and youth develop relational skills and more abstract developmental concepts like creativity and imagination. The ability to create an imaginative play space allows children to take on roles, explore identities, work through issues, and build empathy (Paley 2004). Teachers often scaffold play to teach a variety of academic and socio-emotional content. For example, while learning about addition, teachers may have students role-play a grocery store, giving students the props they will need to succeed, such as grocery lists and receipts to help students to practice adding prices.

Lev S. Vygotsky, a developmental theorist, argued that play is fundamental to the learning process because it allows children to perform "a head taller" than their actual level of development (Vygotsky 1978). This means that play does not simply show us where children are developmentally and what they can do on their own but enables children to perform ahead of their developmental level. Play is the place where they can try on new identities, take risks, and explore concepts that they don't yet understand. Play provides children with the opportunity to explore different ways of being in the world and construct new knowledge through the creative production of new play worlds, goals and motivations, tools, and ways of being. It is a process through which youth quite literally *create* their worlds and themselves. In the Vygotskian sense, play and making are intricately linked.

Making emphasizes learning through doing by using material tools, such as art supplies, gears and motors, and found objects (material tools can relate to any object or series of objects that can be manipulated). Making can be playful, but it can also be serious and focused. As with play theories, making creates the conditions under which youth develop and explore their agency and power by creating an authentic product from their experiences, understandings, and collaborations. Contemporary maker culture emphasizes informal, peer-led, and shared learning experiences. Making provides the opportunity for youth to explore their ideas and their experiences through the manipulation of material tools. Youth are in control of the process from ideation to the final project. Although adults may scaffold and help youth, ideally making goes beyond the activity of creating a predetermined object (e.g., creating a craft that has a predetermined end). Making and tinkering in their various forms remain "fundamentally human, historical and cross-cultural" (Vossoughi et al. 2013). The youth in your local library have likely already experienced these processes but perhaps with different materials, purposes, and contexts (e.g., family traditions, 4H Club, etc.).

Makerspaces are becoming increasingly popular in informal learning spaces, such as libraries, museums, and after-school programs, particularly when they relate to STEAM fields. These spaces tend to veer away from the traditional structure of school and learning by giving youth the power to explore, manipulate, and challenge their understandings and themselves. Many researchers focus on libraries' efforts to establish makerspaces, highlighting subsequent positive outcomes for community engagement and improved library image (see Brady et al. 2014; Sheridan et al. 2014; Slatter and Howard 2013). One of the most well-known examples of a library learning lab is the YOUmedia digital learning initiative for teens implemented by the Digital Youth Network and the Chicago Public Library and supported by funding from the MacArthur Foundation. The project exists both physically, with designated spaces, staff, and materials at a public library in downtown Chicago, and virtually, with a website for participants to interact and share their work. YOUmedia and many other makerspaces organize their offerings around principles of Connected Learning (Ito et al. 2013), which seeks to bridge youth's interests, peer mentorship, and academic achievements across contexts. Libraries, with their open mix of space, people, and resources are a natural node in connected learning activities (Hoffman et al. 2016).

Foundational to both play and making is the need for imagination. This means imagining what is and what could be. Imagination becomes the means through which we understand one another and our experiences without having to have the exact same experience (Vygotsky 1978). Take, for example, reading a book. We use the text and story line to imagine the lives of the characters. Through this active use of our imaginations, we can experience something second-hand that we otherwise may never have known. In making activities, youth quite literally imagine as they work with the materials supplied to them: What happens if we connect this gear to that gear? What happens if I mix red with blue and then add on a button? They may even imagine the end result and focus their process toward achieving that result. Although the process of creation is integral, it is imagination that drives the process. It is the great workhorse of learning (Egan 2015). The ability to imagine correlates directly to the creative problem-solving required both in employment and in life.

HOW DO CHILDREN PLAY?

Play can take many forms depending on the age and developmental ability of the child. Very young children, from birth to age five, engage in exploration, then dramatic play, and then social and physical play (Jones 2011, as cited in Nespeca 2012; Lerner and Greenip 2004), as they begin to learn about the world around them. Children build oral skills, such as communication and vocabulary, as well as socio-emotional and problem-solving skills by interacting with others and acting out their experiences using the tools of toys, games, and dress-up clothing. Children's brains receive a boost, too, when they play in nurturing environments (Diamant-Cohen et. al. 2012). Play enables a child-constructed learning space in which they develop and revise their own rules of play (Paley 2004). Constructive play, using implements such as blocks and LEGOs and Play-Doh, is also important for this age group (Nespeca 2012). During constructive play, young children can engage in dialogic practice as they work with others to build the structures and build a play pattern around the structure, which sparks curiosity and creativity. Children also can hone their physical abilities by using both fine and gross motor skills as they build with blocks and move around their structures during their play.

The public library is well-suited to support play for young children. Through both orchestrated storytimes and open-ended programs that use blocks and toys, the library can be a door to crucial, critical learning development through play for young children. And the children's librarian is a crucial piece of that development process, as the facilitator and mediator of the play experience (Diamant-Cohen et al. 2012).

As children enter and progress through school, they are able to focus for longer periods of time and engage in more complex play activities (Stanford n.d.). Play becomes increasingly social, and children must navigate bigger groups and use more complicated social skills. Competition comes into the picture as children this age learn about themselves in relation to others. They are also learning self-regulation and self-discipline. To support this, libraries can offer maker-based programs that enable school-aged children to work together toward a common goal, building cooperation and collaboration. Programs can feature STEM-related material as well as art and music to encourage creative expression. This continues into the tween and teenage years, eleven to eighteen, as teens move into sports and other group-organized activities, while at the same time developing their own individual interests and working to form their own identities (Child Development Institute n.d.). Library programs can help to cultivate these emergent group and individual interests through play and making programs that are widely varied and open-ended, without the barriers and stresses of standards and outcomes typical of school-related projects.

Through the careful consideration of spaces, people, and resources, we believe that libraries are ideal places for engaging youth in these ways. In the following section, we explore what it is that libraries already do with play- and making-based practices, why libraries are uniquely positioned to do this work, and ways in which librarians can think differently about their role in creating play and making programming.

PLAY AND MAKING AT THE LIBRARY: A LOOK AT THE SPACE, PEOPLE, AND RESOURCES

Libraries structure people, resources, and space in ways that are inherently different from traditional learning institutions like schools. We will first explore some of the ways that libraries currently and commonly offer play- and making-based programming. We will then describe what it is that makes the people, resources, and spaces of libraries different from those at other learning institutions and how they might plan for and create unique play- and making-based programs.

Types of library programs. Traditionally, participation in libraries is self-directed and voluntary, with resources such as books, toys, puppets, puzzles, and child-friendly technology distributed across the designated children's and teen areas, awaiting their attention. Through programs, librarians mediate the play and making experience for children, providing environments and materials rich in learning potential. This is often done through passive programs, librarian-directed programs, and youth-directed programs.

In librarian-directed programs, there is a continuum of adult interaction that is dependent upon what can meet the demands of the activity and the needs of the child and family. For example, during a storytime aimed at babies and their caregivers, the librarian

■ Program types

Passive programs—materials (toys, art or building materials, etc.) are laid out in the youth space to be used by anyone whenever they choose.

Librarian-directed programs—scheduled programs that are designed and led by the librarian.

Youth directed programs—scheduled programs that are designed and led by the youth with guidance and support from the librarian.

will actively model (often by holding a doll or some other prop to direct attention) reading, talking, and playing with a baby, asking adults to imitate them. Yet during an afterschool LEGO building program, the librarian is more likely to ask questions and make suggestions to encourage youth agency instead of giving direct instructions to be followed.

Adolescents typically enter the library and pursue activities driven by personal needs, whether these are academic, entertainment, or social. Not infrequently, young people may attend a program simply because they happened to be in the building when the librarian announced it was starting. There is almost always a high degree of participant input and choice within the program activities. High-quality library programs for anyone from young children to older adolescents happen when librarians attend to the interests and needs of their patrons, then provide resources and activities accordingly.

While we do not promise to offer an extensive list, the following examples are some of the more common programs that involve play and making that we have seen across our work:

Storytimes. Typically involving young children and their parents, family members, and other caregivers, these programs focus on providing literacy-rich experiences. They may include a librarian reading books to the children, interspersed with physical activities and rhymes, and often end with sensory activities, music, art, movement, or playtime using special toys.

Gaming. For older children and teens, the librarian provides games to play. These can be board or video games. Older classics, such as chess, are often as popular as video games. Sometimes the librarian will play if one of the youth needs a partner or to encourage participation.

Crafts. Craft-oriented programming can vary from knitting circles to sessions focusing on a specific craft, such as duct-tape wallets. During these programs, the libraries provide the materials, directions, and resources necessary to complete the project. The librarian may demonstrate the process in the beginning and then help the participants create their own.

Cooking. Similar to craft programming, a cooking program is usually directed toward creating a specific final product, for example, chocolates. Libraries supply the materials and directions to accomplish the end goal. Again, the librarian may demonstrate the process in the beginning and then help the participants create their own products.

Theme program. This type of programming can be centered around a book, series, movie, or popular television show. Although all programming can be connected to a theme, specific-theme programming often involves many play elements, such as trivia, a related game, encouraged costumes, and so on.

Coding. Increasingly, libraries are providing the resources for youth to learn coding via a specific software or manipulative, such as Minecraft, Scratch, or Makey Makey. In addition, robot-building activities span both the coding and the building program categories as youth engage in the making activity.

Building. Programs that focus on building are used for all age groups. These might include building with specific items, such as LEGOs, robots, or even popsicle sticks. In these instances, the librarians provide the materials and usually display a finished product or demonstrate the process.

Program categories may overlap. For instance, a library might have an entire month dedicated to one book series or exploration of a subject, during which time parts of the programming follow that theme. Although this is not an exhaustive list of all the ways libraries plan for play and making, many of these examples span age groups and interests. Within these programs, librarians typically combine space, resources, and their own practices to engage babies, children, tweens, teenagers, and families in play and making.

Library people, resources, and space. Learning in libraries, even within a specific program, is often self-directed, which is one of the factors that makes library learning so unique. Research findings about voluntary learning situations are marked by persistence across a self-selected period of time, learning through repeated trial and error, and plenty of envisioning time during which individuals ponder, imagine, and plan (Bevan et al. 2013; Heath 2004, 2012). These markers align with those of play and maker movements. To understand better the potential that exists to engage with play- and making-centered programming, we must first explore what it is that makes the library so well-suited to this kind of work.

People. Librarians' training and experience in a wide range of information resources prepares them to be the perfect play and making program designers. They can identify youth's interests and offer concrete resources for the next step in the play and making journey. Librarians are natural connectors who quickly recognize that their work fits within the theoretical and practical framework of Connected Learning (Hoffman et al. 2016). Yet connection alone cannot fully capture the multiple and often overlapping ways in which librarians connect the young to one another, to resources, to conversation and its norms, and to on-going curiosity. Youth services librarians understand that simply giving a child the name of a book or website is unlikely to scaffold that patron into a critical thinker, effective lifelong learner, or democratic citizen. Through their relationships with young people and knowledge of a wide range of resources, librarians provide *connections with context* (Evans 2017). It is this skill that turns the act of providing information into a sustaining support for continued learning.

In addition, youth bring with them their own funds of knowledge around play and making. At the heart of the "funds of knowledge" concept is that "[p]eople are competent, they have knowledge, and their life experiences have given them that knowledge" (González, Moll, and Amanti 2005). The idea stemmed from researchers and teachers working together to understand the home and community lives of students. We would argue that youth bring to the library a variety of ways that they play and make within their day-to-day lives and that librarians are uniquely positioned to engage students' funds of knowledge. Librarians who spend time with youth and families, thus finding out more about their interests, can deepen learning for those individuals, and also discover community-based resources their own library patrons can offer.

Resources. Play and making can be stimulated through access to a variety of resources. Libraries are the ultimate resource centers for curious youth. Many other places that youth visit (e.g., museums) can offer materials for exploration, and may even feature special youth exhibits or programs. However, libraries, by their very nature, are different from community spaces where resources are highly curated and directed at a narrow range of topics (e.g., local history, fine art, dance classes, etc.). In contrast, a library's scope of content for which it can provide material is broad, and with the addition of computers connected to the internet, nearly limitless. Libraries of course have books, but also may offer zines, access to the internet, computer games, toys, arts and crafts materials, or group activities. Additionally, there is far less adult-directed "curriculum" than in after-school activities in other contexts. Librarians are trained to uncover individual interests and needs through reference interviews, then provide resources targeted to meet those interests and needs. A librarian would never respond to a child's request for information related to skateboarding by saying, "No, today we are focusing on tennis, so I can give you information about that instead." A library's curriculum, or resources for learning, is individually centered and youth directed in ways that other community organizations can rarely accommodate. Such freedom to explore varied interests invites a diversity of youth to participate.

People also become resources accessible within the library. All patrons, young or old, bring their own funds of knowledge to their participation in library activities. Additionally, librarians create context for youth around materials by embedding questioning in regular discourse. When youth are curious about topics, or have special interests or needs, they seek the after-school company of peers and supportive adults with the type of conversational openers that a librarian offers. By being genuinely interested in what youth think, want, and do, librarians create a space for back-and-forth, ongoing conversations. Such talk flows throughout a library program as librarians, youth, and sometimes whole families play or make together. The dialogue extends even further when librarians and youth ask follow-up questions to elicit each other's thoughts at subsequent meetings. Children and teens answer eagerly because they know these are not tests or a trick questions as may be the case when it might be coming from other adults in other situations. Thus, the librarian becomes a safe and trusted resource for engaging in extended conversation, which is a valuable skill for future academic and employment settings.

Space. Libraries are some of the last places in society where people can spend time free of charge. They provide physical space to explore as well as unstructured time. As societal demands increase, many children are as overscheduled as their parents, and lose precious opportunities for the unstructured thought needed for creativity and well-being. Library spaces can restore these opportunities to both youth and adults.

Room design influences the extent to which people can come together and encounter new ideas and experiences (Aabø and Audunson 2012; Alistair and Simon 2012). Most libraries employ flexible furniture arrangements to support a range of activities from individual relaxation to focused group work. The modern library staff focuses less on shushing and more on maintaining an inviting atmosphere. Even if a separate multipurpose room isn't available, you may designate special times and library sections where youth can be as loud as they like during play or product construction.

The particular nexus of people, resources, and space in the library creates fertile ground for librarians to expand their play and making programming, and to consider the implications of each of these on their programs. In the following section, we demonstrate how librarians might critically examine their assets, objectives, and the power of youth's initiative and imagination to create programs that extend their missions and goals and deepen their connections with their constituency.

A PLAY AND MAKING PROGRAMMING FRAMEWORK FOR LIBRARIANS

The practices of library staff and patrons create a socially constructed community plentiful with learning potential. Every day in libraries across the nation and the world, activities bring together people, resources, and space to create lasting learning connections. Yet we argue that there is little in the field on how to do this critically with play and making at the center. Furthermore, by considering the nexus of space, resources, and play, librarians may be able to develop the kind of programming that goes beyond traditional types of play and making and move toward more creative and equitable practices. To this end, we created the following framework for librarians considering expanding their play and making programming and practices. Practitioners can use the framework to identify patterns, consider current practices, generate ideas, and reflect.

Although there are several factors to consider when designing programming for play and making, we argue that there are four, foundational and central tenets to this kind of work: Participation, Process, Agency, and Collaboration. In the framework, we explore how librarians can design for play and making programming by leveraging and thinking critically about their unique resources, people, and space.

1. **Participation differs across age groups and with individual kids.** Familiarize yourself with the developmental stages to gain a sense of what participation might look like for a three-year-old, as compared to that of an adolescent. Design play and making spaces on the fundamental notion that there is no "right" way to participate.
2. **Process often involves failing, making a mess, frustration, exuberance, and ah-ha! moments.** By considering process, you can move away from a focus on the end product, which enables youth to stay in the moment and to develop at their own pace.
3. **Agency signifies power.** When designing for play and making, you must acknowledge and make space for youths' prior experiences and knowledge, positioning them as experts, with you and their peers functioning as co-learners.
4. **Collaboration looks different among individual youth.** If a young person is playing alone, it does not necessarily mean they are not engaged or collaborating. However, by providing a space for kids to share their knowledge and experiences, your collaboration can help them solve problems, develop life skills, and encourage relationships.

The following table sets out these four central tenets to assist you in planning programs that take advantage of play and making. There is no right or wrong way to adopt this framework. It is intended to inspire critical thinking about what you regularly offer your patrons: people, resources, and space. But your choices will differ based on current objectives. For example, after preschool storytime, the librarian may direct young ones to manipulate specific objects or make a simple craft, with their attention focused on modeling for the children. Or they could put out various toys for the children to play with independently and focus their attention on discussing parenting resources with adults, some of whom may be from underserved communities. One approach isn't better than the other; each choice supports equally valuable purposes. The key is to consider your program activities over time and how they fulfill your institution's service goals to meet community needs. As you explore

	PEOPLE	RESOURCES	SPACE
Participation	• Identify who will participate in this activity. Anyone and everyone? Certain subgroups (teens, babies, etc.)? • Delineate the objectives for working with these people in this program.	• Make a list of your library resources. Which of these resources facilitate participation? Are there rules around the resources (i.e., will computers be available for the required amount of time?).	• Reflect on the ways that your library's physical and virtual spaces are designed to enhance participation. Do they prohibit participation?
Process	• Consider those who will be involved in the imaginative phase. • If needed, who will supervise or demonstrate the use of materials?	• Use library materials to encourage imaginative thinking. This might involve creating connections between books and play and making programming, or it could also include providing whiteboards for brainstorming. • Decide which materials are you will provide for youth to work with. Do the materials relate to the program in some way? • If your library has gallery space, consider using it to display student projects.	• Think about the ways that the library is a space that activates imagination and use those observations to design initial programming. • Stay away from critiquing youth while they are coming up with ideas, no matter how absurd those ideas might seem. • Use the library's space to tell stories and encourage imaginative thinking. • Consider what materials the library can provide. • If you plan to create a product, think about whether it could be housed within the library. What implications might that have?
Agency	• Ask students what they know about a topic before inserting yourself. • If students need help making something, find ways to support them instead of taking over. • Encourage your volunteers or visitors to trust the youth.	• Engage student expertise and curiosity around the resources. In a book-based activity, how can you encourage youth to share interpretations be brought forward? If they are playing make-believe with kitchen supplies, can you allow the children to direct the work?	• Consider how you present yourself within the space and how the space allows you to present yourself (i.e., do you have an urge to control behaviors and products?) Where can you create space for youth ownership balanced with objectives?
Collaboration	• You become the connector between youth and experts.	• Create opportunities for peer connection and peer coaching through resources and with materials.	• Structure the actual space, e.g., the placement of chairs and access to spaces, to promote co-play and collaboration.

the framework and consider the capacity of your library, you can clarify your objectives for utilizing play and making in your programming.

The table on the previous page should help you to think about all the different options available to you, so that you can choose which components would be appropriate to apply in your local context. You can apply the four tenets to the elements of people, resources, and space to find additional ways to deepen learning and connection. But there is no one right way to conduct a program. Each of us must localize activities to best serve the needs of our patrons. The table simply offers a way to think more deeply and critically about the many ways play and making permeate your library.

As a final note, we would like to acknowledge that just as public schools tend to have inequalities based on neighborhood, public libraries, too, have different financial and material support available for youth activities. Library programming can also vary and not all are directly related to play and making. They can include everything from artist performances to console-gaming competitions to crafting activities. Planning for programming often requires both time and money, especially if you are dreaming of new spaces and technological materials. We created this framework for librarians to use when planning for play and making programming to work with their existing resources and space. However, regardless of the resources and space, a thoughtful and committed librarian is the irreplaceable element when designing and delivering meaningful library programs that promote and encourage play and making.

REFERENCES

Aabø, S., and R. Audunson. 2012. "Use of Library Space and the Library as Place." *Library and Information Science Research* 34 (2): 138–49.

Alistair, B., and P. Simon. 2012. "From Civic Place to Digital Space: The Design of Public Libraries in Britain from Past to Present." *Library Trends* 61 (2): 440–70.

Bevan, B., P. Bell, R. Stevens, and A. Razfar. 2013. *LOST Opportunities: Learning in Out-of-School Time.* New York: Springer.

Brady, T., C. Salas, A. Nuriddin, W. Rodgers, and B. Subramaniam. 2014. "MakeAbility: Creating Accessible Makerspace Events in a Public Library." *Public Library Quarterly* 33 (4): 330–47.

Child Development Institute. n.d. "Play and Developmental Stages." https://childdevelopmentinfo.com/child-development/play-work-of-children/p12/#.Wi3BZLT80Wo 1/7.

Diamant-Cohen, B., T. Prendergast, C. Estrovitz, C. Banks, and K. Van Der Veen. 2012. "We Play Here: Bringing the Power of Play into Children's Libraries." *Children and Libraries* 10 (1): 3–10, 52.

Diamond, J., J. J. Luke, and D. H. Uttal, 2009. *Practical Evaluation Guide: Tools for Museums and Other Informal Educational Settings.* Lanham, MD: AltaMira Press.

Egan. K. 2015. "Preface to the First Edition." In *Engaging Imagination and Developing Creativity in Education,* 2nd ed., edited by K. Egan, G. Judson, and K. Madej. Newcastle Upon Tyne, UK: Cambridge Scholars.

Evans, S. A. 2017. "Sparking and Sustaining Adolescent Learning: Embodied Values, Contextualized Literacies, and Developing Identities at the Public Library." PhD dissertation, University of Washington.

González, N., L. C. Moll, and C. Amanti. 2005. *Funds of Knowledge: Theorizing Practice in Households, Communities, and Classrooms.* Mahwah, NJ: Lawrence Erlbaum Associates.

Heath, S. B. 2004. "Risks, Rules, and Roles: Youth Perspectives on the Work of Learning for Community Development." In *Joining Society: Social Interaction and Learning in Adolescence and Youth,* 41–70, New York: Cambridge University Press.

_____. 2012. *Words at Work and Play: Three Decades in Family and Community Life.* Cambridge; New York: Cambridge University Press.

Hoffman, K., M. Subramaniam, S. Kawas, L. Scaff, and K. Davis. 2016. *Connected Libraries: Surveying the Current Landscape and Charting a Path to the Future.* College Park, MD: The Connected Library Project. https://papers.ssrn.com/sol3/papers.cfm?abstract_id=2982532.

Ito, M., K. Gutierrez, S. Livingstone, B. Penuel, J. Rhodes, K. Salen, J. Schor, J. Sefton-Green, and S. C. Watkins. 2013. *Connected Learning: An Agenda for Research and Design.* Irvine, CA: Digital Media and Learning Research Hub.

Lerner, C., and S. Greenip. 2004. "The Power of Play: Learning through Play from Birth to Three." *Zero to Three.* https://www.zerotothree.org/resources/311-the-power-of-play.

Myck-Wayne, J. 2010. In Defense of Play: Beginning the Dialog about the Power of Play. *Young Exceptional Children* 13 (4): 14–23. doi:10.1177/1096250610376616.

Nespeca, S. 2012. "The Importance of Play, Particularly Constructive Play, in Public Library Programming." ALSC White Paper. http://www.ala.org/alsc/sites/ala.org.alsc/files/content/FINAL%20Board%20Approved%20White%20Paper%20on%20Play.pdf.

Paley, V. G. 2004. *A Child's Work: The Importance of Fantasy Play.* Chicago: University of Chicago Press.

Sheridan, K., E. R. Halverson, B. Litts, L. Brahms, L. Jacobs-Priebe, and T. Owens. 2014. "Learning in the Making: A Comparative Case Study of Three Makerspaces." *Harvard Educational Review* 84 (4): 505–31.

Slatter, D., and Z. Howard. 2013. "A Place to Make, Hack, and Learn: Makerspaces in Australian Public Libraries." *Australian Library Journal* 62 (4): 272–84.

Smith, P. K. 2009. *Children and Play: Understanding Children's Worlds,* 1st ed., vol. 1. New York: John Wiley and Sons.

Stanford Children's Health. "The Growing Child: School-Age (6 to 12 Years)." www.stanfordchildrens.org/en/topic/default?id=the-growing-child-school-age-6-to-12-years-90-P02278&sid=.

Vossoughi, S., M. Escudé, F. Kong, and P. Hooper. 2013. "Tinkering, Learning and Equity in the After-School Setting." Paper presented at FabLearn 2013, October 27–28, 2013. https://pdfs.semanticscholar.org/ab32/38c335e8a325760c83c370386fa98171dc20.pdf.

Vygotsky, L. 1978. *The Role of Play in Development.* In *Mind in Society* 92–104, Translated by M. Cole. Cambridge, MA: Harvard University Press.

Whitebread, D., M. Basilio, M. Kuvalja, and M. Verma. 2012. *The Importance of Play: A Report on the Value of Children's Play with a Series of Policy Recommendations.* www.importanceofplay.eu/IMG/pdf/dr_david_whitebread_-_the_importance_of_play.pdf.

Whitebread, D., P. Coltman, H. Jameson, and R. Lander, 2009. "Play, Cognition and Self- Regulation: What Exactly Are Children Learning When They Learn through Play?" *Educational and Child Psychology* 26 (2): 40–52.

RECOMMENDED RESOURCES

González, N., L. C. Moll, and C. Amanti. 2005. *Funds of Knowledge: Theorizing Practice in Households, Communities, and Classrooms.* Mahwah, N.J.: Lawrence Erlbaum Associates.

Honeyford, M. A., and K. Boyd. 2015. "Learning through Play: Portraits, Photoshop, and Visual Literacy Practices." *Journal of Adolescent and Adult Literacy* 59 (1): 63–73. doi:10.1002/jaal.428.

Honnold, R. 2013. "Library as Makerspace." *Voice of Youth Advocates* 36 (3).

Koh, K., and J. Abbas. 2015. "Competencies for Information Professionals in Learning Labs and Makerspaces." *Journal of Education for Library and Information Science* 56 (2): 114–29.

Loertscher, D. V., L. Preddy, and B. Derry. 2013. "Makerspaces in the School Library Learning Commons and the uTEC Maker Model." *Teacher Librarian* 41 (2): 48–51.

McGowan, V. M., Ventura, and P. Bell, P. 2017. "Reverse Engineering." *Science and Children* 54 (8): 68–72.

Nespeca, S. 2012. "The Importance of Play, Particularly Constructive Play, in Public Library Programming." ALSC White Paper.

Open Education Database. A Librarian's Guide to Makerspaces: 16 Resources. http://oedb.org/ilibrarian/a-librarians-guide-to-makerspaces/.

Paley, V. G. 1992. "You Can't Say You Can't Play." *Programming Librarian*. www.programminglibrarian.org/.

Ralli, J., and R. G. Payne. 2016. "Let's Play at the Library: Creating Innovative Play Experiences for Babies and Toddlers." *Library Trends* 65 (1): 41-63.

CHAPTER 4

Librarians as Media Mentors

Building Media Literacy with Programming, Advisory, and Access

Amy Koester and Claudia Haines

INTRODUCTION

In many ways, the landscape in which librarians now find themselves with regard to technology programming first emerged in 2011, when the iPad—the first tablet device to hit the consumer market—debuted in 2010, and librarians and other youth-serving professionals began to experiment with this new technology tool. One of these librarians was Cen Campbell who, in November of 2011, decided to begin documenting her explorations into digital storytimes on a personal blog, which she called Little eLit (https://littleelit.com/). As Campbell explained in her early posts, she saw the potential of this new medium to serve as another tool in the toolkit for supporting children and their literacy development. Campbell continued to test out digital storytime strategies and other iPad programming ideas in libraries and museums, and other librarians across the country were doing the same. A cohort of those early adopters gathered under the banner of Little eLit, both to learn from the trials of colleagues and to share their own experiences on the growing website. By 2014, when Little eLit combined efforts with the Association for Library Service to Children (ALSC) and the iSchool at the University of Washington to survey the field to get a firmer grasp of current library practice of new media use, 71 percent of the 415 libraries surveyed reported using one or more kinds of new media in their children's programming (Mills et al. 2015). The use of technology in programming was already quite widespread.

What was clearly an emerging core practice was also about to receive the name by which it has since been known: *media mentorship*. The term *media mentor* was coined by Lisa Guernsey, Director of the New America Foundation's Early Literacy Initiative, in her 2014 TEDx Talk "How the iPad Affects Young Children, and What We Can Do about It." In the talk, she explored the landscape of new digital media and children—young children in particular. Citing the relative newness of this landscape and the sometimes contradictory recommendations for parents regarding their children's technology use, Guernsey presented the hypothetical that resonated across librarianship: "What if we were to commit to ensuring that every family with young children had access to a media mentor? Truly, what if every child—every family—had access to a person who could act as guide and resource with regard to emerging media and technology?"

This question served as a call to arms for many youth librarians. The underlying sentiment resonated with what we already understood about our roles in libraries serving youth: that we are experts in books for children—the original library medium—and it is fundamental to our jobs to cultivate high-quality collections; to connect children to the best books for their interests and needs and help their caregivers to do so as well; and to create opportunities for children to engage with books and literature in a manner that supports their curiosity and development. This role is central to library service to youth and has been since Anne Carroll Moore insisted that libraries are designed for children, too (Walter 2004). Now, over 100 years later, youth librarians remain dedicated to this role—only now, media encompasses much more than books. All types of technology are in play, and both access and experience benefit children. How is a youth librarian—a media mentor—to respond?

> **New media** refers to any media that uses text, sound, images, and video in a digital setting. It can include e-books, apps, digital music, Makey Makeys, websites, robots, digital audiobooks, computer programs, paper circuits, movies, and more (Haines, Campbell, and ALSC 2016).

Media mentors, as defined in the 2015 white paper from the Association for Library Service to Children, have two core roles. First is the responsibility to "support children and their families in their decisions and practice around media use" (Campbell et al. 2015) Second, media mentors also have access to, and share, "recommendations for and research on children's media use (Campbell et al. 2015). So library staff in the service of youth—media mentors—are, by the nature of their positions, people who introduce children and their families to quality media in any format. Library media mentors use promising and research-based practices to share this media with all families, knowing that an important part of their work involves bridging potential access and skills divides that may exist because of limited resources.

Following the publication of the white paper, the revised ALSC Core Competencies (2015) reflect the ideas of media mentorship throughout: supporting all families by assessing and meeting their information, media, and literacy needs. Media mentorship is specifically addressed in parts II, "Reference and User Services"; III, "Programming Skills"; and IV, "Knowledge, Curation and Management of Materials." Including technology, digital media, and new media in these sections represents the three common types of media mentorship: programming, media advisory, and supported access (Haines, Campbell, and ALSC 2016). Considering new media an essential resource alongside traditional media, instead of an afterthought or an extra, allows library staff to serve both new and familiar families in new ways. By incorporating the newest media into reference interviews, the resources available at the library and online, and programs like storytime, summer learning, and outreach, youth services staff are fully embracing the role of media mentors and in the process increasing the effectiveness and connectedness of their services.

WHAT DOES MEDIA MENTORSHIP HAVE TO DO
WITH YOUTH PROGRAMMING?

If *media* in the *media mentorship* refers to the types of media that are generally consumed (e.g., books, audiobooks, videos, apps), how does media mentorship relate to youth programming? The answer lies in the skills and abilities of a core goal of library programming: literacy. It can be argued that every aspect of the work we do, materials we provide, and programs we offer in the youth library feed into our overarching goal of supporting the literacy development of the children in our communities. The broad concept of literacy is multifaceted; it refers not only to the ability to decode and comprehend the words on a page, but to the myriad other abilities fundamental to school and life success in the twenty-first century. To recognize and understand letters and the sounds those letters make is early literacy. To interpret and apply information about how the world works is science literacy. And to be able to access, make meaningful sense of, and apply information from technological and media sources is media literacy. So, if media mentors are those who support the media literacy of the children and families we serve, the youth librarian's role as media mentor entails the practice of engaging our patrons in programming and other learning experiences in pursuit of greater media literacy.

Media mentorship in libraries will look different depending on each community's unique needs, but there are commonalities across practice. Since the widespread adoption of mobile technology and new media, much of what librarians do as media mentors can be grouped into three categories: supported access to curated content, media advisory (an evolved form of reader advisory), and programming (Haines, Campbell, and ALSC 2016). Although programming is the focus of this book, it is important to consider it as one aspect of media mentorship taking place in the broader context of a library that supports the media, literacy, and information needs of families through all three.

Since the launch of the iPad in 2010 and the many new media tools that have since become available, a plethora of research about digital media and kids has emerged. Organizations like the American Academy of Pediatrics, the Joan Ganz Cooney Center, the Fred Rogers Center, the National Association for the Education of Young Children, the United States Department of Education, Zero to Three, the New America Foundation, and the Association for Library Service to Children have published information regarding using new media with children, and in some cases they have included recommendations based on recent findings. Librarians can use available research and expert recommendations to guide their work.

FRAMEWORKS FOR APPLYING MEDIA MENTORSHIP
TO TECHNOLOGY PROGRAMMING

When considering the goals and implications of technology-based programming for youth, three main frameworks provide guidance and structure to the role of the library staff, as well as the format, content, and setting of the program or activity. The first two frameworks—the principles of media mentorship and the librarian's strategies for supporting development of media literacy—are broadly applicable across the full range of ages served by youth-facing library services. The third, known by the acronym HOMAGO, is focused more toward the older end of this age spectrum.

Basic Principles of Media Mentorship

The mantra of the media mentor is foundational to technology programming for youth: to "support children and their families in their decisions and practice around media use" (Campbell et al. 2015). The framework of media mentorship defines two core functions for library staff who provide technology programming opportunities. The first is the function as guide, specifically in regard to providing guidance in accessing (and even deciding whether or not to access, or how much to access) any given technology. This role of media mentorship helps youth and families to answer "what?" questions about technology. What technology might they use? What can they do with that technology? If applicable, what are the recommendations for best practices for the particular age and abilities of the child who might use it? When providing technology programming for the children on the younger end of the age spectrum, library staff will guide caregivers just as much as the children themselves.

The second function of library staff is to model—more specifically, to model ways of utilizing, effectively, the technology at hand. In this capacity, media mentors assist youth and families in answering the "how?" and "so what?" questions surrounding different technologies. First, how does it work? How does a user put the technology into practice? Moving beyond the basics of competency in operating a technology, the question becomes "so what can you do or create with this technology?" If the media mentor as guide opens the door for patrons to see what is available and to determine what, if any, technology they would like to pursue, the media mentor as model actively throws open that door to show the potential uses of the technology. When thinking about applying this framework to technology programming, it is vital to recognize that the best programs will include both aspects: introduce youth to a tech tool, and then show them the possibilities for creating with it.

Three Ways Librarians Support Media Literacy Development

There are three important ways in which media mentors support the development of media literacy in their patrons. The first is through direct programming designed with the child audience in mind. These types of programs should be created with a view toward what is developmentally appropriate for the intended participants. When a potential program involves screen media or other technological elements, media mentors investigate the recommendations and research of experts that focus on the best use of the technology they plan to use. When a potential program involves children manipulating media tools independently, media mentors consider the fine motor skills of the children in the intended audience as well as their ability to navigate the technology in the program intuitively and confidently. Media mentors do not design media and technology programs blindly, but rather use their existing knowledge of developmentally appropriate programming, supplemented with research and best practices.

Youth librarians also support media literacy development through media evaluation, in which they apply their traditional expertise in assessing children's media to a range of formats. Much like picture books have different evaluation criteria than audiobooks, story apps and programmable robots have unique characteristics that define their use. Regardless of format, however, content must be of excellent quality. It requires time to explore, for example, what apps use a dyslexic-friendly font, or which electrical circuit kit is preschool-friendly, but not every librarian needs to be an expert on every tool. Similar to the book reviews published in *School Library Journal* and *Horn Book,* librarians and digital media experts are sharing reviews of the newest media formats and titles. Librarians and library systems have also created rubrics, like the *Evaluating Apps and New Media for Young Children: A Rubric* (Media Mentor Resources n.d.), to evaluate apps for storytime and other uses. The Kids Inclusion and Diversity Media Action Project (KIDMAP), formerly #DiversityinApps, created the *DIG Checklist* (2017), an extensive list of questions librarians, reviewers, and even families can ask about the quality of a wide range of digital media, including factors of diversity and inclusion in content and design.

A common way to provide hands-on media advisory is through supported access to curated content. Librarians who provide Minecraft access on their public computers, provide mounted iPads with featured apps, or circulate STEM kits in-house have used their evaluation skills to pull together resources that support kids and their families. Providing free access to high-quality digital media ensures that income level, geographic location, and other traditional societal barriers are not factors that influence which kids can play, learn, and explore with these tools. Access isn't the only factor contributing to the digital divide. In the same way that giving preschoolers an alphabet book won't teach them their ABCs, simply providing physical access to technology does little to address the digital divide that affects children from different backgrounds. The digital divide has at its heart a skills gap, rather than an access gap, and so libraries that provide supported access—or access that is both mediated and mentored—are intentionally guiding youth in how to meaningfully and purposefully use different media for learning, exploration, and creation.

Finally, media mentors support media literacy development for children and families by supporting children's caregivers so they may act as media mentors. As models and educators, librarians provide experiences and access to resources that empower families to make the right decisions for their kids and teens. Just as with traditional media and initiatives like early literacy, if librarians are including high-quality media in programs, modeling its positive use to support learning and relationships, and sharing tips on digital media use and evaluation, caregivers benefit.

Hanging Out, Messing Around, and Geeking Out (HOMAGO)

When considering older elementary and teenage youth, any ventures into technology programming cannot be disentangled from this age group's socio-emotional needs—thus the continued relevancy of the HOMAGO framework first shared by Ito et. al. in 2010 when considering programming for these ages. *HOMAGO* is an acronym for "hanging out, messing around, and geeking out," a three-pronged framework for understanding and supporting the social behaviors of tweens and teens. When considering possible technology programming, library staff must first keep in mind what is often the primary goal of any interactions for older youth: to hang out and socialize with their friends. Research cited by Ito and colleagues demonstrates that this desire to be with friends is paramount: a library can offer the coolest program on the most popular topic among teens, but if the program does not offer opportunities to socialize throughout, its chances of success are low. *Hanging out* is the basis on which any program for tweens and teens, including technology programming, is built.

The next layer in the framework is *messing around*—the opportunity for youth to explore something new and try it out in a noncommittal, low-risk manner. *Messing around* is just as it sounds; it's about trying something out for fun rather than for any specific (read: academic) purpose. Especially for tweens and teens for whom access to a range of technologies is not consistent, messing around gives them opportunities to fiddle, tinker, and experiment without risk of appearing to fail at a new skill or tool. Messing around is about experimentation and play. From the perspective of the library staff creating a program, messing around means providing easy access to technologies in a non-rigid atmosphere. It requires providing the technology and describing a few possible uses, as opposed to mandating a single particular activity or mandatory project. If hanging out is about structuring a program so that socializing permeates the program, messing around is about providing multiple, low-stakes on-ramps for trying out new tech within that same program.

The final component of HOMAGO is *geeking out*—the deeper dive into specific skills development and goal-oriented tasks using technology. Think of programs for kids who self-identify as interested in coding; they're primed to geek out in their area of interest and to jump into a more structured coding activity or challenge. Geeking out concentrates the level of broad engagement demonstrated by tweens and teens messing around and funnels it into focused activities that promote both further exploration and discrete skill development. If messing around gives youth access to five different possible uses of Arduinos, geeking out centers on one particular use and encourages interested youth to build and develop their skills around that challenge. Although geeking out is at the tip of the HOMAGO pyramid, representing the highest levels of demonstrated interest and engagement, it's important to recognize that geeking out will ideally happen concurrently with hanging out and messing around. Even for youth with clear, deep interest in a topic, the basic principles of a social setting and opportunities to explore freely remain vital.

TECHNOLOGY PROGRAMMING IN PRACTICE

While specific programs are shared elsewhere in this book, we thought it important to articulate some clear examples of technology programming in practice as it relates to the HOMAGO framework. The following programs, divided broadly by age and type of audience, come from our own practice or from those with which we are personally familiar.

Ages Five and Under

Recognizing the widespread use of new media by families, including young children, librarians across the country are integrating new media into the programming they offer their youngest patrons (Rideout 2013). Although research has demonstrated that high-quality digital technology can complement learning and literacy when it is used intentionally, the use of new media with young children remains the most discussed and debated aspect of media mentorship (NAEYC and Rogers Center 2012). Due to the intense ongoing dialogue around digital media use with young children, we felt it important to include a wider range of examples to illustrate excellent practice.

New media is integrated into storytimes at the Homer Public Library (Alaska) to engage new learners or engage learners in new ways. We share iPad story and play apps that relate to the program's theme and extend learning. For example, we use Miximal, a deceptively simple app offered by Yatatoy, which is based on the timeless flip book format, with children's songs to help children hear the sounds that make up words (in this case, animal names). Being able to hear the sounds of individual syllables, in any home language, is a skill children will use when they formally learn to read.

Short "asides" about the digital media in use provide opportunities to pass on tips to grown-ups to support both early literacy and positive digital media behaviors like joint media engagement. Also known as coviewing, joint media engagement enhances learning for young children, and shared experiences keep the focus on fostering positive relationships. In addition to sharing these tips verbally, we share the information in written form throughout the library, on our website, and in a monthly early literacy article (Takeuchi and Stevens 2011).

As with programs across the country, the Homer Public Library's storytimes also incorporate movement and dance using digital music created by well-known children's musicians from around the world. Using apps like Sound Cloud, Pandora, Apple Music, YouTube, and Spotify, rhythms and lyrics are accessible that both reflect the many backgrounds of diverse storytime families and offer others a window into a new experience or world (Bishop 2015). The variety of languages and styles of music broadens children's understanding of the world and its many cultures. Using shaker eggs, scarves, and rhythm sticks as props during the movement activity helps children play with the beat and appreciate the cadence of music and the spoken language. Digital media that includes diverse characters, languages, settings, and experiences complement the library's book collection by filling gaps left by traditional media.

High-quality digital images, short video clips, and sound recordings of unfamiliar places and animals are also shared along with traditional storytime tools to extend the learning associated with shared books. Seeing video of lions and meerkats in their natural habitats or viewing a tuk tuk in motion on the streets of an Indian city helps young children appreciate stories like *Monty's Magnificent Mane* by Gemma O'Neill and *The Wheels on the Tuk Tuk* by Kabir Sehgal and Surishtha Sehgal in new ways. The images, video, and audio help increase background knowledge about places, cultures, people, and animals unfamiliar to some and, in combination with popular picture books, feed curiosity and stimulate rich conversation—particularly when these resources are explored together.

Stories and group activities are followed by developmentally appropriate arts-and-crafts projects or science experiments that align with the program theme. By including projects and experiments in a program, families gain access to unique or inaccessible supplies and are exposed to new ideas that they can replicate at home. Along with watercolors, markers, scissors, and glitter, new media is included when applicable. For example, Squishy Circuits and Makey Makeys are used to teach about electricity with conductive dough and even bananas. A photo booth with a cityscape background and an assortment of comic-book-style props offers a fun activity for children and their grown-ups during a superhero storytime. All these examples reinforce the role of media mentors as guides, evaluators, and curators, and models of the variety of excellent uses of media.

Youth Aged Six to Eleven

When engaging school-age children (i.e., approximately grades kindergarten through five) in technology-based programming, an overarching goal of media literacy typically translates into a program in which a type of equipment or skill is introduced to the children, followed by opportunities for them to engage with the technology in challenge-oriented activities. Media mentors are essential for making this approach successful. Programming that combines access to the tool and access to mentors who can help young people gain the experience and know-how needed to use the tool successfully addresses the root problem of the digital divide. Integrating access and opportunity ideally motivates young people to continue exploring the program topic or other technology topics and skills beyond the initial program and fills at least some of the gaps that might otherwise keep young people with a range of societal barriers from successfully utilizing these technology tools in their education and in their lives.

At the Skokie Public Library (Illinois), many technology-based programs take the form of boot camps—that is, multi-day programs that engage a core class of children in developing skills around a specific technology over a series of successive meetings. Originally, tech boot camps explored digital comics creation, by which children learned both the basics of visual storytelling and how to create their own stories using Comic Life software; and explorations of 3-D printing that included instruction about and self-directed design using free Tinkercad software in conjunction with the library's 3-D printer.

Most recent boot camps have focused specifically on core concepts of coding. For children in grades kindergarten to two, three-day Scratch Boot Camps have provided introductory exploration of the concepts of coding and hands-on tinkering with Scratch Jr. software, resulting in the creation of coding "stories" that children share in the final program session. For children in grades three through five, a three-day Robot Dance Boot Camp has focused on understanding the basics of coding as well as the timing components associated with creating a finite program. Using Ozobots and their color-based coding language, children explore the abilities of the technology by creating programs that are "choreographed" to music. All these boot camp technology programs share core goals: to introduce children to a technology they might not otherwise explore; to facilitate basic skill development in the technology; to allow children to create something personally meaningful using their newly acquired skills; and to inspire further explorations of coding and technology.

These are all programs in which library staff serve as both guides and models for ways that youth can explore different technology available to them at the library. Designed with the abilities and needs of the target age range in mind, the programs also involve opportunities for sharing what has been learned with caregivers and family members so that a child's support system may continue to encourage exploration and skill development around technology.

Youth Ages Twelve and Older

Programs for teens, just like teens themselves, are more complex and sophisticated versions of those for younger children. Their longer attention spans, broader background knowledge, and greater independence enable teens to participate in maker programs, app design challenges, social media scavenger hunts, and music recording at libraries big and small. These technology programs are generally more in-depth, longer, and can involve more expensive equipment. The most effective teen programs, regardless of the technology used, consider teens' interests and how teens learn best in out-of-school and informal learning experiences. Giving teens space to play, experiment, and collaborate is an important facet of technology programs for teens that ties directly to the HOMAGO framework.

Teen programs do not need to be large-scale or rely heavily on purchased equipment to be effective. The 2016 summer Pokémon GO craze sparked a flurry of pop-up programs that fed off the interests of teens. Teens, and even families, went on "Pokémon GO safaris" offered by libraries in Illinois, Ohio, Alaska, and Maryland, among others. Groups met at libraries with their mobile devices and hunted for the fantastical creatures known as Pokémon at Poké Stops, virtual locations in the digital game found at real locations around town, including libraries. Enjoyed by novices and experts alike, the safari programs provided both librarians and players opportunities to talk about the technical aspects of how augmented reality games work, discuss street safety, and discover what the library has to offer teens. Although the popularity of Pokémon GO may have waned, library staff continue to look for what's popular with teens to spark ideas for programming and create opportunities to model positive uses of digital media.

Teen tech programs all start with two core ingredients: teens' interests and their desire to socialize. Like their younger counterparts, teens use a variety of digital technologies at school and in their personal lives to stay connected and create. Integrating the tools teens already use is a natural strategy for planning and hosting engaging teen programs. Library programs that introduce or utilize technology tools in a cooperative environment provide teens with important skills—logical thinking, collaboration, design theory, and problem-solving—that support their media literacy, lifelong learning, and workforce preparedness.

Families

Many parents and caregivers bring their children and teens to the library to learn, but they are also looking for tips and suggestions themselves. They seek advice to help them be successful in their roles. Public libraries are successfully offering services for entire families, often in multi-generational programs. Across the United States, libraries host programs about digital technology with children and teens and capitalize on digital media's widespread use and technical features to support families in new ways.

The Madison Public Library (Wisconsin) hosts the Supper Club, an evening program in which library staff introduce families to a menu of high-quality apps for kids while the families enjoy a picnic-style dinner together. Staff walk the families through the apps' features and model joint media engagement. After the story and toy apps are shared with the group, individual families have time to explore the apps more intimately on multiple devices or to work on a related craft. Families who cannot attend the program can read more about the shared apps on the library's blog. Recommended apps and an explanation about why they are of high quality can also be found in the "App Finder" database hosted on the library's website (Madison Public Library n.d.).

The Homer Public Library (Alaska) offers special literacy programs for Coast Guard families and other families whose parents are away from home for long periods of time. Inspired by the Brooklyn Public Library's Telestory program, the Bridging the Distance program empowers families to use the tools they have available in new ways to support the literacy needs of their children and teens and to strengthen relationships, even across great distances or over long periods of time. Real-life examples of how to use email, smartphones, photos, DVD players, books, audiobooks, and videogames to spark spoken conversation and written storytelling before and after a parent's deployment or separation are shared along with current research on literacy and digital media use. The program successfully provides valuable information that supports parents and attracts new families to the library. They discover that whatever community they move to, its library will be a valuable resource. Media mentorship and family engagement go hand-in-hand in the digital age.

CONCLUSION

Although digital media and technology have relatively recently become significant components in the lives of children, and thus the purviews of the youth librarian, there is no shortage of examples of ways in which librarians across the United States and the world combine their professional knowledge of children and access to research-based practices to support literacy development among children. The iPad may have revolutionized what technology means in the lives of children and families, and the term *media mentor* may only be a few years old, but librarians have affirmed that providing access to, instruction in, and guidance about media and technology is a core component of what it means to be a librarian serving youth.

This chapter has aimed to provide an introduction to information about the role of the youth librarian as media mentor, as well as to the types of programming that libraries have implemented in service of media literacy and technology skill development. Examples of dynamic, developmentally appropriate programming centered in media and technology emerge just as quickly as new technologies are created. Many of the librarians developing and leading these programs opt to share their programs on blogs, through journal articles, and at conferences. For librarians who wish to develop their own skills as media mentors and providers of technology-based programming for youth, the first step can be as simple as perusing library blogs, partaking of resources from the Association for Library Service to Children, and reaching out to fellow professionals via Twitter or Facebook to begin conversations about research, best practices, and ideas. It is important to remember that, in our capacities as media mentors, we aim also to serve and support our fellow librarians. Looking to our colleagues across the profession for examples of positive media mentorship and engaging programs is a great strategy for serving the youth in our own communities through media and technology.

REFERENCES

Bishop, R. 2015. "Mirrors, Windows, and Sliding Glass Doors." *Reading is Fundamental.*
https://www.psdschools.org/webfm/8559.

Campbell, C., C. Haines, A. Koester, and D. Stoltz. 2015. *Media Mentorship in Libraries Serving Youth.*
Chicago: Association for Library Services to Children.

Guernsey, L. 2014. "How the iPad Affects Young Children, and What We Can Do about It."
TEDxMidAtlantic video, 13:14. Posted April 27, 2014. https://www.youtube.com/watch?v=P41
_nyYY3Zg.

Haines, C., C. Campbell, and ALSC. 2016. *Becoming a Media Mentor: A Guide for Working with Children and
Their Families.* Chicago: ALA Editions.

Ito, M., S. Baumer, M. Bittanti, d. boyd, R. Cody, B. Herr Stephenson, H. A. Horst, P. G. Lange, D.
Mahendran, K. Z. Martínez, C. J. Pascoe, D. Perkel, L. Robinson, C. Sims, and L. Tripp. 2010. *Hanging
Out, Messing Around, and Geeking Out: Kids Living and Learning with New Media.* Cambridge, MA:
MIT Press.

KIDMAP. (2017). DIG Checklist, https://www.joinkidmap.org/digchecklist/.

Madison Public Library. Appfinder. www.madisonpubliclibrary.org/kids/apps/appfinder.

Media Mentors Resources. n.d. nevershushed.com.

Mills, J. E., E. Romeijn-Stout, C. Campbell, and A. Koester. 2015. "Results from the Young Children, New
Media, and Libraries Survey: What Did We Learn?" *Children and Libraries* 13 (2): 26–32, 35.

NAEYC and Fred Rogers Center for Early Learning and Children's Media at Saint Vincent College. 2012. "Technology and Interactive Media as Tools in Early Childhood Programs Serving Children from Birth through Age 8." www.naeyc.org/content/technology-and-young-children.

Rideout, V. 2013. "Zero to Eight: Children's Media Use in America 2013," *Common Sense Media.* www.commonsensemedia.org/research/zero-to-eight-childrens-media-use-in-america-2013.

Takeuchi, L., and R. Stevens. 2011. *The New Coviewing: Designing for Learning through Joint Media Engagement.* Joan Ganz Cooney Center, 15. www.joanganzcooneycenter.org/wp-content/uploads/2011/12/jgc_coviewing_desktop.pdf.

Walter, V. A. 2004. "The Same, but Different." *School Library Journal* 54.

ADDITIONAL RESOURCES

ALSC Core Competencies. www.ala.org/alsc/edcareeers/alsccorecomps.

Campbell, C., C. Haines, A. Koester and D. Stoltz. 2015. *Media Mentorship in Libraries Serving Youth.* Chicago: Association for Library Services to Children.

Guernsey, L., and M. Levine. 2015. *Tap, Click, Read.* Jossey-Bass.

Haines, C., C. Campbell, and ALSC. 2016. *Becoming a Media Mentor: A Guide for Working with Children and Their Families.* Chicago: ALA Editions.

KIDMAP. 2017. DIG Checklist, https://www.joinkidmap.org/digchecklist/.

The Five-Step Outcome-Based Planning and Evaluation Model for Children's and Young Adult Program Assessment

Melissa Gross

INTRODUCTION

Rhonda wants to apply for a Library Services and Technology Act (LSTA) grant to support a new program idea she has for teaching middle-schoolers to code. The grant application guidelines require a plan for outcome-based evaluation. She loves her idea, but she doesn't know how to write a plan for an outcome-based evaluation!

Even though Sophie's storytimes are extremely popular, her director has asked her to demonstrate their effectiveness as part of the argument for the library's proposed budget. Sophie would like to describe her storytimes in terms of what they mean to the local community rather than just providing attendance figures. She has heard that outcome-based planning and evaluation is a good approach for collecting this kind of data but wonders if it can be used with an already established program.

Elsie really enjoys evaluating library programs and services. A position as a program evaluator has opened up that she would like to apply for. The only catch is that it requires knowledge of outcome-based planning and evaluation and she hasn't done this type of evaluation yet. She wonders how difficult it will be to gain a working knowledge of this approach.

■■■

All these scenarios point to the continuing need for librarians to become familiar with outcome-based evaluation. Luckily, the Outcome-Based Planning and Evaluation (OBPE) model provides an easy-to-understand process that clarifies step by step how to incorporate outcome-based thinking into the program development life cycle.

The OBPE model was developed in the early 2000s as part of Project CATE (Children's Access to [and use of] Technology Evaluation) (Dresang, Gross, and Holt 2006).

Project CATE was one of the first studies to consider how children use computers in public libraries. Because Project CATE was funded by the Institute of Museum and Library Services (IMLS), the co-principal investigators were very much immersed in outcome-based thinking and decided to use outcomes not only to evaluate the project but as a guide to designing and developing technology programs for children. The result was the Outcome-Based Planning and Evaluation (OBPE) model. Working with St. Louis Public Library administration and staff, the OBPE model was incorporated into the planning, development, marketing, and evaluation of technology programs and services delivered to children as part of Project CATE. The OBPE model was very well received, not only in St. Louis but through a variety of presentations given at professional association meetings. In 2006, *Dynamic Youth Services through Outcome-Based Planning and Evaluation* was published by the American Library Association, providing youth librarians with a guide for incorporating the OBPE model into their work with their communities (Dresang, Gross, and Holt 2006).

Since the publication of *Dynamic Youth Services,* interest in outcome measurement has remained strong and awareness of the OBPE model has expanded beyond the children's room to include all public library programs and services. OBPE has been a popular topic at workshops held by library systems and at professional association conferences. Over the course of eleven workshops held between 2013 and 2015 for library managers, the original OBPE model was expanded and the new five-step OBPE process was published by the American Library Association in the *Five-Steps of Outcome-Based Planning and Evaluation for Public Libraries* (Gross, Mediavilla, and Walter 2016). An overview of the new, expanded version of the OBPE model is the focus of this chapter. The new five-step OBPE extends the use of the model beyond the children's room but still includes youth services. It also includes a new fifth step (labeled Phase V in the model) that focuses on increasing the visibility of library programs and services in the community and beyond. The new fifth step also serves the needs of youth librarians who are interested in ensuring that their programs and services are responsive to community needs and aspirations.

WHAT IS MEANT BY OUTCOMES?

Outcomes describe how programs and services benefit the people who access, attend, or use them. Outcome-based planning and evaluation go beyond assessing the success of a program based on the widely accepted output measure approach (such as counting the number of program attendees) by assessing what participation meant for the people who attended. It answers the question of whether program attendance improved their lives in some way. Types of outcomes are categorized by IMLS as changes in skill, knowledge, attitude, behavior, condition, or life status (IMLS n.d.).

A *change in skill* can be about being able to do something that an individual couldn't do before. An important skill that libraries spend a lot of time promoting is the ability to read. A change in skill may entail acquiring a new skill or improving an existing skill. For example, once people have basic computer skills, they can go on to learn the various uses of computers that they are interested in. Programs that are designed to help people gain or improve their skills typically focus on teaching participants how to do something (e.g., searching the internet, planting seeds).

A *change in knowledge* concerns acquiring or expanding command of a topic or subject area. Gaining knowledge can entail learning about new concepts or facts, theories, current events, literatures, cultures, technologies, and more. The list of things that we can know is virtually endless. Knowledge can be developed through both formal and informal learning as well as through personal experience. In the library, some programs that increase participants' knowledge may include book clubs, author visits, and storytelling.

Attitude is about opinion, feelings, and thoughts. Programs that are designed to affect attitudes usually seek to change opinions, dispositions, or point of view. Examples of library programs that seek to change attitude include those that promote reading as a fun activity or demonstrate that healthy food can taste good.

Programs that seek *to impact behavior* are concerned with what people do. These programs are designed to affect how people act or behave. Common examples of this type of program are Read-to-Me and Grandparents and Books programs that seek to promote reading aloud to children. Another example is a program that seeks to impact security behaviors online.

Changing condition or life status is about wanting to help people improve some aspect of their personal, social, or professional lives. Library programs of this type include programs that help people see themselves as readers, computer users, or citizens.

The five-step OBPE model embeds outcome-based thinking into the full planning, development, and evaluation cycle such that desired program outcomes are defined and agreed upon ahead of time. The five-step OBPE starts with the process of understanding what kind of outcomes the community wants and then focuses on meeting those needs through the provision of programs and services. Desired outcome(s) are the goal of the program(s) and provide the basis for program evaluation.

WHY SHOULD LIBRARIES USE THE FIVE-STEP OBPE MODEL?

Over the years in which the OBPE model has been developed and adopted, the benefits of applying the OBPE model to programs and services have become clear. One of the main advantages of outcome-based evaluation is that it goes beyond numbers in allowing libraries to describe the impact of programs and services by focusing on how libraries help people achieve their goals and enrich their lives. One complaint that librarians have had about outcome evaluation is that it seems difficult to understand and use. One of the strengths of the five-step OBPE approach is that it simplifies the process and incorporates outcome-based thinking about program ad service development into the full cycle of planning, program development, and program evaluation.

One of the benefits of OBPE that was realized early in Project CATE is that outcome-based thinking can help the entire staff to understand the library's goals and to work toward them in ways that are intentional, resulting in more reflective and effective practices. At the same time, outcome-based thinking puts the library user first in library operations, provides data that informs managerial decision making, and keeps library stakeholders in the loop in terms of how the library is meeting the needs of the community.

Outcome-based thinking provides a solid and systematic framework for the development of new programs and services and invites us to rethink existing programs to ensure that they too are contributing to the outcomes desired by the community. And, when reporting is needed to satisfy grant funders or to leverage the library's accomplishments, the five-step OBPE model ensures that the data is available and relevant and clarifies the importance of the library in the life of the community.

HOW TO INCORPORATE THE FIVE-STEP OBPE IN LIBRARY PROGRAMS FOR YOUTH

The Five-Step Outcome-Based Planning and Evaluation (OBPE) model outlines how to incorporate outcome-based thinking into the library's planning and evaluation practices. A graphic of the model is provided in figure 5.1. However, if you are new to OBPE, the recommendation is to first use OBPE on a new program or service to gain a full understanding of each step by working through the process once. Existing programs and services can also be reviewed and renewed using the five-step OBPE process to incorporate target outcomes. It is not suggested that you evaluate outcomes for programs and services that have not had their outcome targets defined. This is called "fishing for outcomes." If you fish, you may be able to determine outcomes associated with a program or service. Fishing will not guarantee that the outcomes you "catch" are the outcomes the community wants. Also, it is unlikely that these outcomes will provide useful data for future planning.

The five steps in the OBPE model are: 1) gathering information, 2) determining outcomes, 3) developing programs and services, 4) conducting evaluations, and 5) leveraging the library's role. These steps are performed in order, but each step informs other steps and the whole process leads back to step 1 to ensure that programs and services always respond to current data about the library's community. This flow is depicted in figure 5.1.

Each of the steps in the OBPE process is further described below. Additional resources are listed under Recommended Resources.

Step 1: Gathering Information

The first step is to understand the community that the library serves. This involves knowing who belongs to the community, what their life conditions are like, and what their dreams and desires are for their children and the community. Understanding the community is foundational to ensuring that library programs and services respond to users' needs and expand the library's reach to nonusers. Information about the community assists in planning and is essential to understanding what kinds of outcomes the community wants that the library can help achieve.

There are many published sources of data librarians can use to begin to understand the local community. These are available through a variety of sources, such as the US Census Bureau and organizations like Kids Count.[1] School districts, the chamber of commerce, realtors, police, and other local organizations are also sources of local data. This data can be very helpful in providing an overview of the community and in identifying trends that reveal what the community is doing and how it is changing.

Published sources are extremely helpful, but they cannot and should not replace local knowledge that is gained from observation and by talking to people. This means that you should get out of the library periodically and have a look around. Take your library book bag (or other items that identify you with the library) and eat lunch at local restaurants, shop in local stores, attend local events, and read the local newspaper. When you are out in the community introduce yourself and talk to people. Much can be learned through a casual conversation about local issues and concerns that can help generate ideas for concrete actions to improve community life and achieve its aspirations. Another benefit of getting to know people in the community is that it helps build personal connections to the library.

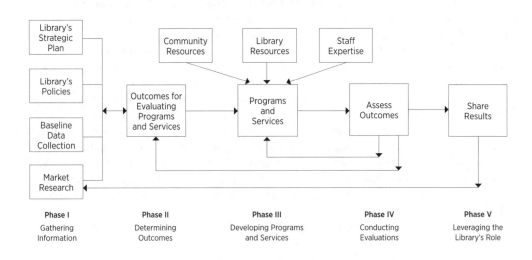

FIGURE 5.1 Outcome-Based Planning and Evaluation Model.

This model is reproduced from Gross, Melissa, Cindy Mediavilla, and Virginia A. Walter. *Five Steps of Outcome-Based Planning and Evaluation for Public Libraries.* Chicago: ALA Editions, 2016, p. 6.

While you are out in the community pay attention to what you see. Where do people shop? How do people get around? What are the neighborhoods like? What languages are used on local business signs? What are the denominations of local churches? How is business doing? Is this a community that has stayed the same for a long time or is it changing? What community agencies or organizations exist, besides the library, that contribute to the quality of life?

Be sure to take what you learn back to the library and have regular conversations about what's going on in the community with your staff. Staff who live in the community will also have information to share. It is important to make sure when gathering information to engage youth and youth-focused people in the community in conversations about what the community is like and what they see as the needs and aspirations of the people living there. Ideally, plan to involve youth and those people interested in youth in all parts of the program-development process, including the informal processes described above as well as formal processes, such as surveys, interviews, and focus groups.

In addition to understanding the community, it is also important to review the library's strategic plan, mission, and policies to be aware of how these might shape program development decisions. It can also be useful to review available statistics on library usage (program attendance, circulation, computer use, etc.) as these may also provide useful information for program development.

Step 2: Determining Outcomes

The data you gathered in step one will provide you with information about what the community considers to be needed and desirable library programs and services, which may give you some ideas about how the library can best respond. When analyzing this information, discuss the findings with staff and other stakeholders for ideas about how the information can be translated into outcomes. The data analysis process is where an understanding of how the library can best serve the needs of children will become clear. Data analysis will also reveal what kinds of outcomes should be the goal of programs and services for the target population. However, sometimes data analysis will reveal gaps in the data you have collected, which may mean that you must collect more data to answer your new questions.

It is important to formally state the outcome(s) that will be the goal of program development, compose a short description of the desired outcome, and identify indicators that will signal that a desired outcome has been achieved. For example, if the goal is for caregivers to read aloud to children, this outcome type is a change in behavior. Indicators that this is happening might include caregiver reports or observations of adults reading aloud to children in the library.

It is also possible to adopt existing outcome statements that have been developed by others for similar circumstances. For example, summer reading outcome statements developed by the California State Library and the California Library Association may be helpful. These are:

1. Children/teens/adults/families belong to a community of readers and library users.
2. Underserved community members participate in the summer reading program (Gross, Mediaville, and Walter 2016, 38).

The Public Library Association is another source for outcome statement templates and standardized data-collection instruments that can be useful (Davis and Plagman 2015; Teasdale 2015).

Identifying desired outcomes, describing them, and specifying indicators are important because they clarify project goals for everyone involved, help keep program development on track, and provide a foundation for later program evaluation.

Step 3: Developing Programs and Services

Developing programs and services is the step that many librarians are most comfortable with and enjoy. It is good practice to involve youth and other community stakeholders in the process both formally as team members and informally as advisors to the project. Stakeholders can confirm the needs or concerns that the project is addressing and provide suggestions. As you develop your program, remember to go back to stakeholders for feedback and to seek advice when you need it. As program development proceeds, continue to check that the program is designed to accomplish the outcomes developed in step 2. If the program design is creeping off-track, it is important to make corrections at the design stage to avoid investing time and money into a program that won't reach the agreed-upon goals.

Collaborative projects are increasingly preferred by funders and can increase the reach of program outcomes. There may be agencies in the community that can help create value and enhance existing services if they share interest in or responsibility for the outcomes targeted by the project. Examples of potential collaborators include local educational programs, health and human services agencies, clubs (4H, Scouts, Girls and Boys Clubs), service agencies, recreational services, and cultural services such as museums.

Step 4: Conducting Evaluations

Evaluating programs is an important process. It demonstrates whether, or the extent to which, desired outcomes have been achieved. It allows you to describe the importance of the program to participants and provides a basis for improving programs going forward. One of the benefits of the five-step OBPE process is that, because indicators of success are identified early on in the process, the basis for program evaluation is clear.

At this step, it is time to develop program objectives. These express the library's goal for the program as a whole. Program objectives need to be measurable, identify a timeframe, and identify the target user group. For example, a program that teaches caregivers how to read aloud to children might have an objective that 50 percent of program attendees will report reading to their children daily one week after the program closes. Notice that the target, 50 percent, is modest. This is purposeful. It is not possible to control all the factors that can affect outcomes, and especially the first time a program is offered it is wise to be conservative about performance targets. If the program exceeds the goal, know you have done well and can raise the target next time. Otherwise, use what you learn from program evaluation to make the program more effective.

There are many methods of evaluating programs.[2] These include observation, surveys, interviews, tests, and focus groups. The method you choose depends on what information you need, and which will work best with your participants. As you think about evaluation methods remember that it can be very useful to know from the participants' point of view what difference the program has made in their lives. For example, you might ask caregivers what benefits they experience in reading aloud to young children.

The results of your evaluation will be useful for future planning, justifying resource allocations, and documenting service improvements. But your results will also help you talk to people and organizations outside the library, as well as to funding sources, about what the library is doing. Program evaluation helps you demonstrate that the library is committed to planning, evaluation, and effectiveness in its service to the community. Within the library, evaluation builds a culture that emphasizes programs and services as a means of achieving outcome goals in which everyone knows not only what programs are offered, but how programs respond to community needs.

Step 5: Leveraging the Library's Role

If you work through the five-step OBPE process, even with a small program, you will learn many things that you will want to share. In the last step of the five-step OBPE process, you will spread the word about what you have learned about the important role the library plays in the community. And there are lots of people and organizations with whom you will want to communicate. One of the results of the five-step OBPE process is that you will have data that demonstrates accountability to funders, management, and government agencies. You should share your successes with all the people who participated in the project as well as with other stakeholders interested in your results. And if things didn't turn out as perfectly as you might have hoped, you will have lessons to share and use to improve the program next time around.

You will have several different target audiences with whom you want to share your findings, so you will need to tailor your communications so that you reach each audience in the most effective way. For example, your report to management will likely look different than your press release to local media or your posts to social media. Libraries that communicate their work and celebrate their relationship with the community and other partners raise awareness of the library and leverage the library's role in the community. When you can demonstrate not only the great programs and services at the library but also how these programs benefit users and improve life in the community, you have a powerful tool for promoting the work of the library and for demonstrating its relevance.

LOOKING FORWARD: CHALLENGES AND POSSIBILITIES

Even with all the benefits of using the five-step OBPE process, you may still be wondering about getting started. There is a natural resistance to doing things a new way that you may face when you bring this idea back to your library. Staff may initially feel that the process will entail extra work or there may be a lack of administrative or other support that may complicate adopting a new approach to planning, development, and evaluation. You may also feel that there is much to discover that you may not have previously considered.

Remember that the five-step OBPE model can be used with any size program and that you don't need to start big. In fact, starting with a small project is a great way to work through the phases and gain confidence with using the model. The model provides a series of steps that you can take one by one, and will reveal a natural progression that makes sense. You will also develop a deeper understanding of how planning relates to evaluation and evaluation to planning.

You may also learn, as was demonstrated at the St. Louis Public Library, that there are other unanticipated benefits of adopting the model (Dresang, Gross, and Walter 2016, xiii–xiv). One result was that the relationship between the library and its users improved. The CATE OBPE process demonstrated to the community in concrete ways the library's commitment to the well-being of young people. The planning and evaluation processes gave library stakeholders and users first-hand experience of the responsiveness of the library to the needs of youth.

A second side benefit of using the CATE OBPE model was that it had an impact on how staff perceived their work. Understanding the outcomes provided a framework for working with youth and allowed staff to consider how they could individually contribute to these goals in their day-to-day interactions with users. This, in turn, led to better relationships among departments, such as technology, marketing, training, and adult services, whose staff all learned to include the desired outcomes with how they thought about their roles in the library.

Finally, the CATE OBPE process was instrumental in demonstrating the benefits of evaluation, which enabled the development of a culture of evaluation. Staff saw the advantages of receiving feedback and realized how access to relevant data can lead to improvements in program and service quality.

Until you start using the five-step OBPE, you will not know what benefits your library and community will experience from engaging in this process. The only way to find out is to give it a try. Chances are that the benefits of OBPE will become clear as you plan, develop, and evaluate programs in your library that are guided by outcome goals informed by community needs and aspirations.

NOTES

1. Kids Count is a project of the Annie E. Casey foundation. See http://datacenter.kidscount.org/.
2. For more detail on methods and analyzing data see Gross et al., *Five Steps of Outcome Based Planning*.

REFERENCES

Davis, D., and E. Plagman, 2015 "Project Outcome: Helping Libraries Capture Their Community Impact." *Public Libraries* 54 (July/August): 33–37.

Dresang, E. T., M. Gross, and L. E. Holt. 2006. *Dynamic Youth Services through Outcome-Based Planning and Evaluation.* (Chicago: American Library Association).

Gross, M., C. Mediavilla, and V. A. Walter. 2016. *Five Steps of Outcome-Based Planning and Evaluation for Public Libraries.* Chicago: ALA Editions, 2016.

Institute of Museum and Library Services. n.d. Outcome Based Evaluations. www.imls.gov/grants/outcome-based-evaluations.

Teasdale, R. 2015. "Project Outcome Launch—Seven Surveys to Measure Impact," *Public Libraries Online* (May 28), Publiclibrariesonline.org/2015/05/project-outcome-launch-seven-surveys-to-measure-impact/.

RECOMMENDED RESOURCES

Dresang, E. T., M. Gross, and L. E. Holt. 2006. *Dynamic Youth Services through Outcome-Based Planning and Evaluation.* Chicago: American Library Association.

Gross, M., C. Mediavilla, and V. A. Walter. 2016. *Five Steps of Outcome-Based Planning and Evaluation for Public Libraries.* Chicago: ALA Editions.

Hacker, K. 2013. *Community-Based Participatory Research.* Los Angeles: SAGE.

Harwood Institute for Public Innovation. "Libraries Transforming Communities: LTC Public Innovators Cohort." 2014. www.ala.org/transforming libraries/libraries-transforming-communities/cohort.

Holt, L. E. 2007. "How to Succeed at Public Library Service: Using Outcome Planning. *Public Library Quarterly* 26, no. 3-4 (2007): 109–18.

Walter, V. A. "Documenting the Results of Good Intentions: Applying Outcomes Evaluation to Library Services for Children." In *Advances in Librarianship.* Vol. 35, *Contexts for Assessment and Outcome Evaluation in Librarianship,* edited by Anne Woodsworth and W. David Penniman, 47–61. North America: Emerald, 2012.

CHAPTER 6

Taking the Library to Unexpected Places

Outreach and Partnerships in Youth Services

Beth Crist

INTRODUCTION

Storm Reyes, daughter of a Native American family of migrant farm workers, was not allowed to have books because they were too heavy for the family's frequent moves. Her family lived in poverty and she had little hope for her future. When she was twelve, a bookmobile came to the field where they were working. She hesitated to go in, but a kind librarian welcomed her and asked about her interests. She left with three well-chosen books. She became a reader—and much more. For the next three years, "The library staff guided my reading, nurtured my curiosity, and taught me to respect myself simply because they respected me," according to Reyes. "It wouldn't have been enough to just introduce me to a world I had never known. The library had faith in me and then led me to a place where I could have faith in myself as well . . . . I was offered hope, dreams and direction . . . . Every day a library is changing and enriching lives, sometimes in the most unexpected places" (Reyes n.d.).

This story is just one of many that exemplifies the need for outreach services and demonstrates the powerful positive impact they can and do have in providing access to materials and to an informative professional to guide the information-seeking experience.

WHY DO OUTREACH?

According to a 2016 Pew Research Study, 19 percent of Americans sixteen and older report never having visited a public library or bookmobile. Additionally, 17 percent of parents of minor children—or one in six respondents—say they have never been to a public library. Furthermore, of the 32 percent of Americans who haven't used a library in the last year, many of whom have earned a high school diploma or below, are living in households earning less than $30,000, and have minor children at home (Horrigan 2016).

Why do outreach? These very groups and other underserved audiences are the ones who need library services the most. Research shows that:

- 71 percent of parents with college degrees read to their children every day, compared with 33 percent of those with high school diplomas or less (ULC Family Learning 2016).
- Unequal access to summer learning during elementary school—including visits to libraries and museums, and simply reading—leads to learning loss, which is cumulative. It results in children from lower-income homes lagging at least two years behind their peers by the time they reach fifth grade, and accounts for up to two-thirds of the achievement gap between ninth-grade students from lower- and higher-income households (ULC Summer Learning 2016).
- In middle-income neighborhoods, there are an average of thirteen books per child; in low-income neighborhoods, the ratio is one book for every 300 children. Increased access to books leads to improved reading and enjoyment of reading and learning; one study shows that children raised in homes with more than 500 books spent three years longer in school than children whose parents had only a few books (Bridges 2013).

Putting these library survey and research findings together, it's clear that those who don't come into the library often are the people who would benefit most from library services, making it critical for librarians to understand how to reach their underserved residents.

There are many reasons why people don't use public libraries. They may not know about the richness of the services available. Others may hold misconceptions about the library, such as public libraries charge a fee for usage, they don't welcome babies, they don't offer materials or services in a community member's native language, or they will require identification that some community members don't have. Some people don't have a family-based, historical, or cultural tradition of library use.

Others face more tangible barriers to using the library. Transportation is a perennial challenge for many, in communities of all sizes. Library hours can be an obstacle—many cannot get to their library when it's open or attend children's programming on weekday mornings. Access to library materials can be another barrier: some parents steer their children away from checking out library materials because they worry about incurring overdue fines or fees for lost or damaged books that they can't afford; some already have charges on their library accounts that prohibit them from checking out materials. Some parents struggle with literacy themselves and don't believe they can help their children in the library. Recognizing the library as a safe and welcome space can be difficult for some community members as well. Residents who feel marginalized in the larger community, such as LGBTQ youth; those who are not fluent in English; teen parents; immigrants; and families currently experiencing homelessness may be reluctant or fearful of using the library. And juggling busy home and work schedules can be a significant and ongoing barrier for many when it comes to getting to and using the library.

Communities are also dynamic organisms that experience increases and decreases of various groups of people depending on a variety of factors. One community may have an influx of new refugees; another may see a rise in its homeless population; and still another may have its library building in a suburb, which was designed to serve rural residents who seldom use it. Communities with a juvenile correctional facility have teens who may receive little to no library services in the facility. It is often these very people who are not visiting the library for whatever reasons, who need library services the most.

JUST WHAT *IS* OUTREACH?

The term *outreach* is sometimes used to include any activity conducted outside library walls, such as presenting a school assembly to promote the upcoming summer learning program or developing a partnership with the local Boys and Girls Club to offer joint programs in their facilities.

The *Online Dictionary for Library and Information Science* defines outreach services more specifically as: "library programs and services designed to meet the information needs of users who are unserved or underserved, for example, those who are visually impaired, homebound, institutionalized, not fluent in the national language, illiterate, or marginalized in some other way." (Reitz 2013). This definition separates *marketing* from *outreach;* although both are critical activities for libraries, outreach specifies delivering library services outside library walls, not promoting in-house services. It also emphasizes the importance of delivering services to undeserved audiences, rather than to general audiences.

To take this concept one step further, it's important to extend this definition to include: "without the expectation that those receiving outreach services will ever come to the library." If people visit the library after receiving outreach services, that's great! But it should not be the end goal of outreach. Outreach is a legitimate, critical service in itself.

Critical components of outreach include:

- Building relationships and trust with non-users, current patrons, and community partners,
- Actively listening to and learning from non-users, current patrons, and community partners,
- Providing authentically inclusive services,
- Respecting and recognizing the strengths of non-users, current patrons, and community partners,
- Avoiding assumptions and stereotypes, and
- Providing equal access to library services for all—including those who never come to your library.

As indicated in the 2016 Pew Research Study, 7 percent of respondents sixteen years and older reported receiving some sort of visit from a librarian in the past twelve months, with another 4 percent receiving outreach in a prior year. Although this demonstrates the presence of outreach efforts, the efforts do not serve all of the 19 percent of Americans sixteen years and over who have never been to a library and the 32 percent who haven't gone in the last year (Horrigan 2016).

HOW DO COMMUNITY PARTNERS AND PARTNERSHIPS FIT WITH OUTREACH?

Collaboration richly benefits communities. By collaborating with community organizations and building partnerships, libraries are able to accomplish more than they could when working in isolation. Through these partnerships, libraries are able to pool their resources with others, leading to improved services that they are also more likely to be able to sustain over time. Each partnership may embody different types of collaboration and resource-sharing, such as cross-training, sharing expenses and workload, sharing facilities, offering connections to groups in the community, and working together to plan and evaluate joint services. Another critical benefit is that, by working together, organizations can cross-promote and offer their services to multiple audiences, thus serving more people than they could individually. Partnerships may be a one-time event or be more encompassing and long-term. The list of potential partners in youth services is long:

Youth and Family Organizations

- Schools, preschools, Head Starts, childcare centers
- Youth programs like 4-H, YMCA/YWCA, Boy Scouts, Girl Scouts, Junior Achievement, Boys and Girls Club, etc.
- Home visitation programs like PAT (Parents as Teachers), HIPPY (Home Instruction for Parents of Preschool Youth), and Nurse-Family Partnership
- Pediatricians' offices and health clinics, especially Reach Out and Read clinics, plus clinics providing services for expecting parents
- Community play and parenting groups, including MOPS
- Early childhood education nonprofits and governmental agencies
- Juvenile correctional facilities
- Groups that support LGBTQ youth
- McKinney-Vento programs (federal funding provided to states to support school district programs that serve homeless students)
- Programs for teen parents and expectant teen parents

Other Community Organizations

- Local Government Agencies, such as the Recreation Department, Police, City Council, Mayor's Office, and so on
- Homeless Shelters
- Other Libraries Within and Outside of Your Library System
- Local, State, and National Parks and Forests
- Supplemental food service programs like the Summer Food Service Program, Supplemental Nutrition Assistance Program (also known as food stamps), Women, Infant and Children (WIC) programs, and food banks
- Migrant education programs
- Religious institutions
- Literacy nonprofits
- Immigrant services
- Service clubs like Junior League, Kiwanis, and Rotary Club
- American Indian tribes
- Post-secondary institutions

HOW DO I START WITH OUTREACH?

1. Get to know your community! As discussed earlier in this section, programming should follow the needs and interests of your community. Providing outreach services is no different. One key step is to explore who is not coming into your library and using your in-house programs and services. Look specifically at children, teens, and families. The answer is likely to be unique to each community. This is of course no easy feat! It requires careful attention to your community and library usage, communicating with and listening to community groups and leaders, and talking with a wide variety of people. The effort will be worth it.

2. Once you discover a group that's underserved in your community, seek out an organization that already supports that community. This is where building partnerships comes in. Meet with representatives of these groups and ask them to introduce you to some of the people you're trying to reach.

3. Next, talk directly with the people you want to serve, and ask them about their interests, goals, and dreams; the barriers they face in using the library; what services they need that aren't provided elsewhere; how the library can best support them; and when and where will work best to provide programming for them. This can entail one-on-one conversations, focus groups, or longer-lasting advisory boards to engage in ongoing communication that will best meet an audience's current needs

■ Some tips for partnering

- Approach potential partners with admiration for their work and outcomes. Point out the goals they share with the library. Invite them to the library for a tour and meeting, and visit their facilities as well.
- Communicate early, often, and clearly with your partners.
- Agree on the role of each partner and document those roles; the more specific they are, the better. You might consider developing a Memorandum of Understanding that each organization signs.
- Be flexible. Even with the best intentions and careful planning, a partner organization may experience an unexpected funding cut or take on a new project, making its staff less able to contribute work or funding to your joint project. In this case, look for an additional partner to fill the gap, or see if your library can contribute more.
- Don't force it. Some partnerships won't work out, and that's okay. If potential partners are reticent about collaborating with the library, talk with them about it and, if it's not a good fit at the time, let it go (though you may wish to reach out again in a year or two to see if the situation has changed). Likewise, if you're currently involved in a partnership that's just not working out, consider a gracious conclusion.

and interests. Advisory boards can also provide broader input to all your library's services. Keep in mind that this is not a one-time effort. Because of the dynamic nature of communities, you will need to engage with community members on a regular basis to understand how the community is shifting and changing.

4. From there, see which barriers your library can remove or ease to enable these community members to use the library. For instance, if low-income parents cite fines and fees as reasons they don't let their children check out materials, try to eliminate at least overdue fines on children's materials. Then, share your new policy with these parents. Many barriers, though, may be insurmountable by your library acting alone, and that's why outreach and partnering are so critical in helping to overcome the diverse range of barriers faced by your community members.

5. Using the information gathered, create a youth services outreach plan that aligns with your library's strategic plan and has measurable goals. Because it's just not possible to reach every underserved group at any one time, a best practice is to focus on one or two underserved groups. Most importantly, carefully consider the input you've gathered from partners and the audience you want to serve and actively include these partners and audience members in your planning process. Look at other services that serve the audience to determine where there are strengths and gaps, think about how your library can add to these strengths or fill some of the gaps, and contact additional organizations that might be potential partners. In formulating your plan, consider what's feasible for each partner organization, even if that means starting out with a smaller program than you'd like. Include evaluation methods for both the planned services and partnerships. Surveys are one type of evaluation that can be useful to determine your success in reaching and effectively serving your intended audience—consider surveying parents, tweens, teens, and partner organizations, depending on your program and goals. Offering surveys on paper and online, as well as in all languages commonly spoken in your community, will make them more accessible and result in higher participation. Convening focus groups is another evaluation method; asking a subset of the intended audience to come in for a conversation is more time-consuming for both library staff and participants (and is not anonymous, which may discourage some potential participants), but can provide much richer, more complete insights into program success and avenues for improvement.

6. Then, go forth and implement your plan!

WHAT DOES OUTREACH LOOK LIKE?
IT'S MORE THAN JUST A BOOKMOBILE!

The bookmobile is the most iconic vehicle, literally and figuratively, for delivering outreach services. These libraries on wheels enable staff to serve community members at diverse locations by strategically selecting bookmobile stops and times using community input, a key to reaching underserved audiences. The Montrose Regional Library District in western

Colorado, for instance, brought its bookmobile to a childcare center in a low-income community during child drop-off and pickup times once a week. This arrangement, in partnership with the school district, allowed busy parents—many of them library non-users—to bring their children to the bookmobile for a storytime and to check out books. Overdue fines were not charged, and prior fines and fees on parents' accounts were waived to enable all families at the childcare stop to make full use of the bookmobile. This program was very successful in increasing access to books for not only the children but also the whole families who used the bookmobile at this convenient location.

But there are many outreach options beyond bookmobiles. Bookmobiles are an expensive proposition and most public libraries don't have one, which should not be a deterrent to providing effective outreach. Here are some innovative examples:

Libraries on Other Wheels—Bicycles!

Libraries across the country are rolling out book bike programs, featuring a pedal-powered bookmobile in the form of a trailer hitched to a bike. Though compact, most still offer a variety of services including materials for circulation, a wireless hotspot, library card sign-ups, and research help. Librarians can take these bikes to housing developments, big box stores, churches, community events, and anywhere else that children, teens, and families may be found—and it's simple to tailor the materials for each event.

Pop-Up Libraries

There are many variations of these mini portable libraries: some are elaborate designs purchased from vendors, such as portable reading rooms; others consist of vans outfitted with library materials and setup gear; still others are simpler, smaller packages that library staff create in-house that can be transported easily in a car. The DIY versions, which can be just as effective, often include a tent, awning, or banner; a collection of books; several iPads or tablets; and fun programming supplies. Whatever the setup, the contents are easily customizable for different venues and age groups. Programming and services, too, can vary appropriately, from afterschool coding workshops for middle-schoolers at a YMCA to a range of services for all ages at evacuation centers during natural disasters.

One example is the Houston Public Library, which partners with the Children's Museum of Houston. The museum's pop-up library provides young children with programming including storytimes, crafts, STEAM activities, free books, and take-home learning activities. Staff members take the pop-up library to afterschool programs, schools, childcare centers, and other locations where there are young children. There is also a pop-up library for children with special learning needs, which incorporates books, technology, and sensory activities.

Another example is the Pueblo City-County Library District's (Colorado) Books in the Park program. This library is one of many around the country that partners with the Summer Food Service Program, a USDA-funded program that provides free lunches and snacks in communities where at least half of students receive free and reduced-cost lunches during the school year. This helps reduce food insecurity for children in the summer. In partnership with the city's Parks and Recreation department, staff members at the Pueblo Library take several book trucks full of books to two city parks where free lunches are served twice a week at each park throughout the summer and provide storytimes, crafts, and outdoor activities. The children—many from low-income households—can also participate in the library's summer learning program at the lunch site.

Pop-Up Programs

Pop-up programs are similar to pop-up libraries but often have a simpler setup. They allow librarians to deliver library services to underserved audiences. These can be one-time events, such as an early literacy activity make-and-take booth at a program for expectant parents at a health clinic; a storytime at a cultural celebration; or a library table at a Pride festival with reading lists for youth and adults, materials to circulate, and rainbow crafts. These programs can be publicized ahead of time or appear as a surprise for those lucky enough to happen upon them. Pop-up programs can also offer recurring visits, like a monthly tech petting zoo at a grocery store or a weekly maker program during the summer at a Boys and Girls Club.

Create grab-and-go kits in sturdy bins that contain everything needed to set up and deliver an outreach program. These can make it so much easier to put on pop-up programs. A library may have, for instance, a maker kit for teens, a creative writing kit for tweens, a STEAM kit for kids, and a pre-writing activity kit for the pre-K set. With all the necessary items thoughtfully preassembled, staff and volunteers who have received training on the kits can easily implement outreach programs for children of all ages. Create kits in languages common in your community; if there's no one on your library staff who speaks the languages well enough to put together the kits and provide the outreach programs, seek help from a partner organization or a community volunteer.

Longstanding, ongoing programs provide the most sustained and in-depth library services to a range of underserved audiences. Just a few of the many possibilities include:

- An ongoing program to provide library services to youth in juvenile correctional facilities that may entail weekly or monthly visits that include book clubs, creative writing workshops, various crafts, re-entry skill workshops, such as resume-building for teens, interview practice for jobs or college admissions, and more. Providing outreach in correctional facilities can be a challenge due to restrictions on the types of technology, programming, and materials that librarians are allowed to bring into facilities, so these visits require careful planning and close communication with the facility staff. However, the effort is worth it because this audience can especially benefit from library services.
- Ongoing library services for teens who are parents or parents-to-be offered through an established school or nonprofit program can take a two-pronged approach: serving the teens' needs and interests with book discussion groups, crafts, music, job and college application prep, and tutoring, as well as meeting their parenting needs with sessions on brain development and early literacy, social and emotional development, and media mentorship.
- Regular outreach to schools of all types enables librarians to provide a large number of children and teens with library services. One option is to partner with the school library staff to provide programming on-site, possibly before or after school or at times the school library would otherwise be

closed. This approach should not usurp the critical teacher-librarian's role but rather provide unique services to students. Another option is to offer library services during student lunch times. The Carnegie Library of Pittsburgh makes such visits regularly to middle and high schools, bringing a collection that students can check out, providing readers' advisory services, issuing library cards, and offering hands-on activities. Other options include showing multimedia presentations paired with book recommendations and providing gaming opportunities.

• Ongoing outreach to unlicensed childcare providers (also known as Family, Friend and Neighbor [FFN] providers) in areas such as child development, early literacy, media mentorship, and STEAM can greatly increase the knowledge and skills of these providers who may have little previous training. Librarians can also foster a community of practice among FFN providers in their communities, creating an additional support system that is beneficial to all parties.

Self-Led Outreach Programs

Also known as passive programs, self-led programs engage residents in library activities in a self-directed, self-paced manner. They also allow for library programming while keeping staff time limited to preparation and maintenance. Deposit collections, for instance, are small collections of books that can be placed in diverse venues, such as childcare centers, Head Starts, juvenile correctional facilities, housing developments, health clinics, WIC offices, and more. Library staff bring a small tailored collection to the venue for a period of time and rotate the collection, with each venue responsible for an informal circulation process. Another option is to supply participating venues with carefully chosen, high-quality, weeded or donated books that don't need to be returned. The Hennepin County Library (Minnesota) offers the Shelter Deposit Program, which provides such books at homeless shelters, which greatly increases access to books for this underserved population.

Little Free Libraries (littlefreelibrary.org/)[1] are another option. These mini-libraries are stocked with books and magazines for anyone to take and keep and, when possible, supply a different item for someone else to enjoy. These are great to install in front of social service agencies, laundromats, schools, and other venues frequented by residents who may not have easy access to books. The best practice for being a good LFL steward is to check on the mini-libraries regularly and add high-quality donated or weeded books when the supply gets low.

StoryWalks (www.bostonchildrensmuseum.org/storywalk)[2] consist of pages from a picture book attached to posts along a trail or road, around the grounds of a library or school, or in other outdoor venues where families may be found. The StoryWalk Project was created by Anne Ferguson of Montpelier, Vermont, and developed in collaboration with the Kellogg Hubbard Library.

Partner-Led Outreach

Partner-led outreach ensures that library staff need not be the only people to deliver outreach library services! Partner organizations can provide tremendous support and extend the reach of your library. When your staff cross-trains with staff from partner organizations, everyone benefits—especially and most importantly, the residents of your community. Depending on the partner organization and your joint goals, library training for partner staff may include Every Child Ready to Read® content, maker activities, library databases and other online resources, digital literacy, and more. It should also include training on all the services that the library provides, not just youth services. As partners interact with their patrons, they'll pass along this knowledge to people of all ages whom they serve.

One example is the partnership between High Plains Library District in northeast Colorado and its local HIPPY and PAT programs, nonprofit organizations that provide home visits to families with young children in low-income households. The library staff trained the home visitors in early literacy and the library's many services for all ages and supplied them with children's books and early literacy activities to give to families they visited. The home visitors incorporated early literacy activities into their visits; they also informed adults about library services they felt might be of interest, such as computer classes, GED classes, or books in their native language, and the like; some families did come to the library after learning about these services. The library expanded its reach through this partnership, especially because the home visitors were able to speak one or more of the six languages spoken by new community members that the library staff could not.

Virtual Outreach

Virtual outreach is possible because computers, devices, and especially smart phones are widespread, even in low-income households, making virtual outreach a viable option to provide library services when and where people already are. Maintaining a robust youth services presence on your library's website and social media is a good first step; going beyond marketing in-house library programs to providing library services virtually is the next level up. For instance, promote early literacy modeling videos like those on StoryBlocks, created by Colorado Libraries for Early Literacy (www.storyblocks.org/), or post videos of book talks that your teen advisory group has made. Provide access for full online participation in your summer learning program. Ensure all your content is mobile-friendly, as some people have easy access only to smartphones.

Embedded Librarians

The concept of embedded librarians brings library services to a group or organization in a very proactive way, and one that allows librarians to become fully engaged and incorporated into the group. To become embedded, a librarian joins a group or organization as a fully participating member that provides key information and library services as needs arise without having to be asked. Youth services librarians may be embedded in PTAs, teacher work groups, a local chapter of PFLAG (a national organization for families, friends, and allies of people who are LGBTQ), a city task force on childcare or services for new immigrants, a program to aid reentry for juvenile offenders, and many other possible situations.

HOW DO YOU MAKE THE TIME FOR OUTREACH AND PARTNERING?

Some libraries have staff or even whole departments dedicated to providing services outside the library, which is great! For small, medium, and rural libraries, however, it can be challenging for a busy youth services librarian to provide meaningful outreach and to partner successfully while at the same time providing high-quality services within the library, especially in the summer. In addition to achieving this already challenging balance, you'll also need to consider your own measures of success—that some communities you touch during your outreach and partnering will wish to connect with you at the library, too.

Here are some ways to do outreach with limited staff and budget:

Advocate to library administration for the importance of outreach and let them know how much time you need to provide outreach services to youth. Keep up to date on community demographics and information on library usage that can help in your advocacy efforts. Whenever possible, connect the need for outreach to your library's mission statement.

Prioritize outreach and partnering in your work; focus on reaching underserved audiences. This includes proactively building time into your schedule for professional development, idea generation, and planning specifically for outreach—and using it.

Remember you're not in this alone! Look beyond library staff to provide outreach services:

- Train volunteers to provide outreach services—and in-house services, too—that can free up time for staff to deliver outreach services. If available, seek high school and college interns; it's a great opportunity for them to gain excellent work experience and provides a rich mentoring opportunity.

- Partners are an excellent resource to deliver outreach services. Cross-train with partner staff; they are resources to deliver services to their existing patrons. For example, home-visitation programs for parents with young children can deliver early literacy instruction, board books, and library cards; staff at an afterschool program can lead children through sessions on basic circuitry using the library's curriculum; staff at a youth organization can provide several sessions of a summer coding camp that's jointly offered by the library to teens. Free up staff time, especially in summer learning programs. Look for inefficient processes as well as programs that are no longer relevant to the needs and interests of your community that you can consider downsizing or eliminating.

When you make a great connection during outreach or partnering with individuals or communities, suggest times for them to come to the library for tours when you'll be there. Seek funding for additional staff hours to provide in-house or outreach services. For local funding, ask for help from the library's Friends group and service clubs like Kiwanis and Junior League. Grants are another potential source of funding that may be available from such diverse sources as local, state, and national foundations; YALSA; ALA; some state libraries; federal agencies; and community-giving arms of national companies, and more.

Providing thoughtful outreach services to underserved communities and partnering deliberately and meaningfully with a variety of organizations are critical components to providing inclusive library services to the children, teens, and families in every community—meeting them where they are with what they need.

NOTES

1. Little Free Library® is a registered trademark of Little Free Library, LTD, a 501(c)(3) nonprofit organization.
2. Storywalk® is a registered service mark owned by Ms. Ferguson.

REFERENCES

Bridges, L. 2013. *Access to Books*. http://teacher.scholastic.com/products/face/pdf/research-compendium/access-to-books.pdf.

Horrigan, J. B. 2016. "Libraries 2016." Pew Research Center. September 2016. www.pewinternet.org/2016/09/09/2016/Libraries-2016/.

Reitz, J. M. 2013. *ODLIS: Online Dictionary for Library and Information Science*. Last updated January 2013. www.abc-clio.com/ODLIS/odlis_o.aspx.

Reyes, S. "Storm from Tacoma, Washington." *I Love Libraries*. www.ilovelibraries.org/storm-tacoma-washington.

Urban Libraries Council. 2016. "Leadership Brief: Libraries Expanding Summer Opportunities." https://www.urbanlibraries.org/assets/Leadership_Brief_Expanding_Summer.pdf.

Urban Libraries Council. n.d. "Leadership Brief: Libraries Supporting Family Learning." https://www.urbanlibraries.org/assets/124-11_ULC_Leadership_Brief_Families_Learning_proof2.pdf.

RECOMMENDED RESOURCES

ALSC Committee for Library Service to Special Population Children and Their Caregivers. 2015. *Library Service to Special Population Children and Their Caregivers: A Toolkit for Librarians and Library Workers*. www.ala.org/alsc/sites/ala.org.alsc/files/content/professional-tools/lsspcc-toolkit-2015.pdf.

Bridges, L. 2013. *Make Every Student Count: How Collaboration among Families, Schools, and Communities Ensures Student Success*. http://teacher.scholastic.com/products/face/pdf/research-compendium/Compendium.pdf.

Diamant-Cohen, B., ed. 2010. *Children's Services: Partnerships for Success*. Chicago: American Library Association.

Stoltz, D. 2016. *Inspired Collaboration: Ideas for Discovering and Applying Your Potential*. Chicago: ALA Editions.

Urban Libraries Council. Summer Learning. 2016. www.urbanlibraries.org/summer-learning-pages-309.php.

CHAPTER 7

The Ever-Changing Library

Advocating for Impact, Value, and Purpose

Judy T. Nelson

INTRODUCTION

In 2016, *Library Journal* identified advocacy as the top skill that library leaders will be looking for in future librarians (Schwartz 2016). In addition, Jaeger et al. state that, "We can no longer hope that one person, institution, program, or policy will save libraries. Nor can we assume a wait-and-see attitude while we turn away in revulsion and refuse to engage . . . We all need to be advocates now" (2017, 363). This strong emphasis on advocacy for libraries is due to the fact that funding for public libraries falls more and more every year. Many believe this is because libraries are not effectively advocating for themselves (Jaeger et al. 2017; Janes 2016).

You, and some of your community, may see libraries as vibrant, bustling places where librarians respond to questions in-person, online, or over the phone; help customers use technology, search for jobs, or learn a new skill; or design programs and go out of the building to visit a classroom or partner with a business. However, a majority of community members may not see the library this way; they may not understand what libraries have become. Google and the internet are being touted as the reasonable alternative to spending precious tax dollars on a public library. Every year there is a legislator somewhere who advocates for the elimination of their local library to save money. The reason? The internet, along with Amazon and Google, provides everything anyone needs for the cost of internet access. Although librarians understand that this reasoning is faulty, they also realize that libraries are now required to show what value they bring to the communities that fund them. Taxpayers want to know where their money is going and what they get for it. Libraries can no longer afford to be passive participants in their community's life. To remain vital and valued, libraries must prove they are worthwhile. We must become effective advocates for our libraries.

WHAT IS ADVOCACY?

The word advocacy can strike fear among practicing librarians. For many, when they hear the word *advocacy,* they envision standing before a large room of decision-makers defending their work and themselves against some perceived negative action. But advocacy is so much more than that and not usually as scary. It does, however, require diligence and ongoing dedication to the cause of library service. Some may think that this kind of advocacy belongs in the hands of library administrators, not those of children's and youth librarians. Others disagree. What is more powerful than the story about the young child who learns to read and becomes a success, or the school-age child who goes to the library every afternoon because they were bullied at school and has nowhere else safe to go, or the teen who enters the library's poetry contest, wins, and goes on to become a published author? It is important to get stories like these, of library impact, out to the community to create awareness of the valuable work the library is doing to support all children and their learning. To do this, children's and youth librarians need to become advocates.

According to Merriam-Webster.com, the basic definition of advocacy is "the act or process of [promoting] or supporting a cause or proposal." A person may be said to champion or advocate for a particular cause or stance. Furthermore, the American Association of School Libraries (AASL) defines advocacy as an "ongoing process of building partnerships so that others will act for and with you, turning passive support into educated action for the library program. It begins with a vision and a plan for the library program that is then matched to the agenda and priorities of stakeholders" (Kachel 2017, 50).

From these definitions, you can see that all children's or youth librarians are not only advocates on behalf of their departments and libraries but also on behalf of the constituencies they serve, the learning outcomes they promote through their programming, the safe spaces they create in their buildings, and the elements of social justice they promote in every aspect of their work with children. You can advocate through the work you do every day. In fact, the Association for Library Services to Children (ALSC) developed an initiative called Everyday Advocacy to explain how to advocate for the work that you do and the communities you serve every day (ALSC, n.d.). Once you understand that you can advocate through the work you are already doing, it is important to realize that you should and need to be advocating every day. Advocacy efforts need to become consistent and systemic. Libraries can no longer rely on one-time efforts.

In your everyday efforts, advocacy will likely occur at many levels and for many reasons, not all of them library-related. You might be advocating for a very specific cause, like building a playground on an abandoned lot versus building a new parking garage, or you might be speaking on behalf of the larger community when transportation departments are looking to cut bus service to your library due to budget constraints. So not every cause or action requires librarians to be involved professionally, but you might be surprised about when you should be an advocate.

KINDS OF ADVOCACY

Typically, youth services advocacy falls into two large categories: internal and external advocacy. Internal advocacy refers to the conversations and presentations you have with your supervisor, the branch manager, or the library director about the work you do every day; the impact of your programs and services on the people who attend and take advantage of them; and the need for sustaining these programs and services when it's time to set the new internal budget. You might talk with peers about the ways in which you're reaching new families with the sensory storytime you just created. Perhaps you propose new programs to reach additional segments of your community and advocate for the need to expand and extend the work you're already doing to make a difference in their lives. Internal advocacy can take place periodically and every day (e.g., talking with families and teens who come into the library and sharing information with them about how to be more engaged and take advantage of all the library has to offer).

External advocacy refers to the marketing and publicity work you do outside of the library, in the community, to raise awareness about what the library does, why it's an important part of the community, and, in the cases of initiatives like levies, why taxpayers should support and continue to fund the work the library does every day. This kind of advocacy might seem necessary less frequently than the internal advocacy, but you can engage in it through your daily work. In writing for school librarians, Kachel provides an Advocacy Continuum as a way to approach external advocacy (2017). She identifies three broad actions in the continuum: Public Relations—"Telling"; Marketing—"Selling"; and Advocacy—"Partnering." These broad actions lead to a "connected set of efforts that become more intense and focused over time, ultimately resulting in lasting alliances and partnerships" (Kachel 2017, 51). Let's think about these three broad actions in the public library:

1. **The public relations phase** is when you are promoting your resources, services, and programs to the broader community and a wide variety of community organizations.
2. **The marketing phase** is when you are making connections between what you offer and the specific needs of community organizations or groups.
3. **The final stage of advocacy** is when you are building the partnership. Programs and services may be part of a partnership, but you are also developing an external advocate who can actively support your work, your department, and your library.

Another aspect of external advocacy is its overlap with outreach work—when you go out of your library walls and reach out to underserved communities, you can advocate for the library through the programs and services you offer to people in these communities. The care you take in creating meaningful outreach programs will resonate with the folks you serve and help to demonstrate the ways that libraries can make a difference in the lives of the families they serve.

WHY SHOULD LIBRARIANS ENGAGE IN ADVOCACY WORK?

Advocacy is crucial for the success of libraries, and in turn, the success of your communities. The most effective advocates are those who understand what the library is doing and the impact that work has on the community. Because of this, effective advocacy will come from all library staff, not just the administration, and community members and organizations who have been impacted by the library. Through your programs and services, you will develop an understanding of how your library is serving and impacting your community. In addition, through those programs and services you are building relationships with community members and organizations who can advocate for the importance of your, and the library's, work in the future. As a result, you are in the unique position to be a powerful advocate on many levels.

Therefore, I contend that every person involved in youth/children's librarianship needs to be an advocate. How you do that and the level at which you act is up to you and the library you work for, but you are the voice for the children, the families, and the community you serve as well as your library and your department. No, you don't have to wave banners or testify before the legislature unless you are comfortable doing so. Being a children's or youth librarian means you care about children and teens and the world they live in. You may also be passionate about reading or gaming. You may be an excellent program designer or book-talker. Having these skills does not overshadow your need to be the spokesperson who promotes and supports the work you do with and for children and youth to promote reading and learning.

GETTING STARTED

How should you start? Here are two things you need to begin:

1. You need to know and understand your library's mission and vision statements and be able to articulate what they mean to you and your community.
2. You need to gain "a seat at the table."

Look at your library's mission and vision statements. Ask yourself questions, such as:

- What does your library's mission statement mean?
- What about your library's vision statement?
- Does your library actively work to make these statements a reality, or are they mere words that are not reflected in the work the library does in the community?
- What does your library stand for and how do the words on paper apply to the work you do every day?
- Whom are you serving and why?

You must be able to articulate your answers to these questions. Write your answers down and practice saying them out loud. Once you understand the values your library is espousing through its mission and vision you are better prepared to be an informed advocate. Your answers are your advocacy talking points, your elevator speech (i.e., short enough to be shared with an influential person in the time it takes to ride the elevator together to your destination).

Here is my approach to answering these questions for my own library system: "The Pierce County Library System's (Washington) vision is to be the community's choice for the discovery and exchange of information and ideas. Our mission is to bring the world of information and imagination to all people of our community." I reflected on these statements and identified what the various words meant to me. I started with the phrase *the community's choice*. Being the community's choice means the community needs to know who we are. Someone needs to be out in the community sharing information about all the services and resources the library has to offer. And don't forget to include community spaces. The simplest opening gambit is to encourage a local organization, such as a preschool co-op, school district, or city parks department to use your meeting room for their monthly meetings. If possible, make sure there is no fee associated with their use and remind the organizations you have free parking! Ask for two minutes at the start of their meetings to welcome them to the building and share one service or resource they might not know about. Bring business cards and make sure you take no more than your allotted time. You are now an advocate for your library. You have informed one segment of your community about some of your services and programs. Now the library can become another choice for discovering and exchanging information and ideas. Repeat this process as often as you can.

The second thing you need to do to become an advocate is to gain a seat at the table. You cannot share information about your services and resources if you do not partner or collaborate with community organizations. Start by having a conversation with your supervisor: Determine how much time you believe you can give to partnerships and outreach, identify which groups you would like to reach out to, and where the greatest potential for success lies. Don't just fall back on the school systems for information; instead, find other community partners that will complement your work and your mission (see chapter 6 for some ideas). Come to this meeting with a plan that includes the names of and specific information about at least two organizations outside of your school systems that you believe should be considered for involvement. Once you have finalized everything with your supervisor, prepare to attend your first meeting. Initially, join community organizations that support children. Once you start participating you may learn of other groups, and as you get out into the community, you will be better able to target a few organizations that will provide you and your library with the greatest level of exposure. Gradually you will develop the connections that align with your library's mission and vision. Just because a group says it supports children and families does not necessarily mean it is a good fit to serve as your library's representative. You will not know that until you get involved and listen. Remember, advocacy is an ongoing effort.

The first two groups I participated in at my current position were very different from each other. The first was the local Childcare Resources group's monthly meeting. For the first few meetings I really did not understand what was being discussed at the meetings, so I did a great deal of listening and asking questions. Gradually I came to learn that local licensed childcares were struggling to meet the state requirements for reading aloud to their children. Many of them participated in our library's outreach program called "Ready for Books," a monthly book-delivery program that brought free library materials to their childcare locations. However, the childcare providers did not know which books were appropriate for the various children they served. They were unaware that certain books were intended for toddlers and others were more appropriate for preschoolers. One childcare provider was so surprised by this difference that she shared the following anecdote: She frequently used the same title with both her preschoolers and toddlers. To maintain the attention of her toddlers, she would speed up her reading so she could turn the pages faster and keep their attention. Imagine her very real delight when, after taking the class we offered on choosing age-appropriate books, she was able to share stories with her toddlers that truly captured their interest and allowed her to scaffold their learning.

Our library system then took the step of becoming certified to train licensed childcare providers, enabling those providers to receive state-required credit for taking a class on learning how to choose a book for a certain age level. The library system started asking about the specific age levels served at the various sites and filled book tubs with developmentally appropriate materials based on these stated needs. Finally, we set up a simple process using the state's early learning guidelines to identify the types and age-appropriateness of every book placed in the Ready for Books containers and shared this information with each childcare provider. This assured the providers that they were working with the right materials for the children in their classroom. Since this had direct bearing on their state evaluations, the providers appreciated our support. The library was able to expand the existing book delivery program by being deliberate about providing training and labeling materials so that childcare providers could easily select developmentally appropriate materials. This made their circle times more enjoyable for everyone, leading providers to expand their work and measure the impact in follow-up surveys. Finally, the library provided childcares with bookmarks to share with parents. Each bookmark included tips for reading aloud and gave childcare providers the opportunity to directly support parents and caregivers. Here you can see how the library's advocacy of the importance of developmentally appropriate read-alouds impacted the children, the childcare providers, and the parents and caregivers.

The second group I joined was a local city's human services coalition. Each month various county organizations attended and shared information about their resources and upcoming activities. I learned a great deal about this community in a very short time and was able to inform a wide variety of agencies, businesses, and organizations—from health-related groups and restaurants to faith-based organizations and juvenile justice agencies—about the services and resources the public library offered free of charge. I exchanged information and ideas at these meetings, I met a variety of people, and I followed up with targeted contacts to start building working relationships. Because of these connections, the library developed a partnership with the county health department and the juvenile court around book clubs and reading. Not everything I learned at these meetings was useful professionally, but being involved allowed the library to tailor services to specific constituents to meet our customer's needs. We would not have known how we could support either the childcare providers work or the work of various other agencies and organizations if we had not been at the table.

Once you start developing partnerships to support and expand your advocacy, you will need to regularly review your engagement activities to determine which ones offer the best payoff. Not every group is going to be a great fit for you and the library. It is okay to disengage from an organization after several meetings. You may only be able to participate in a couple of partnership opportunities regularly and some organizations may not fit the bill at the time. But if you participate, be sure you follow through on any assignments you agree to. You represent the public library, so don't over-promise. By making connections, the community will start to see the library as a potential partner. Over time there will be an expectation that the library will be part of the community's solution, which means you are becoming the community's choice.

Now that you have thought about your library and its role in your community, think about when you should be an advocate. You should be able to participate in any discussion and ask yourself what the role of the library is in the solution to a problem. Once you have determined whether you, as the library representative, have a role to play (and I contend that you will almost always see a role for you and your library, even if it is only to provide a meeting-room facility), then you should think about what that role is. Be specific. Are you willing and able to provide library staff and resources, or only facilities? Although all are valuable, it is critical to not over-promise. Make sure you can articulate why you should be involved. You will need to be able to do this with your own supervisors as well as with the partner group or organization.

PUTTING THIS INTO PRACTICE

Knowing the why, how, and when of advocacy will help you determine your role as an advocate. Let's look at three different scenarios and decide if they are legitimate advocacy situations for you as the children's or youth services librarian, and what your role might look like.

1. The administration of your library is reviewing the collection budget to determine whether the current allocation of dollars for books and magazines is correct. One area under review is the size of the children's/youth budget. Is the existing budgeted allocation appropriate for the various children's and youth collections too high or too low? You have been asked for your input.
2. Your library offers a county-wide reading program for adults each spring. It culminates in an all-community reading event and author visit. So far there has been no discussion of adding any children's or youth activities to this program. Should you recommend that there be youth or family programming as part of this adult initiative?
3. The local high school is discussing plans to add family-focused ESL classes in the evening. Should you be attending those meetings to advocate for how your library can be involved?

These three situations all require advocacy, but should it come from someone in children's or youth services or even the library? Each one involves a different group of people. Do they all need a children's and youth advocate? Keep the why, how, and when in mind as you consider these scenarios:

Scenario number one: A library is reviewing its collection budget allocations, which involves how much gets spent on picture books, teen novels, magazines, and nonfiction to name only a few youth categories. Yes, this situation needs an advocate speaking for children's and youth services. Your collection is one of your core services. Your supervisor needs your input. You should be able to speak to collection usage, condition, and collection needs based on requests from your customers. What is missing from your collection? What is dated or unused? You need to do your homework.

Here are some suggestions for specifics to consider before you attend the meeting to share your recommendations about the allocation of dollars for the children's and youth materials budget (note that this list is not comprehensive):

*   Know the turnover rate for your various collections and how these rates compare to other collections in the library, such as adult fiction, graphic novels, or any special collections that are funded.
*   Know how old your nonfiction collection is and when you were last able to do a picture book replacement.
*   Know how many children and youth are in your community, what school assignments go unfulfilled or partially filled each year, and if there are databases that should be considered for addition to your collection to meet assignment needs.
*   Know how much you will ask for and be able to defend your request.

The more data you provide to support your request, the better. Your support for the collection benefits every child and family in your community. You must be the advocate here.

Scenario number two: Your library's county-wide reading program for adults has not included any discussion about adding activities for children and youth to the program. Should you be an advocate for including either intergenerational programming, a parallel title for children to read, or specific programming for youth that pertains to the title being read? I say yes. Many adults have families. Regardless of whether their children are still at home or grown and living elsewhere, adults will engage in the program to an even greater degree if they can include their families. It is true that not every adult will want to engage with children, so don't oversell your support role, but suggesting the addition of one program aimed at families of the very young, for example, will strike a positive chord. Again, you should be targeted and specific.

At my library we hosted a prominent author and five of his novels for our Pierce County Reads program. He had just launched his first picture book. With the support of his publisher, we provided every librarian and storyteller (our smallest branches are staffed with an Every Child Ready to Read®-trained early learning paraprofessional called a storyteller) with a copy of the picture book, and they committed to doing one storytime featuring the new title. The librarians and storytellers were allowed to use it in whatever context they determined was right for their communities as long as they promoted the adult reading initiative as part of their storytime. When the final survey asked customers where they learned about the program, many mentioned the storytimes they attended with their children. This is where knowing your library's mission and vision comes in. My library wants to be the community's choice for the discovery and exchange of information and imagination. The county-wide reading initiative is aimed at adults, but by adding this small component to the overall program offerings we stretched the audience and invited parents and caregivers with small children to participate. Part of advocacy is promoting a cause. Adult reading is as important as storytimes. Children who see their parents and caregivers reading will be more likely to copy that behavior and read by their selves.

Scenario number three: The first two scenarios involved library-related activities. The third scenario involves the community and an activity that may or may not be library-related. You have learned that your local high school wants to offer family ESL classes in the evening. Should you attend those meetings and advocate for the ways that your library can be involved? Absolutely! Ask yourself these questions:

- Since the high school is considering sponsoring family ESL classes, who will be in attendance?
- If the class will be targeting the parents, what will happen to the children in the families?
- Are these parents currently library users?
- If they come to the library, are they coming only for their children or are they using the library's resources for themselves?

Already you now have two possible additions to offer to the ESL program being planned. You can offer to come and do a short presentation on the public library and its resources for adults during one of the classes. If possible, bring a bilingual staff member, and don't forget to bring library card applications. Invite the class to take a field trip to the library. Next, ask if there will be childcare provided or some sort of program for children that will run at the same time as the ESL class. If so, you can offer to present a storytime or a craft program.

At one of our branches the storyteller noticed that she suddenly had zero attendance at her bilingual storytime. Since this had been a well-attended program, she made it a point to reach out to one of the parents who came to the library to ask what had changed. She learned that the high school, in conjunction with one of the community colleges, had set up a family ESL class specifically for parents of students in the district. The class ran four afternoons each week, including the time of the previously successful storytime. Instead of being in the library at storytime, all those parents and children were now in a classroom down the road. After reaching out to the community college that was providing the ESL class, this branch was able to provide a storytime once a month for the children of the attendees. The bilingual storytime at the library was cancelled due to lack of attendance and instead the storyteller visited the children at the high school during the ESL class. The library branch also invited the class to an open house and tour. Most members of the class attended, and for some of the parents this was their first visit to a free public library. Having bilingual staff on hand helped the parents learn about the resources they could access for free, and the library issued several dozen new library cards. This connection is now being built into the ESL class as they go forward and is considered a valuable part of the program. Other ideas being considered by the branch include holding programs for parents to come and practice their English in a neutral setting, as well as offering technology classes in Spanish. The library lived its mission and demonstrated how it would bring the world of information and imagination to all people in the community regardless of the location. We advocated for the library to have a role in this program and demonstrated our worth to the community.

Advocacy is about championing your library's mission and vision, and it should be happening at every level and in every environment, every day. These examples demonstrate that any arena has the potential to be an opportunity for advocacy. You and your library are limited only by the amount of staff and time you have available to dedicate to this endeavor and your ability to think creatively about how your library can be integrated into your community.

REFERENCES

Association for Library Services to Children. n.d. Everyday Advocacy. www.ala.org/everyday-advocacy/.

Jaeger, P. T., E. Zerhusen, U. Gorham, R. F. Hill, and N. G. Taylor. 2017. "Waking Up to Advocacy in a New Political Reality for Libraries." *Library Quarterly* 87 (4): 350–68.

Janes, J. 2016. "Knowledge for the Win: Expanding the Notion of Library Advocacy to Help Combat Ignorance." *American Libraries* (9–10): 24.

Kachel, D. 2017. "The Advocacy Continuum." *Teacher Librarian* (3): 50.

Merriam-Webster.com. s.v. "advocacy." www.merriam-webster.com/dictionary/advocacy.

Schwartz, M. 2016. "Top Skills for Tomorrow's Librarians." *Library Journal* 141 (4): 38–39.

RECOMMENDED RESOURCES

Advocacy and Activism. Young Adult Library Services Association. www.ala.org/yalsa/advocacy.

Advocacy Resources. Center for Nonprofit Excellence. https://www.centerfornonprofitexcellence.org/resources/advocacy?gclid=CIXQ206RqdECFYZlfgodoVUFCw.

Advocacy University. American Library Association. www.ala.org/advocacy/advocacy-university.

Everyday Advocacy., Association for Library Service to Children. www.ala.org/everyday-advocacy/.

Office for Library Advocacy. American Library Association. www.ala.org/abouala/offices/ola.

PART II

Program Profiles

N ow that we have taken a deep dive into the critical domains of today's children's and youth programming, we will explore broadly what these domains look like when put into practice at libraries big and small around the country. Our vision for part II is to provide you with a holistic view of library programming for children and youth.

To do this, we asked the following questions:

1. What would current library school students and future children's librarians like to know about the cognitive and sociocultural development of children at different stages of life?
2. What are libraries offering in terms of innovative, radical programming for children and teens and how are they incorporating one or more of the critical domains we highlighted in part I?
3. What are the major studies and publications in the library and information science field that pertain to, support, and expand upon current practice in the field?

We then broke this part into three age divisions:

- **Early childhood** (ages birth to five)
- **Middle childhood** (ages six to twelve)
- **Teens** (ages thirteen and up)

Each age section is further composed of three elements that are designed to answer these questions. We have given you a review of the major developmental and learning theories that pertain to children in each age group to establish an informed foundation from which librarians can plan and offer developmentally appropriate programs; a variety of profiles of library programs and strategic approaches to providing learner-centered, informal, meaningful opportunities for children and teens that exemplify both the developmental tenets for each age group as well as many of the critical domains covered in part I; and finally an overview of timely and influential research on libraries and children and teens that provides snapshots of the work that is ongoing and the areas that continue to need growth and further innovation.

Let's talk about each of these pieces and why they're important to your work.

What would current library school students and future children's librarians like to know about the cognitive and sociocultural development of children at different stages of life?

The developmental chapters are meant to provide an overview of relevant research and findings in the areas of culture, learning, and development for a particular age group. We intend each chapter to feature information that can help you understand how to develop meaningful, age-appropriate programs for each age range. The reason we're approaching these particular chapters from the standpoint of culture, learning, and development is that we want to focus on the sociocultural ways children learn rather than just focusing on ages and stages. As we mention above, we have separate chapters for young children, middle childhood, and teens. It's important to us that these chapters focus on not just the child as a learner but also on the social and cultural contexts in which that child learns. Consider the child as a learner in society. By focusing on culture, learning, and development, we highlight not just learning milestones but also the cultural and social influences and structures that shape that learning. We provide an overview of how children develop, learn, and grow across a particular age range in a sociocultural context as it relates to informal learning settings like libraries.

Here we ask, "what do librarians need to know about how children of particular ages grow, learn, and socialize in the world to develop meaningful, age-appropriate programs for them?" To provide this information, we considered the major milestones for learning and development in the particular age range; the family and community's role in helping children grow and develop and socialize in this age range; how children develop their own sense of self; the role of culture in the development and socialization of children in this age range; how the adults in a child's life provide a safe, supportive space for learning and social growth; and the research trends in culture, learning, and development for children in this age range that librarians should take into account when developing programs and services. There is a developmental overview for each age range in part II.

What are libraries offering in terms of innovative, radical programming for children and teens and how are they incorporating one or more of the critical domains we highlighted in part I of the book?

The profiles of library programs for children and youth are intended to provide a foundation and expand your understanding of today's programming for children and youth. This section will help library students and practitioners develop relevant, effective, youth-focused programs in their current and future positions by providing them with a better understanding of library programs for early childhood, middle childhood, and teens, and what their young patrons need to support their learning and development. They reflect and embody many of the critical components of children's and youth librarianship that were covered in part I of the book, through program design, delivery, and assessment.

An important thing to remember when you read the library profiles is that you can follow and adapt them to fit your library's size and budget and the type of community you serve. Think about how a similar program might work at your library for your community—would it be smaller or bigger? Would you have a similar budget or a different funding source? Perhaps the program might need to be longer or use different materials or maybe even be offered for an entirely different age range, depending on what needs your community has. For instance, a block play storytime at one library might work well as part of your toddler storytime because you need some time to talk with parents or to model interactive behavior between young children and their caregivers.

We asked our contributing librarians to consider the following questions:

- What sorts of programs are you developing and delivering at your public library for the particular age group?
- What do today's library school students need to know to be able to develop and deliver similar programs in their future positions?
- What are some of the trends you're seeing and what are the tried-and-true guidelines you use to develop programming in your library?

Within each library profile you will see a little information about the library system, followed by descriptions of some of the programs it offers for the age group. In some cases, the librarians chose to provide additional developmental and learning theory introductions to frame their program approaches and support the learning outcomes they set in place for their programs.

Each chapter concludes with a narrative that describes its author or authors' overall approach to programming, how the library develops and delivers its programs, and their future program plans. We believe that as you read these program profiles, you'll make connections back to the critical domains that were presented in part I of the book and see those domains made manifest in the programs you see in part II. The program profiles cover a range of themes, including equity, community, inclusivity, STEM, literacy, empowerment, leadership, and partnerships.

What are the major studies and publications in the library and information science field that pertain to, support, and expand upon current practice in the field?

The final chapter in each age range section of part II is an overview of relevant research findings and initiatives for a particular age group. This overview is intended to provide librarians with information on library-related research that can inform and guide the development and delivery of meaningful, age-appropriate programs for each age range.

Because libraries are increasingly being considered as valuable sites of informal learning, the latest library-related research and initiatives can provide valuable findings and contributions to the field. But are practitioners and, perhaps even more importantly students, aware of these findings and initiatives? How can we as a discipline leverage this work to put research into practice? The authors of these chapters provide an overview of relevant and timely library-related research and initiatives that can impact and influence practice and benefit the children and families who attend your programs now and in the future.

OUR RECOMMENDATIONS FOR READING PART II

We suggest employing both a linear and a radical approach to reading part II and making use of the information it contains. Perhaps you are already in a position where you are developing programming for children ages birth to five and you need insight into what their learning milestones might be and how others are working to prepare these young children for success in school. Perhaps you are a graduate library school student and you're not yet sure which age range most interests you, and you want to be sure to be prepared because many children's and youth librarians interact with and prepare programs for children of all ages. Maybe your youth services department is considering current strategic trends across all ages in a new plan. For any of these scenarios and for many more, this section will enable you to dive in and absorb at any level, learning from the peer community that's been shared and explained throughout these pages.

Enjoy the variety, flavor, and uniqueness of these profiles; be heartened by the similarities between them because you don't have to reinvent the wheel; and find things that resonate with you, that you want to "steal" and adapt to what you need in your current or future work. Celebrate how creative and innovative children's librarians are providing familiar programs in new and varied ways.

CHAPTER 8

Early Childhood Decoded

An Introduction to Development, Sociocultural Theory, and Early Learning

J. Elizabeth Mills, Kathleen Campana, Emily Romeijn-Stout, and Saroj Ghoting

INTRODUCTION

Have you ever seen a baby just gaze at you, intently observing with those big eyes everything you say and do, and how you move? What is that baby thinking about? How are they making meaning of their world from what they observe? We now know that babies are learning every day, every minute. Brain development research has shown us that learning and development are intertwined from a child's first day of life. What can we as librarians do to support and encourage that early meaning-making process through the programs and services we offer? This chapter will introduce readers to the major research findings in child development, sociocultural theory, and early learning for our youngest patrons and discuss what you can do to help support this critical learning period.

EARLY CHILDHOOD

Children from birth through age five do an incredible amount of developing, learning, growing, and processing (Gopnik, Meltzoff, and Kuhl 1999). The brain is "profoundly flexible, sensitive, and plastic, and . . . deeply influenced by events in the outside world" (1999, 8). At birth, an infant's brain is less than one-quarter the size of an adult's brain, with a similar number of neurons. However, babies need to develop their synapse connections—the way that the neurons are linked. These links send information between the neurons. As children learn, they build more and more synaptic connections. Each connection is related to the experiences that children have and the language(s) they hear (Institute for Learning and Brain Sciences 2016). Thus, the language development that begins at birth (Kuhl et al. 2014) continues for our entire lives as we build our vocabulary and comprehension even as adults.

Babies can be understood to be scientists (Gopnik et al. 1999), constantly taking measurements and observing the world around them, not just in terms of cause and effect with the material world but also with the other humans around them, and this empirical work impacts their language development (Gopnik et al. 1999; Kuhl 2015). The first five years of a child's life are crucial for building a set of important skills that will set the stage for the child's later development (Rankin 2016). This period of early learning is socially influenced and perhaps most strongly guided by the presence of caregivers interacting with the baby as they learn language (Kuhl 2004; Rankin 2016). Children's librarians have the unique opportunity to impact a child's developmental period during the first five years in an informal, play-filled way. Moreover, it is vital that they understand the theory behind how to support and encourage this development. By providing storytimes to children during this period, librarians can facilitate children's language and cognitive development while also modeling practices and helping caregivers to understand how to support this process.

SOCIOCULTURAL THEORY

There are many intersections between the work of children's librarians in the design and delivery of their programs for young children and the major tenets of sociocultural theory. As a subset of learning theory, sociocultural theory is concerned with discussing, describing, and conceptualizing the social and cultural aspects of how we as humans learn. Our environment and the context in which learning takes place as well as who is around us all play a role in how and what we learn (Nathan and Sawyer 2014; Bronfenbrenner 1994). Sociocultural theory therefore offers a framework by which to understand the social nature of how children learn. There are several prominent theories whose tenets support and thus illuminate the work children's librarians do every day in the design and delivery of storytimes and other programs.

Child-centered learning begins with the child and considers what the child is interested in and understands in their world (Dewey 1937; Mooney 2013), knowing that children learn by interacting with the world around them. Children's natural curiosity sparks that learning, so children should have the opportunity to act out the concepts they are learning and be engaged in social activities around that learning (Dewey 1937; Mooney 2013). One approach to understanding early development is as a progression through a series of stages, moving from simple concepts to more complicated systems (Mooney 2013; Piaget 1969), in which children construct their own knowledge, especially through play. Children move through these stages at different rates, influenced by the world around them, which is why it is important to consider the social and cultural aspects to this developmental process, which can influence what and how a child learns. The tools a child uses—language, objects, etc.—are socially constructed and used to facilitate communication and interaction in this world that children are discovering every day (Vygotsky1987). This world is multilayered—made up of family, education, community, and culture—and these layers are all interconnected and extremely influential on children's learning (Mooney 2013; Vygotsky 1987; Bronfenbrenner 1994). An ecological approach to understanding this multilayered world states that children interact with and have an impact on the world around them through repeated interactions in social activities that take place in that world, which over time become more elaborate. The social interactions that facilitate learning for children can be understood as proximal processes that are integral to their learning. Furthermore, building on what was stated above, the extent to which these proximal processes can impact a child's learning is a combination of various influences, including the child, the child's surroundings, and what sort of development the child is working on at that moment. Thus, the immediate world of the child—home, preschool—represents a microsystem that is of direct importance to the child and the family unit (Bronfenbrenner 1994). The library can have a greater or lesser influence on this microsystem depending on the level of interaction of that family with the library. Offering relevant, interactive, learning-based programs that support and extend a child's learning can enable a library to sit within that microsystem and have a greater influence on a child's developmental process.

It is therefore important for librarians to understand the entire ecology in which children learn, from home, to school, to the library, to the larger community, valuing their prior knowledge, as part of meaningful program design and delivery. Librarians, parents and caregivers, and other adults need to actively facilitate and nurture a child's sociocultural learning and inquiry process. Furthermore, librarians and parents or caregivers have opportunities to collaborate, through programs such as Every Child Ready to Read® @ your library® (ECRR), 1st and 2nd editions,[1] to build a deeper understanding of their young children's development and learning process. In this way, the librarian becomes a partner in a family's learning journey, creating a tripartite relationship among librarians, adult caregivers, and children as co-participants in a social setting (Campana 2018; McKenzie and Stooke 2007).

Librarians can impact the early learning development of the children who attend their programs by creating a zone of proximal development—the distance between what children can complete independently and what they can complete with the help of an adult or peer. The adult identifies what the child is in the process of mastering and guides the child toward that mastery:

> What the child is able to do in collaboration today he will be able to do independently tomorrow. Instruction and development seem to be related in the same way that the zone of proximal development and the level of actual development are related. The only instruction, which is useful in childhood, is that which moves ahead of development, that which leads (Vygotsky, 1987).[2]

In programs for young children, a librarian can provide activities, play moments, and verbal encouragement, to give a young child the confidence to try something new and learn and grow in the process. Similarly, adults should use their own experiences to help build on and enhance the experiences of children in the learning process (Dewey 1937; Mooney 2013). This initiates a sociocultural understanding of the role of the librarian as a leader—someone who draws on previous experience to inform a child's learning and provides opportunities for social, interactive experiences. Thus, the role of the librarian should not be to impart knowledge but to support the childs learning process, to help them identify relationships between pieces of information. To enable this, Wood, Bruner, and Ross (1976) developed the concept of scaffolding: an adult can support the child's learning by breaking down an activity that would otherwise be beyond the child's independent skills into smaller pieces to make the activity more manageable. The child can work to complete the elements of the activity that are within their current skill set. With the guidance of the adult, the child can then work on other, more difficult elements of the activity until they have mastered an activity independently. This helps the child to build on information they may have already learned to extend their knowledge. Scaffolding is strongly related to Vygotsky's concept of the zone of proximal development in that adults can use scaffolding to support children in moving through the zone of proximal development so that they can master the next level of skill or task.

LEARNING THROUGH PLAY AND DISCOVERY

Learning for young children can take very different forms than the learning that occurs for school-age children in formal educational settings. The importance of learning in early childhood can often be overlooked, but it is in fact crucial because, once again, what children learn during this period helps to lay the foundation for school-readiness and lifelong learning. It is important to incorporate processes that allow children to take an active role in learning—such as discovery, play, and hands-on activities—into library programs for young children. Bruner's theory of discovery learning (1961) emphasized the importance of facilitating a child's thinking and problem-solving skills, which they can then use in other situations. Learning by discovery, or "figuring things out," allows the child to construct, transform, and organize information so that it is readily available for future application and problem-solving.

Early childhood experiences should employ play as a key element for supporting and encouraging learning. Play and hands-on activities can provide experiences that encourage learning through discovery for young children. When young children engage in play, they build important skills and knowledge that will help to set the stage for later academic and learning success, including self-regulation, oral language abilities, social skills, and cultural information. Ultimately, play and learning by discovery are two of the most important learning processes in which a young child can participate, to help them get ready for school.

DEVELOPMENTALLY APPROPRIATE PRACTICES

What does all this theory mean for your work in your library with your community? When working with young children, it is important to consider whether your practices are developmentally appropriate. You can do this by assessing:

1. What child development and learning theory emphasizes for the target age.
2. Your knowledge of the capabilities of the children in your programs.
3. Your knowledge of the variations in their abilities.
4. Your knowledge of their sociocultural contexts (NAEYC 2009).

In addition to using developmentally appropriate practices (DAP), you might consider scaffolding your storytimes in a couple of ways. Because you may get a variety of ages in a storytime, or your storytime might skew toward different developmental levels depending on the day, it is important to be intentional in your knowledge of child development and the ways you can scaffold your storytime content to be responsive to the children in attendance. Another way to scaffold in storytimes, if you have a fairly regular group, is to include more difficult material over time to make your programs meaningful for young children of different ages through the use of themes as a framework for understanding. In this way, a librarian can create a zone of proximal development that enables children to accomplish tasks or comprehend concepts with the help of an adult that they would not have been able to do on their own. While you are scaffolding for children, you are also modeling early learning practices for parents and caregivers. When you provide familiar as well as unfamiliar materials and stories and you practice child-centered planning, you are putting this research into practice, which enables you to impact the learning of the children you serve.

A CULTURAL APPROACH TO STORYTIME

When we talk about a sociocultural approach to learning, we emphasize both social interactions and the cultural aspects of learning. Culture is social, multifaceted, and experiential, and refers to a set of traditions, beliefs, and interactions shared among a group of people. What makes a storytime cultural? Each aspect of a storytime can be considered culturally laden; the activities, the materials, and the interactions all inhabit and embody cultural understandings and traditions. A sociocultural way of delivering storytime facilitates a co-construction of learning between the librarian, the children, and the parents and caregivers. And the social nature of storytime leads to significant opportunities for learning (Rankin 2016). It is important that librarians understand that children come to storytime with prior knowledge, their own culture. Moreover, this cultural knowledge will always be in flux as children go through the ritual of storytime, informing and being informed by the ritual itself. Storytimes should offer children an equalizing boost, a chance to level the early learning playing field before they enter school. However, when you examine the selected materials, the songs and rhymes, and the very culture itself of storytime, does your practice present any barriers to some who attend or hinder your library's ability to reach your community members effectively? Are your library's doors open to all who wish to enter, and do you reach out to those who are not coming in? Do people feel welcomed by your library's staff, programs, and spaces?

So how do we put this all together? Librarians can best use storytime and other programs for young children to meet the learning and developmental needs of all the children and families they serve by paying close attention to the following:

- Understanding community needs and cultural backgrounds
- Providing both traditional early literacy and early learning opportunities in storytime and other programs for young children, but also looking for ways that those programs can support multiple literacies in young children
- Supporting the intrinsically social and cultural nature of learning and the importance of structured and unstructured social play time for young children to develop language and interpersonal skills
- Recognizing the role of the librarian as a guide and facilitator of this social learning
- Acknowledging the importance of parents and caregivers as part of this learning process
- Understanding that storytime and other programs for young children represent a unique opportunity to help give all children who attend a positive outlook on reading and learning, and being mindful of how to reach those who haven't yet entered the library

The library profiles that follow this chapter embody many of these points in their planning and delivery of early childhood programs. Through a careful assessment of community needs, a thoughtful selection of materials, and an eagerness to make learning fun, librarians can approach learning from a sociocultural perspective and provide safe spaces for inclusive development in a variety of areas for the youngest learners.

What More Can You Do?

While scholars have yet to agree on what specifically constitutes school readiness and lifelong learning, they do agree that certain areas of learning and development are important for young children. In the book, *STEP into Storytime: Using StoryTime Effective Practice to Strengthen the Development of Newborns to Five-Year-Olds* (2014), Ghoting and Klatt present four areas of development and growth that children go through in their early years: social and emotional, physical, language and literacy, and cognitive (which includes math, science, and other subject-specific information). The following brief explanations of each area will give you a general understanding so that you know how to incorporate aspects of each area into your program planning.

Social and Emotional

Social interactions with peers, librarians and other library staff, and parents and caregivers are integral to the learning process for young children and contribute to an atmosphere in which children feel comfortable, supported, and ready to learn. Ghoting and Klatt define social development as "interacting with people. This skill involves the capacity to form relationships with other people. It is external. Children need to learn the skills necessary to communicate their feelings in appropriate ways." When librarians are intentional about interacting with children and allow opportunities for children to interact with each other they help to support social learning. Ghoting and Klatt then define emotional development as "understanding and controlling our emotions. It is internal." A child's mastery of both social interactions and emotional control begins with that first relationship between the parent or caregiver and the child and then grows outward to the family, to peers, and then to the community. Librarians can label the feelings that fictional characters are facing and talk about a range of emotions to prepare the child emotionally to be ready to separate from their parents or caregivers and develop their independence.

Physical

Research has shown that children learn about their world through their senses, and one of the strongest senses for exploration is touch. As a result, physical development (e.g., gross motor skills, fine motor skills, and sensation and perception) has an impact on a child's learning development. The term *gross motor skills* refers to large body movements, which in storytime includes active play songs that get kids up and jumping, waving, twirling, and more. Children learn about balance and coordination through these kinds of movements. *Fine motor skills* include strengthening the muscles in the hands and arms through activities, such as fingerplays, writing nametags, drawing, using scissors. *Sensation and perception* refer to how children understand their bodies in space as well as what's going on inside their bodies. Because children are constantly interacting with the world around them, incorporate physical times (dancing, yoga, jumping, etc.) into your storytimes and other programs for young children to provide them with crucial opportunities to learn with their bodies.

Language and Literacy

Early literacy refers to what a child knows about reading and writing before they are actually able to read and write (Roskos, Christie, and Richgels 2003). Librarians have the privilege of interacting with children while they are building early literacy skills and preparing to learn to read. Early literacy has become a common part of public libraries' programming for children, through initiatives such as ECRR. Therefore, it is important for librarians to emphasize various early literacy skills, including oral language, vocabulary, phonological awareness, print concepts, letter knowledge, and background knowledge, as a part of the singing, playing, reading, writing, and talking they do in every storytime (Dresang et al. 2011; Meyers and Henderson 2004). Most importantly, all of this learning is wrapped up in the fun of storytime so children are learning as they have a good time!

Cognitive

Children amass great amounts of information as they interact with the world around them, information they are trying to synthesize with what they already know and have already experienced. They gain much, if not all, of this information through social interactions with peers and adults, and children enhance their vocabulary through their social play. Children also develop abstract thinking, another aspect of cognitive development, which helps them understand that one thing can represent another and imagine things that are not physically present. Sorting and classifying are further cognitive tasks that children build during this early development period. You can support children in this development process through the stories, activities, and songs you provide that emphasize similarities and differences, opposites, patterns, and new vocabulary.

This might seem like a lot to learn and keep straight as you plan your programs. The important thing to remember is that you know your community best—these are just tools you can use to design and deliver impactful programs that encourage children to develop a love of learning. These domains of early learning can serve to enrich and enhance the work you already do to promote this learning.

NOTES

1. Every Child Ready to Read® @ your library® is a joint initiative between the Public Library Association and the Association for Library Services to Children, two divisions of the American Library Association. The initiative is designed to enable librarians to build awareness of, and demonstrate, early literacy activities for parents and caregivers to use with their child outside of the library.
2. Gendering here is in the original text and therefore is repeated here verbatim.

REFERENCES

Bronfenbrenner, Urie. "Ecological Models of Human Development." In *International Encyclopedia of Education*, vol. 3, 2nd. Ed. Oxford: Elsevier. Reprinted in: Gauvain, M. and Cole, M. (Eds.): *Readings on the Development of Children,* 2nd ed. (1993): 37–43. NY: Freeman.

Bruner, J. S. 1961. "The Act of Discovery." *Harvard Educational Review* 31, 21–32.

Campana, K. 2018. "The Multimodal Power of Storytime: Exploring an Information Environment for Young Children," PhD dissertation, University of Washington.

Dewey, J. 1937. *The Child and the Curriculum.* Chicago: University of Chicago Press.

Dresang, E. T., K. Burnett, J. Capps, and E. N. Feldman. 2011. *The Early Literacy Landscape for Public Libraries and Their Partners.* White Paper, University of Washington.

Ghoting, S. N., and K. F. Klatt. 2014. *STEP into Storytime: Using Storytime Effective Practice to Strengthen the Development of Newborns to Five-Year-Olds.* Chicago: ALA Editions.

Gopnik, A., A. Meltzoff, and P. K. Kuhl. 1999. *The Scientist in the Crib: What Early Learning Tells Us About the Mind.* New York: HarperPerennial.

Institute for Learning and Brain Sciences (producer). 2016. Module 2: Why the First 2,000 Days Matter: A Look Inside the Brain [online module]. Available at: http://modules.ilabs.uw.edu/module/first-2000-days-matter/.

Kuhl, P. K. 2004. "Early Language Acquisition: Cracking the Speech Code." *Nature Reviews Neuroscience* 5, 831–43.

_____. 2015. "Baby Talk." *Scientific American* 313 (5): 64–9.

Kuhl, P. K., R. R. Ramirez, A. Bosseler, J. L. Lin, and T. Imada. 2014. "Infants' Brain Responses to Speech Suggest Analysis by Synthesis." *Proceedings of the National Academy of Sciences of the United States* 111 (31): 11, 238–45.

McKenzie, P. J., and R. K. Stooke. 2007. Producing storytime: A Collectivist Analysis of work in a Complex Communicative Space. *Library Quarterly* 77 (1).

Meyers, E., and H. Henderson. (2004). "Overview of Every Child Ready to Read @ your library." Accessed at http://www.everychildreadytoread.org/projecthistory% 09/overview-every-child-ready-read-your-library%C2%AE-1st-edition.

Mooney, C. G. 2013. *Theories of Childhood: An Introduction to Dewey, Montessori, Erikson, Piaget, and Vygotsky* (2nd ed.). St. Paul, MN: Red Leaf Press.

Nathan, M. J., and R. K. Sawyer. 2014. "Foundations of the Learning Sciences." In *The Cambridge Handbook of the Learning Science,* 2nd ed. Edited by R. Keoth Sawyer 21–43. New York: Cambridge University Press.

National Association for the Education of Young Children. 2009. *Developmentally Appropriate Practice in Early Childhood Programs Serving Children from Birth through Age 8.* Washington, DC: National Association for the Education of Young Children. https://www.naeyc.org/sites/default/files/globally-shared/downloads/PDFs/resources/position-statements/PSDAP.pdf.

Piaget, J. 1969. *The Science of Education and the Psychology of the Child*. New York: Viking Compass.

Rankin, C. 2016. "Library Services for the Early Years: Policy, Practice, and the Politics of the Age". *Library Trends* 65 (1): 5–18.

Roskos, K. A., J. F. Christie, and D. J. Richgels. 2003. "The Essentials of Early Literacy Instruction." *Young Children* 58 (2): 52–60.

Vygotsky, L. S. 1987. *The Collected Works of L. S. Vygotsky: Problems of General Psychology including the Volume Thinking and Speech*. Translated by N. Minick. New York: Plenum.

Wood, D., J. S. Bruner, and G. Ross. 1976. "The Role of Tutoring in Problem-Solving." *Journal of Psychology and Psychiatry* 17.

CHAPTER 9

Prioritizing Community, Literacy, and Equity in Programming for Children from Birth to Age Five at the Pierce County Library System

Susan Anderson-Newham

INTRODUCTION

Pierce County is a geographically large, mixed rural-suburban area that includes Mount Rainier National Park. 72.6 percent of our population is White, 10.2 percent Hispanic or Latinx, 8.1 percent Asian, Native Hawaiian, or Pacific Islander, 7.4 percent African American, and 1.7 percent Native American. We are a medium-sized system—twenty community branches serving almost 600,000 customers, about 60,000 of them under the age of five. We also serve the Puyallup Tribal Nation. The Pierce County Library System (PCLS) surrounds the city of Tacoma and the Tacoma Public Library in Washington State.

BACKGROUND

When developing programming for young children ages birth to five, our system uses three lenses:

1. A system-wide focus on the categories of *learning, enjoyment,* and *community:* all library activities should fall into one of these categories.
2. The Every Child Ready to Read® frameworks: The six skills of early literacy—*print awareness, letter awareness, phonological awareness, vocabulary, narrative skills,* and *print motivation*—underscore all our programming (Every Child Ready to Read 1996). And our librarians make sure the Five Practices of Early Literacy—*talking, singing, reading, writing,* and *playing*—are modeled and promoted in all our programs (Every Child Ready to Read 2005). Every Child Ready to Read® skills and practices are

also used to evaluate our programs, handouts, and web information so that we know learning is present in all we do.[1]

3. Equity: We examine our policies, practices, and cultural perspectives in an effort to celebrate the rich diversity of our county. This helps ensure that we offer the highest-quality programming and contribute to building a healthy and caring community.

PROGRAMS

Storytimes are the most common program that we offer for babies, toddlers, preschoolers, and families. We also offer bilingual English-Spanish and Spanish-only storytimes. The types of storytimes and their frequency is dependent on the branch and the community it serves. Our larger branches might offer all age ranges of storytimes; our small branches might offer only one catch-all family storytime for all ages at once.

There are probably as many ways to present a storytime as there are librarians who do so. But one good rule of thumb is to begin every storytime with the same greeting and end with the same farewell. This consistent bookending helps create a predictable, familiar storytime structure that your families will come to recognize and expect. The familiarity of structure and routine helps children relax. The content of the storytime will vary depending on the age of the children attending, but each program should incorporate rhymes, songs, and movement. Using the Five Practices as an assessment framework can be very helpful in planning. Ask yourself, if you have a conversation with the children in storytime, are you intentionally seeking ways to encourage the *children* to talk? Are you singing and rhyming? Reading? Writing and drawing? Playing? If you look at your storytime plans through the Five Practices lens, you can almost guarantee participation, fun, and learning. There are many ways to incorporate the practices. Some librarians might include yoga or dance. Others might include flannelboard stories or poetry. Some might use apps in a developmentally appropriate way. The content will depend on your interests and areas of expertise as well as the interests of the children and families who attend.

I have found it helpful to introduce a stuffed animal "helper" at storytimes (you could also use a doll or a puppet). Dewey, my bear helper, shakes each child's hand at the beginning of the storytime (this helps me learn the children's names!). Dewey sometimes introduces literacy activities, such as sharing a poem or song, focusing on one particular letter and exploring its sound (letter awareness and phonological awareness), or counting aloud the number of children at storytime (mathematical learning). You could use a helper to introduce a flannelboard story or assist in the telling of a story. A helper can put anxious children at ease until they come to know the librarian better. It is also a useful tool for modeling rhymes and bounces at baby storytimes.

I have witnessed so much creativity at storytime and so many librarians who have successfully brought unique bits of themselves to their programming that I always encourage my staff to examine what they love and brainstorm how to bring that to storytime. I ask, "If you love gardening, how can you share that in the program? If you love dance, can you incorporate some movement and rhythm?" We are always enthusiastic about the things we love, and when we bring our enthusiasm to storytimes, the programs become more joyful. I encourage everyone to sing! Children do not care if you can carry a tune. I worked with a wonderful children's librarian, Avis Jobrack, who could not carry a tune, but sang at *every* storytime! She told me once, "I like to sing at storytime because no one sings worse than me, so I give adults permission to sing with their kids no matter what." So sing together!

When I train new librarians, I encourage them to be intentional about their storytime planning. When planning for a whole session, ask, "Why did I choose those particular books? Are they inclusive and diverse? What skills do I hope the children learn over the course of this session? Are all five practices built into the programs? Are there opportunities for interaction? Am I helping to develop math and science learning?" An intentional approach to planning enables you to focus on incorporating interactive fun into your programs that will encourage children to participate and learn through play.

Babytimes. These storytimes are for our youngest customers and their caregivers. The age range might be divided into "pre-walkers" and "walkers" up to age two; if your community does not have enough of an audience to separate these ages, you might designate this storytime as appropriate for birth through age two. Though infants will find this program filled with enjoyment and fun, babytimes are equally directed at parents and caregivers. We model reading and singing to babies as well as cuddling them! We hope to fill their ears and brains with language and love.

I like to sit on a blanket on the floor for my programs with this age group. I generally share one or two beautiful, age-appropriate books featuring simple text and simple illustrations or photographs (which babies especially love). The subject matter for these books centers on familiar topics—family, routines, food, animals, and so on. There are many ways to share books with this age group:

- Read one book aloud, showing the illustrations to the group as you read.
- Pass out many copies of one book for everyone to read at the same time (choral reading).
- Distribute a selection of appropriate books for caregivers to individually share with their children.

However you share the books you choose, this is an excellent way to promote our wonderful library collections and start children on the road of loving books and reading.

Between books, we fill babytimes with very simple fingerplays, songs, cuddling rhymes, and gentle movement rhymes—rocking, softly bouncing, and caressing the baby while singing or chanting the rhyme. There are hundreds of resources in print and online with appropriate *wiggles* and *bounces* for this age group. Simple sign language can be very effectively introduced at these storytimes as well.

Babytime programs are fairly short, given the attention spans of the customers—perhaps fifteen to twenty minutes at the most. They are usually followed by an open-ended play period in which blocks, balls, washable toys, and books are made accessible for babies to explore. (Babies also learn an incredible amount from exploring each other!) An open-ended play time also gives caregivers a chance to socialize and share information and enables the librarian to build relationships and share library resources. And open-ended play provides a rich environment for social-emotional and cognitive learning.

Babytimes are often filled with unexpected moments. I have always used Dewey to model the gentle bouncing and cuddling rhymes. He would sit on my lap like the babies do with their caregivers. Once the babies got to know me, often one would crawl onto my lap and take Dewey's place—thus becoming my new model. At one babytime, after one baby did that, another crawled over and climbed into my lap as well. And before long, my lap was overflowing with babies! The storytime ended in laughter and cuddles, and I moved right into the play period making sure that each baby had sufficient time on Miss Susan's lap.

Toddler Times. Generally, toddler times focus on two- to three-year-olds and their parents and caregivers. I generally sit in a chair at this storytime, but many parents and caregivers will sit on the floor with their toddlers. This is a very active and busy age group with limited attention spans, so I share two or perhaps three short and simple books, interspersed with active fingerplays, songs, and movement rhymes. Because toddlers are very mobile, movement rhymes include independent activity for the child. This is one example: "Stretch up high! Touch the ground. Nod your head. Blink your eyes." These activities help build vocabulary and spatial awareness for children and they harness a toddler's natural energy, keeping them engaged in the storytime.

Similar to babytimes, toddler time books will have simple text and simple illustrations. The content of the books still focus on familiar themes—home and family, neighborhood, animals, food, concepts, numbers, counting, shapes, and so on. We like to model dialogic reading when sharing books with this age group—asking open-ended questions to continuously appeal to the active toddler brain. These questions also demonstrate a way of sharing books that is more engaging for children and more effective in developing their language and literacy skills.

Preschool Storytimes. This storytime is planned for three- to six-year-old children and their parents and caregivers. Because preschoolers are developing their attention spans, these programs can be longer. Of course, it's good to remember that the length and content of storytimes could vary widely depending on the customers and the interests of the librarians presenting them. Any combination of storytelling, the flannelboard, dance, yoga postures, puppetry, poetry, math, science, games, and apps is a welcome part of a storytime. Other languages might also be introduced during the program as well. Some of our librarians incorporate tactile elements, picture cards, and toys, bringing sensory learning and more inclusion into their storytimes. As with all our programs, we want *every* child to feel not only welcome, but celebrated. The books shared at a preschool storytime can be longer and more complex, with a wider variety of content and busier illustrations.

Family Storytimes. Our smaller branches don't generally have the population to warrant storytimes geared to many different age groups. So, we offer a catch-all family storytime for all ages. One week, we might see four babies, seven toddlers, five preschoolers, and a six-year-old. The next week might be all babies and toddlers. Since we do not know precisely who is coming each week, we over-prepare, bringing many more books than we could ever share at one program, guaranteeing that we will have developmentally appropriate materials for whomever shows up. Family storytimes draw on the contents of all the other storytimes, depending on who attends.

SUMMER STORIES AND CRAFTS

Our staff is busy during summer with the Summer Reading program, yet we still want to offer storytimes, so we created a series of kits that we call Summer Stories and Crafts. These kits center on a theme (e.g., "Beach,") and can include:

- Books
- Flannelboard stories, including the text or lyrics to the story or song
- Music on CD
- Fingerplay and rhyme sheets
- A science activity and supplies

- Craft idea and supplies
- Recommended apps to use in storytimes
- Various realia: puppets, seashells, and so on
- Evaluation forms

The kits are stocked with enough supplies for many branches to use over the summer and are rotated throughout the system. This allows the staff to present wonderful programs with a minimum of preparation and planning. All the kits are created by librarians and then evaluated and tweaked after each summer.

Outreach Storytimes. Pierce County Library also ventures out into the community to present storytimes for children in childcares. We have a designated librarian who presents eighteen to twenty-two storytimes each month in childcare centers and Head Start and ECEAP (Washington State's version of Head Start) programs around the county. These take place in preschool or toddler classrooms and the programs look very much the same as library storytimes but with a few additions. Because we want parents to know that the library is out in the community (advocacy!), we created twelve simple bookmarks that indicate which library visited their child's school that day. The bookmarks also contain a literacy or STEM activity for the family, as well as a couple of recommended book titles. Each librarian brings enough bookmarks for each child at the school to take home and keep. Then, at each monthly visit, the children receive a new bookmark. On the first visit, the librarian provides a notebook supplied with some literacy resources for the teachers. At each subsequent visit, the librarian hands out a storytime sheet listing the books shared, the rhymes used, the songs that were sung, and perhaps some additional activities that could extend the learning from the storytime. These sheets allow the teachers to end the year with a collection of storytimes ideas and resources for their own use.

Block Parties. Because our system is closely associated with the early learning community of Pierce County, we are constantly learning about the opportunity gaps and specific needs of the children in our county. A few years ago, it was brought to our attention that our incoming kindergarteners were faring well in terms of literacy skill development but were lacking in math skill development. We did some research and brainstormed with partners, which led us to invest in sets of unit blocks for each of our branches. These blocks are used at special building programs using LEGOs, straws, and connectors, and so on, as well as after many storytimes. Some branches have introduced "block parties" open to the public. A large part of our block-play programming is an ongoing partnership with several Head Start and ECEAP classrooms. We pair a classroom with a library branch. Once per month, beginning in January and ending in May or June, the class visits the library for a short storytime and open-ended block play. Each child receives a set of wooden blocks to take home and keep, an information sheet for parents on supporting block play (available in both English and Spanish), and a free book at each visit to add to their home libraries. The library fundraises to cover the blocks, the books, and the transportation to and from the branch. Some of the branches hold Head Start parent events at the library to sidestep the transportation costs and to connect parents more directly with what we have to offer. At the end of each year, we encourage the teachers to complete a survey about their experiences. This helps us improve the program from year to year. This has been an extremely popular program in our community.

Block play enables children to work on fine and gross motor skills, build vocabulary and communication skills, and work on social-emotional skills such as problem-solving and empathy. Some children build from their own imaginations; others use books for inspiration, (see figure 9.1), so be sure to provide print materials with your blocks. Walk around the block play space, talk with children and parents and caregivers about what they're building—by doing so, you're modeling for parents and caregivers how to carry on their own conversations with kids during their play, which builds a strong relationship between the parents and caregivers and the child but also facilitates interactive play.

Outside Performers. In addition to the programming created and presented by our staff, we maintain a budget for hiring outside programmers: puppeteers, musicians, storytellers, and other professionals who work with very young children. We keep a database of potential performers and occasionally attend performer showcases so we are able to offer high-quality independent programs for our customers. This can take the pressure off to provide regular programs and give your audience a breather. You can even build off these programs for your next storytime, using similar themes and activities. You never know where your ideas will come from!

FIGURE 9.1 A Block Party Masterpiece!

PARTNERSHIPS

Because we work closely with the early learning community of Pierce County, we are able to identify any gaps in our service and find ways to help fill those gaps. Sometimes this involves the creation of partnerships.

LIL Readers. One example is our LIL Readers partnership (part of United Way's Launch into Literacy initiative). Because our staff is so busy, the library will never be able to present regular literacy-based programs for the home childcares in our county. But we still want to reach out and support this population, so the library and United Way created a partnership that places volunteers into home childcares to present storytimes. The library can provide the home childcare contacts because we have a book delivery system to childcares, so we have a relationship with them. The library also trains the volunteers on early literacy and sharing books with young children. We provide the kits—librarian-created bags of selected books, flannelboard stories, rhymes, songs, and activities centered on a theme—and we circulate them to the volunteers through our branches. United Way solicits the volunteers, supports the Memorandum of Understanding with the home childcare providers, processes the background checks, and acts as the volunteer liaison. This partnership allows us to support literacy and language learning for many more children in our community.

Community Readers. Our area has a yearly pageant for high-achieving high school senior girls who become "Daffodil Princesses" for the annual spring parade. Most high schools nominate a princess who becomes a sort of ambassador in the community for charity and volunteerism. We have a partnership with the program every year where we train the princesses on how to share books with young children and then offer Read with a Princess programs in branches all over the county. They make their appearances in full princess regalia, which makes this program extremely popular with our youngest customers. And because we have a large military base in our county, this year we are adding a similar program on Armed Services Day called Read with a Service Person.

RESOURCES FOR PROGRAM DEVELOPMENT

We use many resources when developing programming. Our library purchases wonderful books filled with rhymes, songs, games, storytime plans, math activities, science ideas, and so on. The American Library Association publishes hundreds of titles that help support programming in library branches. Additionally, we are fortunate to live in an age with an abundance of online resources: library websites, association websites, blogs, online publications, and social media. When you begin to develop your own programming, be sure to take advantage of all these resources; they will help you to get started as well as give you ideas for keeping your programs fresh and exciting! And don't forget conferences! If you have the chance, try to attend local and national conferences—they are a wonderful place to participate in workshops or sessions that offer opportunities to share what works, what doesn't, and what might be trending.

CONTINUING TO LEARN AND GROW

At the Pierce County Library System, we have an ongoing peer-to-peer coaching program. During the autumn and spring storytime sessions, we pair up all our youth services staff. They arrange to observe each other's storytimes at some point during the session. At the end, we hold a youth services meeting where everyone shares what they observed: great books, wonderful activities, unknown rhymes or songs, as well as ideas they plan to "steal." This has proved an excellent way to support new staff, re-inspire experienced staff, and promote strong team building. The robust nature of this sharing time, as well as the extensive nature of the resource file that we keep, demonstrates the success of this program. While you may not have a peer-coaching program in place at your current or future library, you can always work to start one or just find a few peers who also want to learn and grow to join you in an informal sharing and feedback process. Watch each other's programs if you can or just talk about them. You will learn so much from hearing about others' practices and sharing your own.

CONCLUSION

We make a point of connecting with the early learning community of Pierce County and partnering with many organizations to inform and create innovative and popular programs to demonstrate our commitment to the Pierce County community. When we align that programming with Every Child Ready to Read® and other relevant research, as well as our mentoring and continuing education opportunities for staff, we incorporate continuous learning into our everyday operations and events. And through our System's commitment to equity and celebrating every child, all the while infusing everything with a spirit of fun, we create welcoming and enjoyable programs for our very youngest customers and their families.

NOTE

1. Visit the ECRR website (http://bit.ly/2DaQ53f) to learn more about the skills, components, and practices of Every Child Ready to Read®.

REFERENCE

Every Child Ready to Read® @your library®. 1996. Public Library Association and Association for Library Service to Children.

Every Child Ready to Read® @your library®, 2nd edition. 2005. Public Library Association and Association for Library Service to Children.

CHAPTER 10

Arapahoe Libraries

Early Literacy All Around

Melissa Depper and Lori Romero

INTRODUCTION

Located in suburban Denver, the Arapahoe Libraries reach approximately 250,000 patrons within Arapahoe County, Colorado. Library services are provided at eight branch locations, as well as through outreach initiatives and bookmobile services. The library service area is diverse in geography, population, community needs, and socioeconomics.

The Arapahoe Libraries take pride in offering creative and forward-thinking programs, services, and learning opportunities, as well as offering cutting-edge technology, excellent customer service, coffee shops, studios, and makerspaces, encouraging a collaborative, "let's find out" spirit.

Due to a strong commitment to early childhood literacy as an ongoing strategic focus, Arapahoe Libraries has a dedicated early literacy department known as Child and Family Library Services (CFLS). The CFLS team is currently comprised of five early literacy librarians and fourteen storytime specialists supervised and coordinated by this chapter's authors. More than sixty storytimes and early literacy programs are provided each week that aim to empower parents and prepare our youngest patrons to succeed when they reach school age.

RECURRING EARLY LITERACY PROGRAMS (AGES BIRTH THROUGH FIVE)

The Arapahoe Libraries Child and Family Library Services Department offers a comprehensive menu of programs for children ages birth through five and their caregivers. Our aim? To provide a rich and thoughtful menu of early literacy opportunities for our parents, caregivers, and children. We hope attendees will feel like partners, so that they leave our programs armed with more strategies and ideas than they had when they arrived. And we want them to come back! We strive to build relationships and, because we know true learning happens over time, our early literacy programming structure features the element of recurring opportunities. In other words, our programs are rarely one-shot events. Instead, we use a series approach and hope that participants build a new network of like-minded friends.

Our nine programs are intentionally structured to support research-based early childhood concepts, including:

- Language and play-focused activities, with child-adult interactions as paramount
- Introducing high-quality, age-appropriate books at every program
- Developmentally appropriate programs tailored specifically to babies, toddlers, and preschoolers
- Literacy messaging and informal education for adults

Our Programs

Literacy-Based Storytimes

Audience: Children from birth to five years and their parents and caregivers.
   ○ Baby storytime (birth to twenty-four months)
   ○ Toddler storytime (two to three years)
   ○ Family storytime (all ages; geared to preschoolers)
About the program: The Arapahoe Libraries offer more than sixty storytimes each week throughout our eight branches and bookmobile service, including three Spanish and a Russian language storytime. Storytimes run approximately thirty minutes and are followed by fifteen minutes of "learning-through-play" time featuring age-appropriate toys and activities designed to encourage parent-child interaction and learning. Each storytime includes engaging books, songs, movement, and participation activities, along with Every Child Ready to Read® (ECRR) literacy messages to spark understandings of ways to promote early literacy at home.

Little Explorers

Audience: Children ages two to five and their parents and caregivers.
About the program: Designed for working families, Little Explorers programs are offered monthly on Saturdays. The hour-long program begins with a literature-based storytime aligned with high-interest STEAM (science, technology, engineering, art and math) concepts and related hands-on extension activities.

Stories & More

Audience: Children ages birth to five and their parents and caregivers.
About the program: Stories & More is an hour-long program offered eight times a month at five of our branches and at one off-site recreation center location. The grant-funded program includes a literacy-based storytime followed by active extension activities related to the reading, writing, singing, talking, and playing strategies demonstrated during the storytime. This popular program offers a special opportunity because each child and

family leaves with a quality children's book, a play-based literacy tool or activity for use at home, and a practical literacy tip handout.

Literacy Make & Take Workshops: *Early Literacy Tools to Go*

Audience: Any adult caregivers who work with children ages birth to five.

About the Program: This grant-funded evening program is a companion to Stories & More. Early Literacy Tools to Go is held twelve times per year. Busy caregivers who are seeking time to create early literacy learning activities and build a community can network with others who work with young children. This community building is supported with supplies and "maker-tools," such as laminators, paper-cutters, die-cutting machines, etc. that are provided for hands-on experimentation, following activity demonstrations by our early literacy librarian. Participants are introduced to great books, and they create tools to use in their childcare setting the very next day.

Family Place Play & Learn Workshop Series

Audience: Children ages one to three along with parents and caregivers.

About the program: This four-week workshop series is the centerpiece of the Family Place Libraries initiative and is offered twice each year at each of our designated Family Place Libraries branches. This hour-long program is set up in a large space with preschool-like stations, including gross motor, manipulative, music, blocks, narrative play, reading, and art center. Parents follow their child's lead and explore and interact at each station. Every session also includes an early childhood expert from the community to answer individual questions and offer suggestions to parents. Our volunteer experts have included speech language therapists, nutritionists, behavior specialists, occupational therapists, literacy specialists and music/ movement teachers.

Building Blocks: A Kindergarten Readiness Program

Audience: Children ages three to five along with parents and caregivers.

About the program: Building Blocks is a home-grown, three-session series rotating to a different branch each trimester. Building Blocks activities and experiences are based on common kindergarten readiness expectations for language, literacy, math, and science that are provided in fun, exploratory ways. The program also features parent tips, a literacy backpack to check-out each week and a quality book to keep in the child's home library.

Reading Readiness Outreach Program

Audience: Teachers at designated preschool and childcare sites in our service area.

About the program: Because we wanted to make an impact with adults who see numerous young children every day, we designed the Reading Readiness

Outreach Program. Our early childhood literacy trainer travels to eight carefully selected, off-site locations to provide library information and unique, ongoing early literacy training, modeling, and coaching for teachers. The trainer offers a demonstration storytime focused on a particular ECRR early literacy skill every two weeks for participating teachers, followed by discussion and coaching sessions throughout the year. Teachers receive literacy tips and practice kits to help replicate the strategies modeled in the storytime, as well as sets of convenient, circulating library bookbags for families to check out and use at home.

Begin with Books

Audience: Home childcare providers who care for children from birth to five years.

About the program: This long running, volunteer-based literacy program brings a monthly storytime to home daycare settings. The program is intended to help childcare providers who want to promote early literacy but may find it difficult to bring their young children to library storytimes. Trained Begin-with-Books volunteers bring a themed storytime and activities to the home environment and leave a bag of quality children's books to read and switch out for new books the following month.

Bright by Three

Audience: Families with newborns to three-year-olds visiting our libraries.

About the program: Bright by Three is a free, statewide initiative for parents and caregivers of children birth to three years. When trained library staff observe parents and young children playing in our early learning spaces and attending programs, they can provide an overview and offer a Bright by Three bag containing valuable child development tools, information, and resources to empower parents. Bright by Three offers follow-up opportunities with families and opt-in Bright by Text messaging services.

OUR PROGRAMMING STRATEGY

We have used several different strategies for developing programs, including borrowing models from other organizations or libraries, designing experiences that help meet our partners' needs, in-house creation, and adapting and refining long-running heritage programs.

For all program development, we first determine that the proposed program meets our library's overall mission as well as our annual strategic goals. Broadly, this means supporting lifelong learning; more narrowly, this means targeting initiatives that will help develop early literacy skills and school readiness in preschool children.

If we are working with a partner, we work to make sure that we are meeting their needs as well. Our certification by the Family Place Initiative requires us to hold a certain number of programs that closely match the Family Place program outline in terms of time, frequency, materials, and community expert participation. For our Make & Take and Stories & More programs, the Arapahoe County Early Childhood Council (ACECC) receives grant money from state and national sources that they in turn share with our library to support these research-based activity programs. These programs must meet certain goals specified by their grant, which is designated for reaching Family, Friend, and Neighbor caregivers.

When creating new in-house programs, we first decide whether our general plans meet library mission and goals, and then we look to see which needs are being met with existing programs and which needs still persist. Is there a segment of our service population that does not have access to current offerings? Do we feel there is an age group that could use more support? For instance, the Building Blocks program, a kindergarten readiness series, was developed using this approach. Once we launched the Family Place Play & Learn series, which serves children ages one to three, we designed a separate program to target the different needs of older preschoolers, ages three to five. Our Little Explorers programs, for ages two to five, were created to showcase curriculum-based learning experiences in music, arts, science, math, and engineering that mirrored state educational standards but were difficult or impossible to incorporate into traditional storytimes.

For longer-running programs, such as our preschool Reading Readiness Outreach program or our traditional storytimes, we focus on continual refinement and adjustments to meet changes in community, goals, resources, or partners. The Reading Readiness Outreach program grew out of a partnership program that over time no longer aligned with our service area, which meant the CFLS Department was able to take a fresh look at the program, redesign a large part of the service, and better reach preschool teachers with on-the-job training in early literacy research and best practices for their classrooms. The core of the program—visiting children and teachers at area preschools—remains the same, but much of the delivery, materials, and outcomes have been recreated. Similarly, traditional storytimes have been offered at our library for decades; however, over the past ten or twelve years, in response to ECRR and new research findings, we have been able to make significant changes to how we deliver them. These changes include the way we hire and train storytime providers; select storytime materials and activities; teach staff, parents, and caregivers about early literacy concepts; and incorporate toys and manipulatives to support play-based learning both during and after storytime.

WORKING WITH OUR PARTNERS AND OUR COMMUNITY

The CFLS Department works with a number of community partners, from other nonprofit organizations to individuals who provide expertise for programs, as well as local volunteers. As mentioned above, the ACECC provides grant money that supports our Stories & More and Literacy Make & Take programs. The library and the ACECC had established a working relationship to deliver outreach programs to early childhood centers, and when the ACECC received additional grant funding, they came to us to talk about developing a new program to reach a broader community of caregivers.

The Family Place Initiative is an overarching national partner for the library, but the Family Place programs offer opportunities for partnerships on the local community level as well. Each session of the Play & Learn series is attended by an early childhood expert. These professionals are often as interested in outreach as the library is! It may take some effort to connect with their organizations, but they are often happy to maintain an ongoing relationship, because it meets their own needs for reaching families in the community.

ASSESSING OUR PROGRAMS

We use various methods for assessing our programs. We value listening to the informal, spontaneous, verbal comments shared with our librarians by our patrons during and after program sessions. We collect information about routine output measures, such as attendance per program and frequency of repeat attendance. In some cases, we use feedback forms provided by our community partners to gather statistics they have requested to satisfy their own grant reporting needs.

From time to time, we have created in-house evaluation forms to collect ongoing or targeted input from our patrons, to help us make minor adjustments to programs, or to gather feedback regarding one-time projects, such as renovation of a children's area. We have plans to create a survey tool to include in the circulating library bookbags offered through the Reading Readiness Outreach Program for parents to complete after using the materials at home.

Pre- and post-program surveys, developed by our department and solicited from parents or caregivers before and after they participate in a session, help us to assess two programs: Begin with Books, and Family Place Play & Learn.

Last year, we also completed an in-depth written evaluation designed and administered by a paid local educational consultant. To create and administer our evaluation, the library hired Clayton Early Learning, a local organization dedicated to early childhood education research, practice, and training. Over a six-month period, they used formal tools, such as child development assessments, family measures, and facilitator quality measures to observe the children, parents, caregivers, and the librarian presenting the program. Because measuring the impact and outcomes of our programs is of high value to our library district, funding for this evaluation was built into the library's operating budget, over and above normal budget items. This demonstrated the deep support by our library directors for our department's early literacy objectives.

Overall, we are working toward more data-driven decision-making, using information from assessments, such as the Clayton evaluation and our pre- and post-program surveys. We are in the process of gathering this type and amount of data for the first time and will evaluate it in the coming year, in the hope that it can guide our program development and resource allocation. *We want to make sure we are not creating and delivering programs simply for the sake of developing new experiences or chasing trends. Rather, we want to ensure that we are providing programs, experiences, and services for the purpose of meeting our local community's needs and having a measurable impact on our patrons' early literacy behaviors and school-readiness outcomes.*

HIGHLIGHTS AND CHALLENGES

Another form of assessment requires analyzing patrons' or partners' anecdotes about our programs. These success stories are highly motivating and point to where particular program outcomes are in sync with larger goals and objectives.

For example, the ACECC considers the Stories & More program to be highly aligned with their goals and it has proven to meet their needs. Therefore, they have proposed working with our library to develop training and materials for other library systems in Arapahoe County. They are pursuing additional grant funding specifically to expand the program—an excellent vote of confidence!

One of the childcare directors, who is part of our Reading Readiness Outreach program, shared that since the beginning of this partnership with the library, she and her teachers have learned about the impact that early literacy skills will have on her young students' lives. Thus, she has begun to incorporate questions about early literacy experience and knowledge into her hiring process for potential teachers. This represents a meaningful shift in her priorities for her staff, one that will have a far-reaching impact on her school community.

The Family Place Play & Learn series has proven to be an excellent, nonjudgmental way for storytime providers to connect families dealing with a child's temporary behavioral or emotional challenges to community experts who may enable them to determine helpful tools or next steps. Sometimes families don't know what professional help is available, or are reluctant to have their children formally assessed, and due to this opportunity we've heard from parents who were able to talk with a nutritionist, nurse, or speech therapist at just the right moment.

Challenges include the ongoing process of matching available resources for a program— budget, staff time, meeting rooms, and materials—with community demand. We want to offer the right number of sessions, from our one-time event programs to our daily storytimes, so that most of the patrons who wish to attend may do so. Conversely, there are some locations that need ongoing local promotion and advertising to drive sufficient attendance to sustain the program long-term. Where we use community experts, we strive to balance our invitations so that no single expert feels that we are demanding too much of their time. We also work continually to keep all program content fresh and research-based.

LOOKING TOWARD THE FUTURE?

In the future, we'd like to do even more with data-driven decision-making to guide our program development. We have a few specific new programs we'd like to explore, including world language storytimes and teen parent support, both of which will help us to connect a greater number of parents and caregivers in our community with library services. We'd also like to continue to develop our "literacy spot" concept, a kind of pop-up, semi-passive programming that provides materials for drop-in early literacy engagement experiences. These experiences are mediated by librarians to help build relationships with and provide early learning support for families outside of storytimes.

We feel fortunate that our past years of intentional departmental planning have led us to a current programming level where we are consistently meeting a wide range of early learning needs for our patron population. As a result, we don't have plans for global or in-depth changes to our programs and services at this time, though we continually work to fine-tune our strategies and offerings.

CHAPTER 11

The Free Library of Philadelphia

Serving Its Youngest Patrons
with a Community-Minded Approach

Sarah Stippich and Christine Caputo

INTRODUCTION

Philadelphia is a city of neighborhoods, each with its own character and strengths. Like other public libraries around the country, the Free Library of Philadelphia offers a diverse set of programs for children and teens that reflect the needs and interests of the neighborhood in which each branch is located. The Free Library has an extensive history of providing programming, materials, and services to children of all ages to support their information, social, and personal needs.

BACKGROUND

Chartered in 1891, the Free Library began offering services and materials to children in 1903. Today, the Free Library is a large urban library system composed of the Parkway Central Library, fifty-two neighborhood libraries, community Hot Spots, the Library for the Blind and Physically Handicapped, the Regional Research and Operations Center, and the Rosenbach Museum and Library, which provide materials and services for children and teens from birth through high school, as well as their families, teachers, and other caring adults. Philadelphia is a diverse city with a total population of almost 1.6 million people. Forty-five percent of the population is African American, 45 percent Caucasian, 7 percent Asian, and about 14 percent are Hispanic or Latinx. Almost a quarter of the population in Philadelphia is below the age of eighteen; a quarter of the residents speak a language other than English at home; and about a quarter of the residents over the age of twenty-five have college degrees (US Census Bureau 2017). This chapter focuses on some of the early childhood programs and services at the Free Library of Philadelphia, some of which are similar to those found across many public libraries while others are unique to Philadelphia.

WORDS AT PLAY VOCABULARY INITIATIVE

On a Saturday morning in June, we gathered around a small tarp on the floor of a crowded meeting room, waiting for our special guest to show herself. Slowly, Camilla the three-banded armadillo uncurled herself, her hunger for bugs outweighing her shyness. As she trundled toward the grubs sprinkled on the tarp, some children ran away screeching, while some nearly picked her up. Nicole Goodsell, Coordinator of Outreach Programs for the Philadelphia Zoo, kept Camilla safe while explaining how the armadillo's shell protects her and lets her curl up away from danger. Two-year-old Aaliyah sat at the edge of the tarp, holding her mom's hand for safety, but her eyes were transfixed on her new armadillo friend. Later, she got to touch Camilla's strong back with one curious, outstretched finger. This is a typical Play Party with the Free Library of Philadelphia's Words at Play Vocabulary Initiative.

Over the last several years, the Free Library has found various methods to work with our patrons and residents to provide programs that are both fun and engaging. As we implement new programs, we use our past experiences, current research, and best practices shared from other libraries to inform our approach and to ensure the success of the project and the people who attend. One of our most successful early childhood and family programs is the Words at Play Vocabulary Initiative, initially funded by PNC Grow Up Great (https://www.pnc.com/en/about-pnc/corporate-responsibility/grow-up-great.html).

The Words at Play Vocabulary Initiative (https://libwww.freelibrary.org/programs/words-at-play/) is a comprehensive, community-wide initiative to support children's vocabulary development before they begin kindergarten. It consists of a portfolio of family programming, a marketing plan, collaboration with partner organizations and community organizations, professional development, and an evaluation plan. Our programming focuses on two neighborhoods in North Philadelphia that are predominantly African American and have a high incidence of generational poverty. This community also has a history of programs that were offered and then ended fairly quickly, so members can be wary of new initiatives.

Planning for the Words at Play Vocabulary Initiative built upon previous projects from the Free Library of Philadelphia, as well as best practices learned from other libraries and community engagement organizations. During the planning process for this new project, the library team decided upon the goals of the project, what the best tactics and strategies to accomplish the goals would be, how we would implement the project, who would be involved in the whole process, and how would we evaluate if the project was successful. The other big question we considered during the design phase was the best way to work with the community members in a respectful and supportive manner. Our goals for the project were:

- To help families support their children's vocabulary development before they begin school;
- to build trusting relationships with families and within the community as a whole;
- to extend the program further into the community to serve hard-to-reach families; and
- to build a successful program that made a difference in the lives of families.

Our funder brought four cultural organizations to the initiative: The Franklin Institute Science Museum, The Kimmel Center for the Performing Arts, the Philadelphia Museum of Art, and The Philadelphia Zoo (see figure 11.1). These partner organizations bring content knowledge, experience, and skills to the collaboration that raise the level of programming and provide rich, content-based activities. These activities can expand children's exposure to new ideas and materials in a way that allows them to more easily understand and internalize new vocabulary.

During the planning, we started with the question: "How do we support parents and families in helping their young children build their vocabulary before they start school?" To do this we turned to the updated Every Child Ready to Read® program (www.everychildreadytoread.org) from the Public Library Association and the Association for Library Service to Children (both divisions of the American Library Association), which has five areas of practice to support children's early literacy development:

Reading
Writing
Singing
Talking
Playing

These practices have influenced how we approach our work. For example, we named our library-centered programs "Play Parties" instead of storytimes to highlight the crucial role of play in building a child's vocabulary and content knowledge.

In a previous special project where we worked with our local housing authority, we hired "resident ambassadors" to help get the word out about the family programming we were hosting at the housing sites, to help recruit families to participate (and attend on the day of the program!), and to help let the residents know that the library is the real deal and

FIGURE 11.1 Nicole Goodsell, Coordinator of Outreach Programs for the Philadelphia Zoo holding a pelt for children to touch.

it is okay to attend the programs—all ways of building trust with the micro-community. Knowing how well this plan worked with this small project, we revised and reworked the idea and hired local residents to become Neighborhood Ambassadors. The Neighborhood Ambassadors have been critical to the success of this project by talking to community members, visiting local businesses and early learning programs, and supporting the programming in the libraries and in the community. They have helped build a bridge between the library, the partner organizations, and the community, and have been instrumental in establishing trust among the cultural partners, the library, the community organizations, and the families we serve. We'll talk more about our wonderful Ambassadors later.

As we mulled over what kind of programs we thought would be most successful, we decided to take a combination approach, going wide and shallow as well as narrow and deep. There are five programmatic elements in the Words at Play Vocabulary Initiative:

- Play Parties
- Pop-Up Play Parties
- Community Events
- Block Parties
- Family Fun Trips

To go more deeply into the community and reach as many families as possible, we participate in community events, host block parties, and offer Pop-Up Play Parties in non-library locations. At community events hosted by a wide variety of organizations, the Words at Play team brings informational brochures, fun literacy activities, and giveaways. The Block Parties are held at the fifty-two neighborhood libraries with the intent of making lots of noise and getting as many neighbors as possible to participate and learn about the program while participating in vocabulary building activities in a fun, relaxing environment. The Pop-Up Play Parties were designed to be a shorter version of the Play Party series to give families a taste of the program in a community setting where they are already comfortable. In addition, there is a Words at Play marketing campaign that goes deep into the neighborhoods to reach as many people as possible, using social media, an email newsletter, and blanketing the community in advertising like flyers, door hangers, and bus advertisements. The more narrow and deep activities include the Play Party series, which is designed to have families return to each program and build their learning week to week, while getting to know other families and sharing the vocabulary activities they have been doing at home between the sessions. The Family Fun Trips also provide an exciting learning experience at each of the cultural partner organizations.

The cornerstone of Words at Play is our series of Play Parties, which we like to call "amped-up storytimes," since they include not just books and stories, but also science experiments, music and performing arts, creative artistic expression, and animal science. Each partner draws upon their own expertise to contribute activities that will enhance and support the children's vocabulary. Each month of Play Parties has a theme that lends itself well to a variety of approaches. For example, one month we explored food: we sang songs about food like "Today is Monday" while sharing Eric Carle's book by the same name; we explored easy recipes to try at home; we discussed how animals' habitats determine what foods they might eat; and we made our own artwork inspired by food-themed pieces in the Philadelphia Museum of Art.

Every other month, we hold Play Parties on Saturday mornings at our two neighborhood libraries—a time that enables more working parents and caregivers to attend than a weekday morning would. These hour-long programs are an opportunity for the partner organizations to collaborate on fun, easily accessible ways to show adult caregivers how to discover, contextualize, and reinforce new words for their young ones. They also offer a time for parents to get to know one other, share resources, and have fun with their children. For each Play Party, we identify two or three vocabulary words and integrate them into stories, science experiments, art projects, songs and performances, and explorations of animals.

We collaborate to construct our Play Parties so that adults are empowered to continue the learning at home. Our structure is similar to a typical storytime in certain ways. We start with a song or rhyme and a quick overview of the initiative, which is typically followed by a fun, interactive book. Rhymes, songs, and movement activities get everyone up and moving. We frequently include activities in which families work together—a shape scavenger hunt, dissection of different kinds of berries, or even just reading a book as a family. We then gather together and share our ideas with each other. During our Play Parties, staff members share not only early literacy tips, but also tips about using binoculars with young children, tips about making art together as a family (see figure 11.2), or about listening to and making music together. These tips are mentioned during the Play Party and also on tip sheets that families take home. We know that building a home library is an important stepping stone toward literacy, so families leave with their own copies of specially selected books along with educational toys that are aligned with the theme of the day's Play Party.

FIGURE 11.2 Family time painting together.

How do Play Parties differ from a typical library storytime? We chose the name Play Parties deliberately to signify that our focus is on play-based learning. Caregivers who might not feel comfortable entering a library and attending a traditional storytime are reassured by the festive, interactive energy of our programs. And although we always include—and give away—picture and board books at each program (see figure 11.3), we spend more time exploring new ideas and ways to deepen understanding, with our goal being increased vocabulary exposure and retention.

Words at Play requires a significant amount of staff time. One staff member from the Free Library coordinates details for each Play Party, orders giveaway books, and ensures alignment with early literacy best practices. The project director manages the budget and statistical reporting and serves as the liaison to funders and grant writers. Still another staff member oversees all community outreach, planning Pop Up Play Parties at community sites and being the touchstone for our Neighborhood Ambassadors. These three positions are based out of the Free Library, and the latter two are grant-funded positions. Each partner organization has staff members who work on Words at Play and contribute their content knowledge to create our programming. While each partner brings their own area of expertise, it can sometimes be a learning curve to figure out the best way to present a program to young children and their families. But each organization is committed to providing great programs and making Words at Play a success.

FIGURE 11.3 An array of giveaway books.

To plan our programs effectively, all partners remain in constant communication with each other. We communicate via email and monthly in-person education team meetings. We at the library advise on early literacy best practices and library-specific planning considerations, and we rely on our partners to contribute their expertise as arts and science educators. For example, when planning our series of Play Parties highlighting the continent of South America, staff from the Philadelphia Museum of Art led families in making Peruvian-inspired fabric weavings after we read *Spicy Hot Colors* by Sherry Shahan, all the while talking about warm and cool colors and encouraging families to make up "looking games" with their children. Free Library staff coordinate this planning and make sure families are notified about upcoming programs.

Since it is a family-based program, Words at Play provides a great opportunity for adults to draw upon their own experience to increase their children's vocabulary. During each program, we pose direct questions to caregivers: How can you explore patterns at home? Where in your neighborhood can you hear music? What foods does your family eat at special celebrations? We pause during read-alouds to ask them to share thoughts with their children and other families. Neighborhood Ambassador Linda remarked, "I think that building vocabulary, building relationships between parent and child, that's the best part."

Our Neighborhood Ambassadors are recruited to spread the word about the program because they live, work, and raise their children in our initiative's target neighborhoods. Neighborhood Ambassador Syreeta started bringing her son Phoenix to Play Parties, and soon started talking to her friends and neighbors about the program and bringing them with her to the library. She is now one of our biggest advocates in her community. For her, Words at Play offers a chance to socialize with other parents of young children and to share ideas and news. Syreeta has inspired us to expand the scope of our programming to include more time for adults to meet and play with their children, facilitated by our Neighborhood Ambassadors. We now provide coffee and snacks and help to offer connections to representatives in schools, healthcare organizations, and recreational organizations.

We also like to draw on each Neighborhood Ambassador's strengths and preferences. For example, Letitia has helped immensely by making phone calls to families before each Play Party and getting our giveaway materials organized. She spends some of her time in our office and some welcoming families as they arrive at each program, usually with the help of her young son Maurice. Linda loves talking to people in the community, so she spends more of her time outside of the library. She says, "The best part [of Words at Play] for me is going out in the field and actually talking to the people, and to see how interested they are, because I get excited when I explain the program to them." This type of outreach has led to a great turnout at our Play Parties and a deeper impact on our families.

Words at Play has also established Book Nooks in eight community businesses, primarily barbershops and laundromats, to help saturate the neighborhood with more print-rich environments. In Philadelphia neighborhoods, a common gathering space—particularly for men—is the barbershop. After scouting neighborhood businesses, we offered business owners a Book Nook that includes a bookcase, small rug, child-sized chairs, and about seventy brand-new books, as well as a short training on early literacy. As children are getting their hair cut, barbers can ask them open-ended questions and introduce them to words like *clippers, trim,* and *shears* to help grow their vocabulary. Our strongest advocate in North Philadelphia is Jasmond Schoolfield, also known as Jazz the Barber. At Creative Image Unisex Salon, Jazz encourages families to select a book from his shelves while they wait, and he will often run deals where children can get a free haircut if they read to him or one of his barbers. He uses his social media to promote early literacy at the same time he promotes his business (Stippich 2017).

COMMUNITY ENGAGEMENT

Words at Play is not the only community-embedded program we offer, but we have learned a great deal about how to absorb community input and create programming based on community needs and desires that takes place both in and out of the library. We are moving forward with implementing intentionally designed play spaces in libraries that are focused on play and learning for preschoolers but are usable by older children. In planning for the transformation of four early learning Play Spaces in libraries, we worked with our design team and local play space experts to hold community input sessions. Families used paint, blocks, repurposed cardboard, and other materials to brainstorm what they wanted their new library spaces to look like. Because of this, our library's families have a real stake in the future of their library.

Another example of our community focus is our devotion to creating a welcoming, safe, and inclusive space for all members of the public. Some of our rock star children's librarians have created programming specifically to welcome children with autism, who may have different sensory needs and social cues. Because of this, their caregivers may feel apprehensive about bringing their children to a space typically viewed as very quiet. Sensory Story Times build upon these children's strengths and address their needs to promote literacy and social interaction in a safe space.

Ann Hornbach of the Torresdale Library holds a monthly Sensory Story Time "for children who have a hard time in large groups, are on the autism spectrum, or are sensitive to sensory overload." She provides fidgets, headphones, and weighted lap pads, and even uses special lamps instead of the harsher fluorescent lighting of the library's meeting room. John Crimmins at the Fumo Family Library is supplementing his Sensory Story Time with iPads and opening up his programming to include children who are not necessarily on the autism spectrum. Both librarians make use of visual schedules, name tags for attendees, and lots of movement activities and songs. Their greatest gain from these programs has been strengthened relationships with the children and families who now know that the library welcomes and celebrates them. The librarians notice increased participation by the children and value the opportunity to get parents together to interact and talk with each other.

Our unique, community-focused approach has also generated the Stories Alive program, in which incarcerated family members can read to their children through live videoconferencing. For these free sessions, all family members receive the same children's books, which the incarcerated parent reads to the child. This has been a great way to reconnect families and to strengthen the bond between parent and child through reading and has been a good opportunity to partner with the Philadelphia Prison System (https://libwww.freelibrary.org/programs/prisonservices/).

One way we take our services outside the library is to offer our experience as librarians to other professions. At the Free Library, we offer early literacy workshops for early childhood educators. Whenever we can, we work with our region's educational providers to make sure educators are able to receive continuing education credits for attending workshops. In the past, we have held workshops on a variety of subjects, including a yearly professional development event tied into the Pennsylvania One Book, Every Young Child (www.paonebook.org/) program, which highlights the importance of early literacy throughout the state. Each year, attendees learn from the author or illustrator of the year's selected book about their bookmaking process and others speak about interactive storytelling, dual language learners, and more. Although some of our staff are active in national and local library professional organizations, we also partner with local educator organizations like the Delaware Valley Association for the Education of Young Children (DVAEYC) to share knowledge. At its annual conference, we conduct a workshop on early literacy and connections between the books we love and research-based learning opportunities in the classroom. Since educators often do not have the time to seek out new books for their classrooms, they especially love our booktalks about new, high-quality books that can support their teaching.

LANGUAGE, LEARNING AND LITERACY

At the Free Library, we try to respond to the diversity of our communities by offering a large range of programs and services. We strive to take a unique approach to our core services and to integrate current and cutting-edge trends in our programming in new and innovative ways. In this way, we are becoming more than just a quiet place to sit and read, but also a vibrant community hub in which families can build, play, and create together.

One of the largest trends in education and in library service is a focus on STEM—science, technology, engineering, and math, sometimes with art included—as key areas in which we can support young children's learning in and out of school. Whereas our Literacy Enrichment Afterschool Program (LEAP) focuses on students in kindergarten through high school through homework help and literacy activities, our programs for younger children also support STEM skills. Over the last few years, the Free Library has introduced more dynamic, interactive, hands-on programming, especially around STEM.

One example is our Wooden Block Parties. Commonwealth Libraries Bureau of Library Development has supplied our libraries with sets of wooden blocks of various shapes, toy cars, animals, and play people of various ethnicities. Each library has found space to store the cabinet of blocks and schedules Wooden Block Parties for children ages three to six and their caregivers. We know that block play supports many aspects of a child's early learning. A child exploring engineering concepts might ask, "How can I make this block balance on top of that one?" As well as basic counting skills, core math skills are developed as children learn about shapes and how they can fit into to each other. But block play also bolsters many early literacy skills. For example, when a family works together to build a tower, they may invent a story about a kitten stuck at the top of the tower and how it could be rescued. Or we can be inspired by The Three Billy Goats Gruff and build bridges, telling the story as we build. Block play supports narrative skills, vocabulary skills, and social skills all at the same time (McCleaf Nespeca 2012).

Conducting a play-based program in a library can pose specific challenges. Staff, patrons, and caregivers may not initially see the connection between play and literacy. Many libraries are small and have little space available for children's programming. Therefore, ensuring that library staff are versed in the research behind play is important. Libraries are also expected to be relatively quiet places, and children at play are simply not quiet! How do we find a balance between all these considerations while still offering high-quality, play-based learning opportunities?

Again, we rely on the flexibility of our library staff and our patrons. Some libraries will offer Wooden Block Parties, with a more casual feel than a typical storytime, as part of their parent cafe series. We also train our staff to conduct a play-based program with intention, asking: "What do you hope to achieve, and how do you establish a framework that encourages controlled chaos?" For example, children are encouraged to pick just five blocks to start out. Then more blocks are slowly introduced, as well as animals, scarves, items from nature, and toy people to enable more complex structures. We keep attendance relatively small at these programs, and caregivers are provided with sample open-ended questions to encourage good block-building conversations. Clean-up time is included as a built-in component of the program so that caregivers can extend learning opportunities while helping to tidy up their children's work areas.

Our summer learning program, branded as the Summer of Wonder, provides possibilities for children to learn in many different ways. The "summer slide," the tendency for school-age children to lose academic skills over the summer, has been well documented and libraries around the country have developed a variety of programs to address this achievement gap (www.summerlearning.org/). But we also want younger children to develop a love of reading and learning early so that they will become more successful when they enter school.

During the Summer of Wonder, children complete activities in five different Discovery Paths, earning a sticker for each Path they complete. Library staff track progress on Passports and offer programming themed around the Paths, such as Sleuth the Truth, Healthy You, and Just Read It. The preschool activities are informed by Every Child Ready to Read®, so there are reading, writing, singing, talking, and playing activities throughout. For example, children can complete the Healthy You Discovery Path by doing activities like pretending to cook, reading a book about feelings, and having a dance party.

Wonder Kits, themed in conjunction with the Summer of Wonder Discovery Paths, are provided to each Free Library location during the summer. Each kit is contained in a canvas bag and includes materials to support both passive and more in-depth programming by our librarians: games, building kits, and basic materials like extra paper and markers, which allow library staff to create their own programs for children. The Sleuth-the-Truth Wonder Kit, for example, includes a magnifying glass, fingerprinting supplies, and instructions on creating secret codes. Each kit is adaptable for patrons from toddlers to teens. Philadelphia's children have a lot of fun with the activities that we provide to continue their learning throughout the summer and leading up to their school years.

COLLABORATION AND PARTNERSHIPS

One of the best ways to extend the reach and enhance the work of the public library is to collaborate with other organizations and community members. Many of the programs described in this section are successful because of the partners and the expertise and resources they bring. Partnering with others is also a great way to enhance and support core services in libraries, like getting library cards in the hands of customers. What better way to give children cards than to go out to where they and their families already are? At the Free Library of Philadelphia, we have partnered with Reach Out and Read Greater Philadelphia to give out library cards during well-baby visits at the doctor's office. Reach Out and Read's goal is to share with parents how important it is for them to read aloud with their children and how the love of books will help them start school ready to learn (https://www.reachoutandreadphilly.org/home/about-us and http://readby4th.org). With shared goals in mind, successful collaborations can help both organizations succeed.

Another national organization that supports children learning to read and reading on grade level after they begin school is the Campaign for Grade-Level Reading (www.grade levelreading.net/). Read by 4th is the name of the campaign in Philadelphia that is being led by the Free Library of Philadelphia. As the backbone organization of the campaign, the Free Library convenes over ninety organizations across the city in a collective impact model to work together on school readiness by making the most of out-of-school time, school attendance, families' teachable moments, high-quality reading instruction, and by creating read-together zones across the city (http://readby4th.org/). The proverb "it takes a village to raise a child" is absolutely true. Many organizations coming together in collaboration to support children's success can make a huge difference.

LOOKING TO THE FUTURE

Public libraries are always looking to the future to see what's next to support young children, their families, and caregivers. Like many public libraries, the Free Library is beginning to focus more on a user-centered design approach in our work with communities and stakeholders in planning and designing programs to meet their needs. This approach puts the customer (child, family, community) in the center of the planning process. Unlike a top-down process with library staff deciding what to offer to the community, the user-centered design process allows us to talk to customers and have them be an integral part of the whole process, rather than an afterthought. As we move forward with new projects, we are working to use this patron-focused process.

In Philadelphia there are several new projects that we are planning, including the "Play-brary"—playspaces for preschoolers in libraries. As mentioned earlier in the chapter, we are using a customer-focused approach in the process of implementing these new intentionally designed preschool play spaces. The four neighborhood libraries chosen for this project are in geographically disparate parts of the city in unique, vibrant, and diverse neighborhoods. The evaluators for this project, led by Kathy Hirsh-Pasek, a Temple University professor and expert on language development and young children's play, are designing a study that will look at how these new spaces affect child- and parent-level outcomes in terms of vocabulary building and "language dancing"—the conversations between children and caregivers that promote healthy literacy development. Look for updated information about this project online in a paper presented at the 2017 International Federation of Library Associations and Institutions (IFLA) conference as well as in articles and online posts.

A related and emergent project is Read, Baby, Read: a holistic initiative to develop, implement, and evaluate infant and young toddler spaces, collections, and programming in model libraries. The project includes specialized baby programming and parent workshops, along with staff development, with the longer-term goal of expanding these model services to clusters throughout the Free Library system. The Free Library is also currently working with a local funder on creating a new approach to working with early learning programs to support teachers' and families' success in working with children from birth to five years on language and literacy development. This approach has multiple categories of activities, including professional development, technical assistance to childcare programs, family engagement and family literacy, and updated literacy spaces in the classrooms. We plan to use neighborhood libraries as "literacy hubs" for the childcares in the neighborhood and to recruit parent ambassadors—modeled after the Words at Play Vocabulary Initiative—to build bridges between families, early learning programs, and libraries. This project will create a literacy buzz throughout the community that will bring people together in support of early childhood literacy.

An additional area of focus in the future addresses media mentorship, families, and young children. We are currently working with a researcher to assess our current work and our role in the community around this topic. Although we are still in the beginning stages of this work, technology is becoming ever-present in our daily interactions, so supporting families in best practices with their young children will be increasingly important. Much has been written in books, articles, and white papers about best practices for this topic, but there is still more to do as libraries refine our roles as media mentors. Directly supporting young children and their adults in literacy and learning is an important role for public libraries. And we are honored and proud to advocate for this critical work.

REFERENCES

"About Us." Reach Out and Read Greater Philadelphia. https://www.reachoutandreadphilly.org/home/about-us/.

Campaign for Grade-Level Reading. 2017. www.gradelevelreading.net/.

"Every Child Ready to Read®. Read. Learn. Grow." www.everychildreadytoread.org/.

Free Library of Philadelphia. www.freelibrary.org/.

McCleaf Nespeca, S. 2012. "The Importance of Play, Particularly Constructive Play, In Public Library Programming." Association for Library Services to Children. www.ala.org/alsc/sites/ala.org.alsc/files/content/FINAL%20Board%20Approved%20White%20Paper%20on%20Play.pdf.

National Summer Learning Association. www.summerlearning.org.

Pennsylvania One Book: Every Young Child. www.paonebook.org/.

"PNC Grow Up Great®—Inspiring Great Futures." https://www.pnc.com/en/about-pnc/corporate-responsibility/grow-up-great.html.

"Prison Services." Free Library of Philadelphia. 2017. https://libwww.freelibrary.org/programs/prisonservices/.

Read By 4th. 2017. http://readby4th.org/.

Stippich, S. "Every Child Ready to Read: Reaching Outside the Library Walls." *Children and Libraries* 15, no. 1 (Spring 2017): 38–39.

US Census Bureau. 2017. "Population Estimates, July 1, 2016, (V2016)." https://www.census.gov/quickfacts/table/PST045216/42101,00.

"Words at Play Vocabulary Initiative." Free Library of Philadelphia. https://libwww.freelibrary.org/programs/words-at-play/.

CHAPTER 12

Cultivating Knowing and Growing at the Scottsdale Public Library

Mariko Whelan

INTRODUCTION

The Scottsdale Public Library is located in Scottsdale, Arizona, and operated by the City of Scottsdale. The library was founded in the summer of 1955 by Lou Ann Noel and Beth Fielder, and was initially run strictly by volunteers with a collection of 300 donated books. Housed in the Adobe House in the Scottsdale town center, the unairconditioned building served as a community center and held library hours two mornings a week for two hours. From these humble beginnings developed the library system that is now a vital part of life in the city of Scottsdale.

BACKGROUND

In 1960, the City of Scottsdale assumed responsibility for the library. In 1963, it relocated the library from the Adobe House into a vintage, 1909, little red schoolhouse that had previously served as City Hall. To meet the high demand for services and the need for more space, the city opened the main, Bennie Gonzales-designed, Civic Center Library facility in 1968. Growth didn't stop there; in 1995, Scottsdale's Civic Center Library celebrated its grand re-opening, doubling its size. The system has flourished over the years and now includes five branches: Mustang Library opened in 1987 and, like Civic Center Library, holds the distinctive title of a Family Place Library™. Palomino Library opened in 1995 and is a shared-use facility located on the campus of Desert Mountain High School. Arabian Library opened in 1996 also as a shared-use facility but later moved to its own building in 2007. Arabian's unique design earned the 2008 International Interior Design Association/Metropolis Smart Environments Award. The most recent branch to be added to the system was the Appaloosa Library, which opened in 2009 and has also won a multitude of awards for excellence in design. This appealing conglomeration of library branches has a total of 194,967 square feet of space. More than 1.1 million people visit the libraries each year. The collection exceeds 1.2 million items with an annual circulation of 2.9 million. Scottsdale Public Library serves a diverse population that runs the gamut from the affluent to those in need, making it necessary to provide a full spectrum of services for our patrons. The City of Scottsdale is one of Arizona's ten largest cities and is located in the Phoenix Metropolitan area. It covers 184 square miles and is home to a population of 231,204 people.

PROGRAMMING APPROACH

Programs at the Scottsdale Public Library have a predominant characteristic: they are created to foster parent-child interactions. From storytimes to early learning programs, all programs seek to provide opportunities for interactions between the caregiver and child. The programs featured in this chapter exemplify this approach, as well as our commitment to these values.

KNOWING AND GROWING

One part of the system's robust early learning focus is the Knowing and Growing program. These are a series of free six-week programs that promote healthy growth and development through literacy and play. They are aligned with Arizona's Infant and Toddler Guidelines, Arizona's Early Learning Standards, and Arizona's School Readiness Framework. Programs also take into consideration Every Child Ready to Read® @ your library® and incorporate the practices of read, talk, sing, play, and write into each and every class.

The primary objective of the Knowing and Growing programs is to provide opportunities for interactions between the child and the adult, emphasizing the importance of supportive and playful interactions and their impact on a child's growth and development. These interactions occur throughout the program in various ways. When we read, we encourage parents to ask their children questions, demonstrate curiosity about the story, and model engaged listening. When we sing, all are encouraged to sing along and participate in any actions that correspond to the words to the song. The words to the songs, rhymes, and chants are posted for parents and caregivers to read as they engage in the activity, and they are encouraged to continue the songs, rhymes, and chants at home. When we play, parents and caregivers are bolstered in their efforts to engage in playful interactions with their children guiding the play. For the practices of writing and talking, we provide suggestions and model them, empowering parents and caregivers to be the guiding force in their children's early development. Together these concepts facilitate the development of each Knowing and Growing program. Each component is vital to creating a successful, impactful, and comprehensive early learning program that meets the specific needs of families who are seeking literature-based enrichment programs that prepare their children for school.

Immense time and effort go into planning the Knowing and Growing programs, starting with the selection of read-aloud books that will define the tone for each week. They are carefully chosen based on quality and content to align with the weekly concepts. The activities are open-ended and emphasize the process of learning rather than the creation of an end product. Children develop skills by adding to their prior knowledge and experiences. Other considerations for program implementation include scheduling: which days, times, and locations will best meet the needs of the families; consistency in the staff who implement the program; and the layout of the environment.

Currently there are three programs written specifically for Knowing and Growing:

1. Books Can . . . ™, which focuses on the social and emotional development of young children and provides parents with strategies to support the heathy growth of their young children.
2. Fun with Math & Science™, which strives to create scientific and mathematical thinkers through a variety of hands-on experiences and the use of open-ended questions.
3. Step Up to Learning™, which focuses on approaches to learning, how children learn to learn, while providing guidance and opportunities for young children to become engaged in social interactions and learning experiences.

Each program offering utilizes two read-aloud books; songs, rhymes, or chants; parent tips, and an opportunity for parents or caretakers to interact with their children in fun and interactive ways. These programs were created based on the needs of the community with the intent to support the journey to school readiness. New program ideas are also inspired by current research regarding parent-child interactive programs and the passion of youth services staff to provide families with programs that are new and innovative.

BOOKS CAN . . . ™

Jazlynn sits on her mom's lap under a giant scarf; together they are reading and acting out a book. Olivia and her grandma roll a ball back and forth as Grandma sings "Twinkle, Twinkle, Little Star" (see figure 12.1). As they roll the ball, Grandma focuses on making eye contact with Olivia to create a secure attachment and positive relationship. These are just two examples of adult-child interactions during Scottsdale Public Library's Books Can . . . ™ program.

Books Can . . . ™ is a six-week program for children ages birth to five that is designed to guide parents and caregivers in understanding the importance of social and emotional development in their children. The program endeavors to supply families with helpful ideas and strategies that can be used at home to support the healthy development of attachment, feelings, security, relationships, and self-regulation skills.

How is social and emotional development defined? For the purpose of the Books Can . . . ™ program, social and emotional development refers to a child's understanding, expression, and management of emotions and the ability to establish positive relationships with others (Cohen et al. 2005). Through various experiences, children learn how to express themselves and

FIGURE 12.1 Ball Play.

gain self-control over their emotions. They need opportunities to practice appropriate ways to interact with others socially. Developing nurturing relationships and engaging children in positive early learning experiences will help the child develop social and emotional skills as well as self-confidence (Ghoting and Klatt 2014). Research consistently shows that young children who experience positive, nurturing encounters are better prepared to be successful in school and in life (Cross and Conn-Powers 2011; Lally and Mangione 2017).

Each week of this program is set up to focus on a specific social and emotional area of growth and development. Since these skills are developed through interactions with others, the program expects parents or caregivers to participate with their children, taking the new information and strategies being discussed and practicing them through playful interactions during the program. Since the program covers a wide range of ages (birth to five years), instructors are tasked with determining and employing the books and activities that are most appropriate for the make-up of that specific class. To foster learning at home, each week families receive a free book that focuses on the week's concept. They can take the book home and add it to their personal libraries. They also receive a tip sheet that reviews the strategies and activities that were presented during the program.

The program is six weeks long and covers the following concepts:

- Attachment (Trust and Emotional Security)
- Feelings (Naming Emotions)
- Self-Awareness
- Self-Regulation
- Relationships and Social Interactions
- Effective Praise

To support school readiness, each program has a routine that is well-established. The routine consists of the following:

1. Introduction
2. Opening song
3. Concept definition
4. Four "tips" that are incorporated throughout the program where appropriate
5. Two books read aloud (one before activity time and one after)
6. Three songs, rhymes, chants, or finger plays (or a mixture)
7. Parent-child activity time
8. Yoga (one pose per week for a total of six poses during the program)
9. Closing song

Each program component serves a specific purpose that together form a cohesive whole in the program.

Opening Song

The opening song is used to establish a warm, inviting environment. Children are each greeted one at a time by name to create a safe, welcoming atmosphere for all who are attending. A simple chant or song to a familiar tune is the easiest way to greet each child, for example, "Hello, [child's name]. Hello, [same child's name]. Hello, [same child's name]. We're glad you're here today," and then repeated for each child.

Concept Definition

The concept definition clearly defines the weekly topic being covered. This definition is explained in friendly terms to help parents and caregivers understand often complex, abstract concepts about social and emotional development.

Weekly Tips

The weekly tips are used to explain and expand upon the weekly concept and to create tangible examples of what the concept means in daily life. These are the strategies we hope parents internalize and implement at home. To help parents remember the tips, we print them on the weekly tip sheet that goes home with parents at the end of each session.

Read-Aloud Books

Books are a tremendous resource and the foundation of the Books Can . . . ™ program. Reading one-on-one with children is a great way to establish a secure attachment between parent or caregiver and child. Teaching social and emotional concepts by using books and modeling book reading for adults and children is an essential learning component that sets the stage, not only for the development of social and emotional concepts, but for acquiring knowledge regarding various concepts linked to early growth and development.

Songs, Rhymes, Chants, Fingerplays

Singing songs, saying rhymes, reciting chants, and performing finger plays are good ways to incorporate learning concepts in a fun, interactive manner. The words to familiar nursery rhymes, such as Pat-a-Cake and Jack and Jill, are displayed and handwritten on a poster and sung together during the program to model for parents and caregivers the value of positive interactions using songs and chants. They also support brain development and help create strong connections in the brain.

Parent-Child Activity Time

Each week, activities that support that week's concept are introduced to the families. Interaction time takes fifteen to twenty minutes and provides an opportunity for parents or caregivers to interact with their children in silly ways. Parents and caregivers are reminded that the class is an adult-child participation program and are encouraged to put their cell phones away to eliminate distractions. Children are provided with various manipulatives, finger puppets, balls, scarves, and books as well as other learning opportunities while parents or caregivers are encouraged to follow their children's lead in what they do or play. Following the child's lead helps build the child's positive self-esteem, and one-on-one activities provide opportunities to practice building a healthy attachment relationship with the child. When parents and caregivers sing songs, read books, and do finger plays with their children, they are not only supporting positive interactions but also setting the foundation for later success with reading and supporting social and emotional growth and development.

Yoga

Each week a yoga pose is introduced with an affirmation that is connected with the weekly theme. Yoga is a great social-emotional tool and can help a child become calm and focused. It can also be a wonderful one-on-one activity that promotes positive interactions.

BOOKS CAN . . . ™ WHAT DOES IT LOOK LIKE?

Before it's time for families to come into the room, the instructor has hung up the agenda and handwritten song posters on the wall; posted the yoga poses; and strategically set up the items that families will be using for the session. Finger puppets, books, playground balls, giant scarves, and connecting beads are all placed in covered wicker baskets on the floor, waiting to be introduced and used during the adult-child interactive time.

Near the door an assortment of plush animals or "lovies" are put out for children to select as they come into the room. The lovies support the creation of a safe, warm environment. They serve as a tool to help eliminate some of the stressors that children feel when engaging in a new situation and provide a familiar, tactile experience for the child. Lovies also provide a quiet diversion for children while weekly concepts are being introduced to the adults.

A colorful array of yoga mats is spread out, one for each family who has registered for the program. As families arrive, children select their favorite lovie and choose the yoga mat they will use for the day (see figure 12.2). Since this is the fourth week of the six-week program, families greet each other and say hello to the children. Everyone has learned each other's name because of the hello song that has been sung each week.

FIGURE 12.2 Yoga mats for children to sit on during the program.

FUN WITH MATH & SCIENCE™

Using the blue strips of tape on the floor and a handful of jumbo pipe cleaners, Christopher tells his mom, "I'm five tape lines tall but I'm bigger than five of the fuzzy sticks!" (see figure 12.3). Then his mom lies down on the floor and asks how many pipe cleaners long she is. Christopher carefully puts down two more pipe cleaners and says to his mom, "You're eight long!" Mom then asks Christopher which of them is taller or longer. He lies down on the floor next to her and says, "You are, Mom!" Mom asks Christopher, "How do you know I'm taller?" Christopher says, "You're eight fuzzy sticks and I'm six. Eight is bigger than six." This is just one example of the interactions that happen in Scottsdale Public Libraries Knowing and Growing program, Fun with Math & Science™.

Fun with Math & Science™ is designed to explore math and science concepts with children ages three to five years old in an enjoyable and interactive manner. Practicing math and science skills with young children helps them connect ideas, develop higher-order and logical thinking skills and investigative skills that help them to better understand the world around them. Parents and caregivers are key to helping their children think mathematically and scientifically. Parents and caregivers can model mathematical thinking for their children by counting items, looking at sizes and shapes, measuring and comparing items, and finding patterns in the environment. They can also model scientific thinking by using their senses to observe the world around them, make predictions, and experiment.

FIGURE 12.3 Family Math Time.

When exploring math and science concepts, it is essential that children have opportunities to be engaged in the learning process through hands-on experiences. Children are born scientists that explore the world around them using their five senses (Gopnik 2001). They touch, taste, smell, look, and listen throughout their day, gaining new knowledge and discovering new things. Each week, interactive learning stations are categorized into four main areas: books, fine motor, gross motor, and manipulatives. The materials at each station are chosen because they provide opportunities for children that foster the development of school-readiness skills through exploring, constructing, and developing an understanding of their environment.

As with many other concepts, books are a great way to introduce math and science concepts to children. Numerous books focus on the five senses and concepts such as counting and comparing, sorting and classifying, measurement, and one-to-one correspondence. These concepts become more tangible when presented in combination with books and hands-on activities that support these concepts.

Beyond books, we also encourage parents and caregivers to use open-ended questions as a tool for facilitating the development of scientific and mathematical thinkers. Open-ended questions are designed to prompt children to both think and respond. Closed-ended questions, which have only one correct answer, fail to facilitate conversation. With open-ended questions, children can elaborate and explain their thinking, which helps to solidify their thinking process. Examples of open-ended questions are posted on the wall at each learning station.

Similar to Books Can . . . ™, Fun with Math & Science™ establishes a consistent routine that contains the following:

- Introduction
- Opening song
- Concept for the week
- Four "tips" that are incorporated throughout the program where appropriate
- Read-aloud book 1
- A song, rhyme, chant, or finger play that coincides with the weekly concept
- Learning stations—parent-child interaction time
- Read-aloud book 2
- Session conclusion, reminders, and closing song

The six-week program covers the following concepts:

- Using Our Senses
- Counting and Comparing
- Geometry and Identifying Attributes
- Sorting and Classifying through Investigation
- Patterning, Sequencing, and Making Observations
- Measurement, Hypothesizing and Experimenting

Each weekly concept builds on the concept covered the week before to create a complete picture of what math and science skills entail. To extend and continue the learning at home, tip sheets are handed out to each family at the end of every class. These contain the weekly tips, songs, and suggestions for supporting the weekly concept through regular daily interactions. All participants also receive a free book that relates to the weekly topic to add to their personal collection.

WHAT DOES THE PROGRAM LOOK LIKE?

It's time for learning stations. The instructor has already uncovered and introduced the items that have been set out for exploration, and the children are anticipating what comes next—the transition song. The instructor begins singing, "It's time to choose a station, a station, a station. It's time to choose a station, which one will you choose?" Children move excitedly around the room. Adults follow their children's lead as they move to the learning station that has piqued their interest (see figure 12.4). Sitting down next to their children,

FIGURE 12.4 Children take the lead, adults follow.

the parents and caregivers engage in joint play using the materials that have been set out. This week's focus is on patterns, sequencing, and observation. Children play with various rocks in a bin, noting their differences with magnifying glasses and flashlights. Some are using tweezers to pick up foam shapes and then gluing them into patterns on strips of paper. Others are at the book station, reading and pointing out the sequence in the story to each other. Still others are practicing jumping from one square to the next on the hopscotch grid, first using one foot and then both feet, discovering patterns with their whole bodies (see figure 12.5). During this flurry of activity, you can hear parents and caregivers using open-ended questions to facilitate the learning that is occurring. Some children stay at the same learning station for fifteen minutes of the twenty-minute time frame, while others move around the room, going from station to station, trying each experience.

FIGURE 12.5 Hopscotch time!

STEP UP TO LEARNING™

Based on the success of the first two Knowing and Growing programs, a third program has recently been created, called Step Up to Learning™. This six-week program, written for children ages three to five years old, focuses on children's approaches to learning in both social and academic settings. Constructed using the same design as the other two programs, Step Up to Learning™ also follows a consistent routine that incorporates the following program components:

1. Introduction
2. Opening song
3. Weekly concept
4. Four "Tips" that are incorporated throughout the program where appropriate
5. Read-aloud book 1
6. Song, rhyme, chant or finger play
7. Play and Learn—parent/child interaction time
8. Read-aloud book 2
9. Session Conclusion, reminders and closing song

The six-week program covers the following concepts:

- Initiative and Curiosity
- Attentiveness and Persistence
- Confidence

- Creativity
- Reasoning and Problem-Solving
- Learning within a Community

Initiative and Curiosity set the tone for all other weeks of the program. Initiative refers to children's ability to demonstrate independence and control over the choices they make. Initiative reflects how self-sufficient and confident a child is while pursuing relationships and interacting with others. Curiosity is the innate predisposition children have to be active learners who seek to understand their environment and the things and people within that environment through exploration. These are the building blocks that lay the foundation for the other concepts covered in this program.

Viewed as one of the most important domains of early childhood development, approaches to learning look at the observable behaviors that indicate how children are engaged in social interactions and learning experiences. How children approach learning contributes to their success academically, socially, emotionally, and developmentally. Providing an engaging environment that allows for independent exploration and creativity sets the groundwork for success in school and beyond. However, how do you teach approaches to learning? Half the battle of teaching these concepts is introducing them to parents and making them aware of what approaches to learning look like and how to recognize them in their children. Children, on the other hand, learn these skills through play and interacting with others.

WHAT DOES THE PROGRAM LOOK LIKE?

It's week three of Step Up to Learning™ and it's time to read the first book. Children move closer to the instructor so they are able to see the pictures. The instructor introduces the book by saying, "Today we are going to read *The Dot,* by Peter H. Reynolds. Parents, we chose this book because at some point all children struggle and feel as if they can't do something. Children can lose their confidence and need a new perspective to help them persist in their endeavors. Children, have any of you ever felt like you can't do something? That it's too hard? Let's find out how the character in the book regained her confidence, how she learned to feel like she could do it, by figuring out how to do something that started out as difficult." During the read-aloud, the children are engaged and listening. The instructor employs shared reading techniques as they tell the story and the children willingly participate.

CONCLUSION

Knowing and Growing programs are just one piece of a comprehensive system being implemented at the Scottsdale Public Library to support early childhood development. The library system works in tandem with parents and caregivers to enable their children to attain the skills necessary to be successful in school and in life. All Knowing and Growing programs are six weeks in duration and the expectation is that families will commit to attending all six weeks of the program. Registration is required, and the classes quickly fill up, making it necessary to add additional programs based on need. Many parents take the classes more than once, enjoying the experience a second time once their children are a little older. Due to the difference in age, a child will get something completely new from each learning experience.

The Knowing and Growing programs are also provided at venues other than the library. Through partnerships with local community centers and family resource centers, families who might not use the library have access to these high-quality programs at alternative locations.

All stakeholders who participate in the implementation of Knowing and Growing programs are provided with extensive training and a co-teaching mentoring support model to ensure fidelity in program implementation. The Scottsdale Public Library staff works closely with Arizona State University's T. Denny Sanford School of Social and Family Dynamics to conduct research on the programs, working to achieve the accolade of evidence-based programming. The Knowing and Growing curriculum has not only served the patrons in the city of Scottsdale but has also had a positive impact on surrounding cities that have implemented the programs. Through partnerships established via grant funds, other library systems have received training, supplies, and mentor support to implement Knowing and Growing programs at their libraries. Pre- and post-program surveys have been used to determine patron satisfaction and to ascertain if community needs are being met. This unique curriculum concentrates on educating parents and children together through playful interactions. The goal of each Knowing and Growing program is to provide families with the tools needed to help their child to be ready for kindergarten and successful in school and life.

Scottsdale Public Library is an important piece of the early literacy puzzle in the state of Arizona. Through working in conjunction with other agencies such as Read On Arizona, the Arizona State Library, local school districts, library systems, and other early childhood agencies we can successfully support the literacy and learning development of our youngest patrons.

REFERENCES

Cohen, J., N. Onanku, S. Clothier, and J. Poppe. 2005. *Helping Young Children Succeed: Strategies to Promote Early Childhood Social and Emotional Development.* Washington DC: National Conference of State Legislatures and Zero to Three.

Cross, A. F., and M. Conn-Powers. 2011. *A Working Paper: New Information about School Readiness.* Bloomington, IN: Indiana University-Bloomington, Indiana Institute on Disability and Community.

Ghoting, S. N., and K. F. Klatt. 2014. *STEP into Storytime: Using StoryTime Effective Practice to Strengthen the Development of Newborns to Five-Year Olds.* Chicago: ALA Editions.

Gopnik, A. 2001. *The Scientist in the Crib: Minds, Brains, and How Children Learn.* New York: HarperPerennial.

Lally, J. R., and P. Mangione. 2017. "Caring Relationships: The Heart of Early Brain Development." *Young Children* 72 (2). https://www.naeyc.org/resources/pubs/yc/may2017/caring-relationships-heart-early-brain-development.

CHAPTER 13

Intentionality, Interactivity, and Community in Early Childhood Programming at Public Libraries

An Overview of Research

Kathleen Campana and Betsy Diamant-Cohen

INTRODUCTION

Although it has long seemed clear to librarians that storytimes and other library programs for young children play a pivotal role in their early literacy and learning development, there was a lack of research that demonstrated these beliefs. Although there has been some research that examines children's literature and collections, the literature is far more limited concerning what is going on in library programs for young children—their content and structure, and the impact that they have on the children and families who attend. There have been many barriers to this type of research. First, librarians did not want to interfere with the privacy of family visitors by asking questions regarding parents' educational and economic status. In addition, since attendance at library programs is not mandatory, the same children might not come to programs on a regular basis. Furthermore, children regularly have many experiences; how could the influence of attending weekly library programs be isolated from all the other experiences a child had in one week?

Virginia Walter, an early advocate for research in children's librarianship, wrote *Outcome Measures for Public Library Service to Children* in 1992. This manual was designed as a practical guide to standardize procedures for collecting, interpreting, quantifying, and measuring the results, or outputs, of public library service to children and teens. Then, in 1997, an article in *Public Libraries* written by Frances Smardo Dowd called for more research on the impact that preschool storytimes have on children's early literacy skills, suggesting the use of pre- and post-test conditions.

Since the late nineties, some research has finally started to focus on library programs for children and youth (McKechnie 1996; Prendergast 2016; Campana et al. 2016; Mills et al. 2015). Then in 2013, Eliza T. Dresang noted, "The roles of public libraries in the information behavior of youth are more research- and evidence-based than they have been in the past" (97). She worked to implement several research projects that helped to provide evidence that library services impacted children. Because of the importance of research and evidence-based practices for this role, this chapter will provide an introduction to the library research that is applicable to programs offered for young children, classified according to three principles: intentionality, interactivity, and community. The importance of these three principles for early childhood services emerged from Project VIEWS2 (Campana et al. 2016; Mills et al. 2018), the first wide-scale study to establish the early literacy impact of storytimes using a quasi-experimental design. The research included here covers the time period of 2000 to 2017 and is still applicable to current library programs.

INTENTIONALITY

The principle of intentionality refers to the practice of being intentional and deliberate in everything you do with children's services, including how you decide what parts of your community to reach out to, what programs and services to offer, and how you design your programs and services to intentionally support *all* children and families in *all* types of learning. The studies detailed here help to highlight the importance of being intentional across all aspects of serving young children and their families.

Campana, K., J. E. Mills, J. L. Capps, E. T. Dresang, A. Carlyle, C. Metoyer, I. Bayo Urban, E. N. Feldman, M. Brouwer, K. Burnett, and B. Kotrla. "Early Literacy in Library Storytimes: A Study of Measures of Effectiveness." *Library Quarterly* 86, no. 4 (October 16, 2016).

As part of the four-year IMLS grant, VIEWS2, researchers observed 240 storytimes offered in forty libraries over two years. The study was designed as a quasi-experimental study with an intervention. In the first year, after observing 120 storytimes, they found that storytime providers are including a wide variety of early literacy content in storytimes and children are exhibiting a wide variety of early literacy behaviors while attending storytime. Furthermore, when they looked at the storytime providers' early literacy content and the children's behaviors, they found a strong correlation, which suggests that the children are responding to the early literacy content in storytime. (The paper for the second year is detailed below. See Mills et. al. "Early Literacy in Library Storytimes Part 2.")

Lopez, M. E., M. Caspe., and L. McWilliams. "Public Libraries: A Vital Space for Family Engagement." Cambridge, MA: Harvard Family Research Project, 2016. www.hfrp.org/librarycta.

Using surveys and site visits, this study explored how libraries are engaging with families. They found that although libraries are engaging families in many ways, they can and should be doing more. One takeaway is that libraries should be intentional about engaging with the families they serve, especially those with younger children, because of the importance of the parents and caregivers as their children's first teachers in early learning.

McKechnie, L. "Opening the 'Preschoolers' Door to Learning': An Ethnographic Study of the Use of Public Libraries by Preschool Girls." PhD dissertation, University of Western Ontario, 1996.

In her dissertation, using observations to understand the library use of thirty preschool girls, McKechnie found that "many opportunities for learning" were provided through library services. Opportunities to learn literacy skills and learn about the library were two of the more significant types of learning observed. Through her observations and reliance on their parents to journal about their experiences as "key informants," she introduced ethnographic observation as a unique way to reflect the perspective of preschool children in the public library. Some takeaways from her work are 1) to be intentional about supporting children's learning (and that of their caregivers!) in all interactions; 2) to provide spaces for children and their caregivers to read together; and 3) to provide programs and toys that emphasize the importance of stories.

L. Mills, J. E. Romeijn-Stout, C. Campbell, and A. Koester. "Results from the Young Children, New Media and Libraries Survey: What Did We Learn?" *Children and Libraries* 13, no. 2 (2015).

To understand technology use in library programs for young children, researchers utilized a survey of library practitioners. They found a high rate of technology usage in programs with an emphasis on tablets and MP3 players to bring music and sound into the program. Although there was evidence of usage, there was less evidence of mentoring for families around these devices. This is important to consider because the field has since adopted media mentorship as a way for librarians to help families understand how they might incorporate media into their own child's life. Some takeaways are that you can expect that media will play a role in your practice, whether you are incorporating it into programs, guiding children and families with using technology in the department, or mentoring families on their usage at home. Therefore, you should work on becoming well-versed in all types of media.

Mills, J. E., K. Campana, A. Carlyle, B. Kotrla, E. T. Dresang, I. Bayo Urban, J. L. Capps, C. Metoyer, E. N. Feldman, M. Brouwer, and K. Burnett. "Early Literacy in Library Storytimes Part 2: A Quasi-Experimental Study and Intervention with Children's Storytime Providers." *Library Quarterly* 88, no. 2 (2018): 160–76.

In year two of the VIEWS2 study, an intervention taking the form of an early literacy training that emphasized intentionality, interactivity, and community was offered to half of the participants. Following the intervention, researchers observed another 120 storytimes. From these observations, the researchers found a statistically significant increase in the early literacy content and the children's early literacy behaviors at the experimental group storytimes, although there was no statistically significant change for the control group storytimes. These findings suggest that an intentional and interactive focus on early literacy can make a difference in the observable early literacy content of storytime and the children's observable early literacy behaviors while attending storytime. A takeaway from this study is that it is important to be intentional and interactive when planning and delivering the early literacy and early learning content of your storytimes.

Naidoo, J. C. "Over the Rainbow and Under the Radar: Library Services and Programs to LGBTQ Families." *Children and Libraries* 11, no. 3 (2013): 34–40.

Naidoo examined library services to LGBTQ families in thirty-nine libraries across the United States. Among other things, he found that most libraries worked to be inclusive of LGBTQ families by incorporating LGBTQ picture books in their programs and services. In addition, a smaller percentage of libraries offered specific programs for LGBTQ families. Some recommendations that he offers are to be intentional about developing inclusive storytimes by incorporating books with different kinds of families, gender-bending characters, and same-sex friendships; or by tweaking the text of other books during delivery to be more inclusive. He also recommends developing partnerships with community organizations serving LGBTQ families.

Prendergast, T. "Seeking Early Literacy for All: An Investigation of Children's Librarians and Parents of Young Children with Disabilities' Experiences at the Public Library." *Library Trends* 65, no. 1 (2016): 65-91.

As part of her study, Prendergast used a variety of methods involving libraries, librarians, and parents of children with disabilities to explore the role of the public library and early literacy in the lives of children with disabilities. She found that, although libraries and librarians could play an important role in supporting families of children with disabilities and meeting their early literacy needs, libraries and librarians had differing capabilities to offer physical and social accommodations for children with disabilities and their families. In talking to the families of children with disabilities, she uncovered that although these families are using the library, they do so in a passive way. They tend to not take advantage of library programs and librarians' services. Takeaways suggested by the librarians in the study are: the importance of training and professional development opportunities to help in being intentional about serving families of children with disabilities in the ways that they need; and the necessity for intentional outreach to build a trusting relationship with these families and understand different ways that libraries can meet their needs.

INTERACTIVITY

The principle of interactivity refers first and foremost to the importance of interacting with children and their parents and caregivers in all your programs and services. With young children, allow them to interact with the information that you are incorporating in your storytimes—this helps to support their learning. As such, you should incorporate continuous opportunities for children to interact with you and their caregivers through all parts of the programs. In addition, you often hold the privileged role of having access to the caregiver for a period of time, so it is important to interact with them to share methods for supporting early learning, while also modeling interactive behaviors in the talking, singing, reading, writing, and playing that you do in your programs. Interactivity can also refer to the work you do to build relationships with the communities you serve—listening, talking, attending community meetings, being present in the lives of the people you serve. The studies below highlight the importance of being interactive in your programs and with your community as well as supporting and modeling interactivity for parents and caregivers and their children.

Celano, D. C., and S. B. Neuman. "Libraries Emerging as Leaders in Parent Engagement." *Phi Delta Kappan* 96, no. 7 (2015): 30-35.

As part of evaluating ECRR2 and working to understand how libraries are engaging with parents, researchers performed a number of phone interviews with librarians from twenty libraries across the nation. From these interviews, they found that the five practices of ECRR2 (talking, singing, reading, playing, and writing) have been adopted by libraries. They are incorporating the five practices into their programs and encouraging the parents and caregivers to use them at home. The ECRR initiative is making an impact with parents and children but libraries still face many challenges in their efforts, such as staffing, funding, and reaching *all* families. One takeaway is that the whole point of the five practices is to get parents interacting with their children, so one easy way to do this is to incorporate and model the five practices in an interactive manner in your programs.

Martinez, G. "Public Libraries—Community Organizations Making Outreach Efforts to Help Young Children Succeed in School." *School Community Journal* 18, no. 1 (2008): 93–104.

Using case studies, the researcher examined how libraries are working to support early literacy through outreach. She found that libraries are using a wide variety of outreach methods to support early literacy in their communities, especially for the neediest populations who may not otherwise visit the library. In addition, she found that many libraries were working with families, schools, and other community partners to support school readiness. One takeaway is the importance of outreach in getting out and interacting with your entire community to support their literacy and learning needs, rather than limiting your services to only those who can come to the library.

McKenzie, P. J., and R. Stooke. "Producing Storytime: A Collectivist Analysis of Work in a Complex Communicative Space." *Library Quarterly* 77, no. 1 (2007).

In this study, researchers used observations, informal conversations, and interviews to understand the work that goes into producing public library storytimes. They found that although the storytime provider performs administrative work to prepare for storytime, all storytime participants play a role in the work that occurs during storytime to co-create the environment. In addition, they identify different types of work that occur at storytime, including literacy work, information work, and caring work. Some takeaways are that it is important to leave time to do the administrative work required of producing storytime; and during storytime you should make space for everyone to participate, interact, and contribute to co-creating the storytime environment.

Neuman, S. B., and D. C. Celano, "Worlds Apart: One City, Two Libraries, and Ten Years of Watching Inequality Grow." *American Educator* 36, no. 2 (Fall 2012): 13–23.

Researchers used a longitudinal ethnographic method to explore two communities, one affluent and one not so affluent, and the libraries that serve them. They sought to understand the relationships between libraries and the individuals who use them and how libraries might or might not be leveling the playing field for those across the socioeconomic spectrum. They found that although access to physical materials may be fairly equal in both libraries, the differences in social and psychological support from adults in early childhood in the two neighborhood libraries led to "a pattern of print and media preferences," with adolescents in the affluent community reading more complex material and adolescents in the non-affluent community reading easier material and turning to media as a way to avoid reading. Some takeaways include: it is not enough to provide resources in the library and in programs. When working with young children it is imperative that you be present and engaged with modeling and sharing with parents and caregivers how to talk, sing, read, play, and write in an interactive manner to best support their child's literacy and learning. In addition, providing more staff whose sole purpose is to get out from behind the desk and interact with children and families in the children's area can help those who support children and their families in their interactions with print and media while at the library.

Stewart, R. A., S. Bailey-White, S. Shaw, E. Compton, and S. Ghoting. "Enhanced Storytimes." *Children and Libraries* 12, no. 2 (2014.): 9–14.

Using pre- and post-surveys of parents and caregivers and storytime providers, this study worked to understand the impact on parents and caregivers of training storytime providers how to incorporate early literacy asides into their storytimes. Early literacy asides are moments in the programs where the librarian interacts with the caregiver to share information about supporting early literacy. The researchers found that, following the training for storytime providers, parents and caregivers felt they increased their knowledge of early literacy and were more motivated to support early literacy skills for their children. However, these increases did not lead to a change in the parents' and caregivers' early literacy behaviors. Some takeaways that they identify are that asides can be disruptive for children and families who are used to the routine of storytime, so it is important to allow for training and practice time to be successful with achieving a seamless delivery of adult early literacy asides.

COMMUNITY

The principle of community refers to two types of community. The first is the community that you serve. Given that public libraries serve the communities in which they are located, it is important to approach your program design from a community-centered perspective. Work to understand what your community needs and what groups in your community you might not be reaching. Find ways to locate programs in and outside of the library to reach and serve *all* your community, including those who currently use your services and those who don't. The second type of community is the community of your peers. Building a peer community, either in-person or virtually, can be a valuable resource for ideas and feedback as you work to continuously develop more effective programs. The studies below together demonstrate the importance of community—both your user community and your community of peers.

Brown, J. A., and J. E. Stefaniak. "The Design of a Cognitive Apprenticeship to Facilitate Storytime Programming for Librarians." *Contemporary Educational Technology* 7, no. 4 (2016): 331–51.

Brown and Stefaniak examined the effectiveness of offering a cognitive apprenticeship framework to train storytime providers in designing and delivering high-quality, early literacy-based storytimes. Some themes that emerged from their findings after the apprenticeship were that the trainees felt more organized and prepared; they valued the modeling aspect; and they appreciated the individualized, adaptive learning. However, they did express a desire to learn from others, including their peer and expert communities, in addition to their trainer. One takeaway is that it is important to build peer communities that you can turn to for training, advice, ideas, and feedback, and work to seek out opportunities for modeling from more experienced storytime providers.

Campana, K., M. Brouwer, I. Bayo Urban, J. E. Mills, J. Capps, E. Feldman, and K. Burnett. "Connecting Collections and Cultures by Creating a Community of Children's Librarians Around Early Literacy Storytimes." *Proceedings of the American Society for Information Science and Technology* 51, no. 1 (2014): 1–4.

As part of the VIEWS2 grant, the researchers used interviews with storytime providers to understand their perceptions of a virtual community of practice that was created as part of the VIEWS2 training. They found that although some storytime providers struggled to feel a sense of community in the virtual space, they found value in being able to share storytime techniques and make connections among their libraries. One takeaway is the importance of having a community where you can share ideas, gain feedback on your storytime techniques, and continuously develop more effective storytimes.

Chen, P., C. Rea, R. Shaw, and C. J. Bottino. 2016. Associations between Public Library Use and Reading Aloud Among Families with Young Children. *The Journal of Pediatrics* 173, 221-27.

By interviewing 200 parents of children six to eighteen months old who were attending their children's well-visits with their pediatricians, researchers examined public library use and shared reading practices of the families interviewed. They found that parents who owned a library card were more likely to use the library and read aloud to their children. In addition, they found that a high percentage of those interviewed wanted more information on public library services to children. Takeaways from this study are that it is essential to go into the community to promote the public library's services to children and to work to get library cards in the hands of families with young children. In addition, the location of the pediatrician's office for this study suggests that doctor's offices serving young children may be an ideal community location for partnering around these marketing efforts.

Clark, L. K. "Caregivers' Perceptions of Emergent Literacy Programming in Public Libraries in Relation to the National Research Councils' Guidelines on Quality Environments for Children." *Library and Information Science Research* 39, no. 2 (2017): 107-15.

This study used surveys to understand caregivers' perceptions of early literacy programs for children from birth to three and whether they align with the National Research Council's (NRC) Guidelines for Environments for Children. The researcher found that most parents and caregivers felt that the programs addressed cognitive and physical development, supported responsive and nurturing relationships, and believed that the librarians helped to facilitate learning for the children attending their programs. In addition, some parents and caregivers felt the program was helping to prepare their children for school and that the appropriate size of the program should be left for the librarian to determine. Finally, Clark found that, for the most part, these programs align with the NRC's Guidelines for Environments for Children. One takeaway is that the community of caregivers values the cognitive and physical development opportunities provided by library programs, and thus it is essential that librarians gain an understanding of the cognitive and physical needs of the children in their communities and work to address those needs.

Czarnecki, E. 2006. *The Carroll County Public Library Emergent Literacy Training Assessment Project.* http://lrsv.umd.edu/abstracts/Stoltz_et_al.pdf.

A study done by Carroll County Public Library in Maryland examined the impact that offering early literacy training for in-home childcare providers would have for the children who attend these in-home childcares. An early literacy assessment was done with the children before and after the training. They found a significant increase in the children's scores on the early literacy assessment following the training, suggesting that offering early literacy training for in-home childcare providers can have a positive impact on the early literacy skills of the children who attend their childcare. One takeaway from this study is that there are many ways to have an impact with early learning in your community. It does not have to be limited to those who come inside the library. Pierce County Library System also recreated this study with similar results, as detailed in Campana and Dresang (2011).

Hughes-Hassel, S., D. Agosto, and X. Sun. "Making Storytime Available to Children of Working Parents." *Children and Libraries* 5, no. 2 (Summer/Fall 2007): 43-48.

This study examined how libraries are adjusting their programming to meet the needs of families with young children when the parents or guardians work full-time. To do this the researchers examined program schedules, methods of program delivery, and interviewed librarians whose libraries were offering a large number of programs during non-work hours. They found that many libraries had adjusted their program schedules to offer programs during non-work hours to meet the needs of their communities. In addition, they also found that libraries were using some other ways to provide "literacy lead-ins" to families who could not attend their programs. Although many libraries are now providing programs during non-work hours, the important takeaway from this study is that it is essential to consider your community's needs when developing programs, including program design, content, locations, and schedules.

McKenzie, Pamela, and Rosamund Stooke. "Making a Difference: The Importance of Purposes to Early Learning Programs." *Children & Libraries* 10, no. 2 (2012): 47-52.

In this study the researchers used observation to examine the goals and purposes across early learning programs offered by libraries and other community organizations in order to understand the links between these programs. They found that all of the programs are making many kinds of differences and identified three takeaways for early learning programs: 1) any high-quality program "develop[s] in context," with program leaders making mid-program adjustments to the current flow of the program to meet the current needs of their community; 2) standardized programs limit program leaders' ability to make these mid-program adjustments, therefore limiting their ability to be user- and community-centered; and 3) in some cases it may be necessary to account for and acknowledge participants' differences or run the risk of making them feel excluded.

Mills, J. E., K. Campana, S. Fullerton, M. Brouwer, A. Carlyle, C. Metoyer, and E. T. Dresang, 2015. *Impact, Advocacy, and Professional Development: An Exploration of Storytime Assessment in Washington State.* http://views2.ischool.uw.edu/wp-content/uploads/2015/11/Dreang-White-Paper-Supp-Doc-1.11.pdf.

In this study, researchers performed interviews with storytime providers and library administrators to explore how libraries are assessing their storytimes. They found that assessment of storytimes is an emergent practice and that libraries use a wide range of activities to assess their storytimes. One takeaway is that most of those who are using some type of assessment find it to be beneficial to their storytime practice, so it is important for librarians to find ways to assess their storytimes that work for them, their storytimes, and their libraries.

CONCLUSION

As this chapter demonstrates, there have been a variety of studies examining children's services at the public library. However, to be able to grow and develop more effective practices and continue to advocate for your role and the role of your department, you must have access to more recent relevant research that is based within your own field and practices. Although you may have very little time for looking at research in the busy days of a children's librarian, you can benefit by staying abreast of findings in our own and other disciplines to inform your own practice and translate them via developmental tips for parents, to assist in the development of the *whole* child. Children's librarians have a unique opportunity to use their storytimes and other programs not only to focus on developing language and literacy skills, but to help in the development of all the early learning skills.

REFERENCES

Campana, K., and E. T. Dresang, 2011. "Bridging the Early Literacy Gulf." *Proceedings of the American Society for Information Science and Technology,* 48 (1), 1–10.

Campana, K., J. E. Mills, J. L. Capps, E. T. Dresang, A. Carlyle, C. Metoyer, and I. B. Urban, E. Feldman, K. Burnett, and B. Kotrla. 2016. "Early Literacy in Library Storytimes: A Study of Measures of Effectiveness." *Library Quarterly* 86, no. 4 (October 2016).

Dowd, F. 1997. "Evaluating the Impact of Public Library Storytime Programs Upon the Emergent Literacy of Preschoolers: A Call for Research," *Public Libraries* 3 (6): 348–51.

Dresang, E. T. 2013. "Digital Age Libraries and Youth: Learning Labs, Literacy Leaders, Radical Resources." In *The Information Behavior of a New Generation,* edited by Jamshid Beheshti and Andrew Large. New York: Scarecrow.

McKechnie, L. 1996. "Opening the 'Preschoolers' Door to Learning': An Ethnographic Study of the Use of Public Libraries by Preschool Girls." https://ir.lib.uwo.ca/cgi/viewcontent. cgi?article=3637&context=digitizedtheses.

Mills, J. E., K. Campana, A. Carlyle, B. Kotrla, E. T. Dresang, I. B. Urban, J. L. Capps, C. Metoyer, E. N. Feldman, M. Brouwer, and K. Burnett. 2018. "Early Literacy in Library Storytimes Part 2: A Quasi-Experimental Study and Intervention with Children's Storytime Providers." *Library Quarterly* 88 (2), 160–76.

Mills, J. E., K. Campana, S. Fullerton, M. Brouwer, A. Carlyle, C. Metoyer, and E. T. Dresang. 2015. "Impact, Advocacy, and Professional Development: An Exploration of Storytime Assessment in Washington State." views2.ischool.uw.edu.

Molz, K., and P. Dain. 1999. "Civic Space/Cyberspace: The American Public Library in the Information Age." Cambridge, MA: MIT Press.

Prendergast, T. 2016. "Seeking Early Literacy for All: An Investigation of Children's Librarians and Parents of Young Children with Disabilities' Experiences at the Public Library." *Library Trends* 65 (1): 65–91.

Walter, V. A. 1992. *Outcome Measures for Public Library Service to Children: A Manual of Standardized Procedures.* Chicago: American Library Association.

CHAPTER 14

Connecting Programs to the Learning and Development of Children Ages Six to Twelve

R. Lynn Baker

INTRODUCTION

As brain research has shown, the first years of life set the stage for later learning, building the connections that are crucial for a successful transition into kindergarten (Center on the Developing Child at Harvard 2016). The elementary and early middle school years (children between the ages of six and twelve) build on these early connections to set the academic and literacy-based foundation that can establish successful learning throughout the rest of a child's life. There are various developmental considerations that must be understood to provide effective library programs and services during the pivotal stage of learning that occurs during elementary and early middle school years.

Thanks to the rapid and crucial development that children's brains undergo during the early years of life, school-aged children are ready to take the next step toward organizing their thoughts and understanding the world around them. Even after this stage of development, the brain is still not finished growing; it will merely be ready to continue its journey toward full maturity, which is not until sometime during the adult's mid-twenties (Siegel and Bryson 2011). During the elementary school years, the child's brain is focused on developing the skills that are necessary to become a successful learner and reader.

READING SKILLS

The successful beginning reader demonstrates an understanding of each of the six early literacy components mentioned in chapter 8, Early Childhood Decoded: An Introduction to Development, Sociocultural Theory, and Early Learning—oral language, vocabulary, phonological awareness, print concepts, letter knowledge, and background knowledge. Paris (2005) classifies these skills into two groups: constrained and unconstrained. Constrained skills include those that a child can master by a certain point, such as letter knowledge and phonological awareness. In other words, there is a finite end to the achievement of these skills. Unconstrained skills, on the other hand, refer to those that develop over a lifetime, such as vocabulary and comprehension. Once the child has mastered the constrained skills of letter knowledge and phonological awareness, decoding is next. Decoding is the child's ability to quickly combine individual letter sounds to read a word (National Institute for Literacy 2007). As children learn to decode, they are also developing comprehension—the child's ability to understand what they have read (Carrier 2009). For a child to comprehend text entirely, there must be some form of real-world reference. A new reader may have difficulty comprehending something that does not have a corresponding personal experience. It is important for beginning readers to be exposed to different cultures, activities, and practices to create a frame of reference for things that may otherwise be unfamiliar to them when they read. Once children can comprehend the content of the text they are reading, fluency is the next skill that begins to strengthen. Fluency of reading occurs when a child can read (aloud or silently) with speed and expressiveness (National Institute for Literacy 2007). With fluency, a child is able to read without many mistakes and is able to make sense of and retain what they have read.

During the early elementary school years, executive function skills emerge. These are higher thinking skills that allow the child to focus attention, act on information, access working memory, self-monitor thoughts, and control responses to distractions—all skills that are necessary for learning to read (Hecker 2017). During the activation stage of reading, the child prepares to focus on the task of reading. This level of concentration is needed for children to experience comprehension of what they are reading. When children already have exposure or background knowledge associated with the content that is included within the text, they have an emotional connection to what they are reading. This connection fosters comprehension. As the child continues to read the text, the child must be able to tap into their working memory (Nouwens and Verhoeven 2017). This means that children must be able to retain what they have already read and connect it to the new ideas presented through the text. As children mature as readers, they become more aware of how well they are comprehending and retaining what they are reading. At this point, children can self-monitor their own reading practices and infer meaning through contextual clues. This higher-level executive function enables readers to build new literacy skills and retain new vocabulary—which are the building blocks of reading.

TWO SIDES OF THE BRAIN

In addition to the executive function skills that are needed for a child to become a successful learner and reader, the child must also be able to make connections between the left and right sides of the brain. Each side of the brain has its own specific purpose (Siegel and Bryson 2011). The left side of the brain is primarily used for logical thinking tasks, such as reading, writing, talking, and problem-solving, whereas the right side of the brain is primarily responsible for emotional and creative thinking tasks, such as imaginative thinking, creating art, and engaging in musical activities. There is a connector between each side of the brain, known as the corpus callosum (Integrated Learning Strategies 2016). The corpus callosum is a band of fibers that transmits information between the two sides. It also acts as a barrier between the two sides of the brain when one side may be interfering with the duties of the other side. Activities that strengthen the corpus callosum can help a child transfer information between the two sides and more easily make the transition between different modes of thinking, such as reading information and expressing creative thinking. Such activities include bringing parts of the body to midline or tasks requiring the coordination of both sides of the body, through athletic activities or music and movement activities to help to strengthen the corpus callosum (Integrated Learning Strategies 2016).

When a child is asked to quickly switch gears between types of learning and experiences, it is difficult to do so without a strong corpus callosum. Therefore, when working with school aged-children, it is important to alternate types of experiences, such as reading, movement, discussion, and creative projects. When a child exhibits problem behavior during transition times, this can often be attributed to the child's inability to quickly switch modes of thinking, which is due to an under-exercised corpus callosum. For children who get "stuck" in one mode of thinking, as might be the case when a child is struggling with a reading or writing task, providing them with a creative thinking activity can boost cognitive reasoning by providing a "break" to the left side of the brain. It is important to understand how the brain works during this stage of development to meet children where they are and offer challenging activities to help them as they continue to develop these skills.

THE SOCIAL LEARNING BRAIN

In addition to creating connections within the brain, children are also busy developing social-emotional skills to help connect to those around them. Children start to develop social-emotional skills at birth and, similar to unconstrained literacy skills, will continue to develop these skills throughout their lives. During this stage children are learning to control themselves and their emotions. Children who can control their impulses and focus on tasks will feel more confident and struggle less with learning (Brooks and Goldstein 2002). The child's ability to focus independently without being distracted impacts their reading development. Confidence, focus, and successful learning is also impacted by social acceptance during the later elementary and early middle school years. Children are beginning to deepen their friendships during this time and grow more independent. Self-awareness begins to develop, and children understand that their choices have outcomes and consequences, which enables them to develop mastery orientation, that is, a personal responsibility for learning (Child Trends 2014). This stage is important for a child to be able to engage in independent tasks.

In addition to social- and self-awareness, children during this stage begin to develop individual learning styles. The child may learn best by seeing (the visual learner), by listening and discussing (the auditory learner), or by doing (the kinesthetic learner) (F. Baker 2015). It is important to offer experiences and activities that incorporate each of these various types of learning because children who attend library programs represent all levels of learning and have varying temperaments. Such rich programs will help children meet their individual learning style needs. Learning styles are often determined by a child's individual personality traits and temperament (Child Development Institute). They may be slow to warm up to others, easygoing and flexible, or strong-willed with many of their own ideas and plans. Therefore, it is important to build a rapport with children to learn about their temperament, likes, dislikes, needs, and strengths. This will help to discover the best way of connecting with each individual child. The biggest part of helping a child become a successful learner is building a relationship through connections.

LIBRARY PROGRAMS

To have the biggest impact, librarians must understand the wide range of development, temperaments, and learning styles represented by the children who attend their programs.

Building a connection with the child goes a long way toward fostering a child's lifelong love of learning and reading. When children understand that reading and learning can be fun and make an emotional connection to the process, they are much more likely to be successful.

Making a connection during the elementary and early middle school years requires some extra effort, because children are often pulled in many directions: sports, afterschool activities, and other community events. It is important for librarians to reach out to children, families, schools, and other organizations to build collaborative partnerships. By keeping in constant communication, librarians can schedule library events at the most optimal times for participation. Using a survey with children, parents and caregivers, and schools to collect information on scheduling and interests can go a long way toward meeting the needs of children in your community (R. Baker 2017). There are many different types of programs that can be offered to best meet the needs of children in the community.

Younger elementary school children often still enjoy reading or story-based programs (R. Baker 2017). The key to a successful story-based program for early elementary grades is choosing books and activities that are developmentally appropriate. This may include reading more advanced picture books, or chapter books that the children are not ready to read yet on their own. Offering booktalks (which is much like presenting a "trailer" or public service announcement for the book) for children who struggle with making their own book choices can help connect reluctant readers with books. Programs like these can help contribute to children's still-developing reading skills, especially comprehension and vocabulary.

Elementary school children may also be interested in attending ongoing "club" programs. Clubs can be scheduled at the same time each week or each month. Reading or book clubs can span a few weeks to give participants a chance to discuss a book and do connected activities after they read the book at home. Clubs can also be focused on an activity, such as chess, knitting, or a craft; or focused on an interest, such as a card game or a collectible item; and can be offered in the library or at schools and other community locations. Clubs can give children a chance to develop some social connections and provide librarians with time to incorporate a wide variety of activities to meet the different ways that children may learn. Libraries and school systems can also collaborate to create community-wide book initiatives, with children in certain grade levels reading the same book. Several in-house and outreach programs can be offered connected to the book with an author visit as the culminating event.

Pop-up and passive programs offer a way to engage library patrons with program activities on their own time and at their own pace. A pop-up program is one that is impromptu, not planned for a specific time or date (Koester 2014b). When there seem to be enough interested participants at the library, the librarian announces that the program will be starting in a few minutes and then leads the program. The pop-up program theme or concept is pre-set but easy to offer at any time with materials at hand. On the other hand, a passive program is planned for a specific span of time but does not require a librarian to lead it. This kind of program invites participants to engage in an activity on their own and then submit something so the library knows that they have participated. The activity might include voting, making a submission to a contest, or contributing to a larger group project (Horrocks 2014). Both pop-up and passive programs offer ways to provide children with a variety of different experiences in the library in a short amount of time, which may help to strengthen the corpus callosum.

Readers' theater programs incorporate reading, storytelling, and drama (Cornwell n.d.). The children who participate practice reading from a script and contribute to planning the production, props, and costumes. At the end of several practice sessions, the children present a performance by reading and acting out the script. Readers' theater programs offer a way for elementary and early middle school children to work on reading skills, including narration, vocabulary, fluency, and comprehension. Such programs help to promote print motivation through encouraging the enjoyment of reading and also help to meet the needs of all types of learners.

Children in this age group also typically enjoy STEAM (science, technology, engineering, art, and math) programs. These types of programs offer a natural way of combining entertainment with hands-on learning through discovery and exploration (Koester 2014a). Examples of STEAM programs might include chemistry or earth science-related experiments, learning how to generate computer code, learning how to design structures, creating clay sculptures, or using geometry to figure out how to build a pyramid. The goal of offering a STEAM program should be the connection between the participants and discovery of new information. A STEAM program typically offers hands-on activities that are ideal for attracting and meeting the needs of all types of learners. Additionally, children could be encouraged to work in groups in these programs, which will help to provide social connections and experiences.

Another way to engage children in this age group is to invite local guests to present, or help present a program, which provides an opportunity to collaborate with members of the community (R. Baker 2017). Reaching out to experts in the library's community helps to build collaborative relationships with members of the community, to build support for library programs through those relationships, and to connect program participants to services that exist in the community. Local guests will often volunteer their time or present for a nominal fee. For larger events with larger budgets, such as summer reading programs or community-wide initiatives, libraries might consider inviting a national speaker, author, or artist to present a program or series of programs. Library systems that are geographically close to one another may consider sharing the cost if the guest's fee is beyond the budget of individual libraries. Travelling presenters will often book multiple presentations over one day or several days. This provides libraries with the opportunity to offer programs that they may not otherwise be able to afford and provide participants the opportunity to attend a program by a guest presenter that they would otherwise not have the opportunity to attend. Guest presenter programs should always connect to the needs and interests of children in the community. This is another way that libraries can connect children to learning, literacy, and new experiences within their community.

Regardless of the type of program and service, it is possible to offer fun experiences while incorporating opportunities for literacy and STEAM learning. Programs and services for children between the ages of six and twelve should aim to combine entertainment with hands-on learning through discovery and exploration to keep children engaged and allow them to see that learning can be fun.

CONCLUSION

When librarians are knowledgeable about child development and are in tune with the children and families they serve, they are able to plan intentional programs for school aged children. Based on the understanding of brain development and stages of learning, children's programming can have a big impact on creating lifelong learners and readers. Through creating community partnerships with other organizations throughout the community, libraries can reach more children and families and serve needs that may otherwise go unmet. Gathering information about the interests and needs of children and families enables libraries to offer programs that are most likely to draw the greatest interest, serve the greatest needs, and fill the most gaps that exist within the community. Through intentionally implementing these strategies and practices across program planning for children in kindergarten through fifth grade, libraries move beyond the walls of their building to help children learn, explore, discover, and become engaged readers and learners.

REFERENCES

Baker, F. 2015. Learning Styles in Children. Kidspot. www.kidspot.com.au/school/primary/learning-and-behaviour/learning-styles-in-children/news-story/2c188e7d8ca8d273b2f441fcae6ae1ba.

Baker, R. L. 2017. *Creating Literacy-Based Programs for Children: Lesson Plans and Printable Resources for K-5.* Chicago: ALA Editions.

Brooks, R., and S. Goldstein. 2002. *Raising Resilient Children: Fostering Strength, Hope, and Optimism in Your Child.* Baltimore: Paul H. Brooks.

Carrier, G. 2009. Comprehension. Reading Rockets. www.readingrockets.org/article/comprehension.

Center on the Developing Child at Harvard University. 2016. *From Best Practices to Breakthrough Impacts: A Science-Based Approach to Building a More Promising Future for Young Children and Families.* https://developingchild.harvard.edu/resources/from-best-practices-to-breakthrough-impacts/.

Child Development Institute. n.d. *Temperament and Your Child's Personality.* https://childdevelopmentinfo.com/child-development/temperament_and_your_child/#.WdeZBWhSzIU.

Child Trends. 2014. *Measuring Elementary School Students' Social and Emotional Skills: Providing Educators with Tools to Measure and Monitor Social and Emotional Skills That Lead to Academic Success.* www.childtrends.org/wp-content/uploads/2014/08/2014-37CombinedMeasuresApproachandTablepdf1.pdf.

Cornwell, L. n.d. What is Readers Theater? Scholastic. www.scholastic.com/librarians/programs/whatisrt.htm#bio.

Hecker, L. R. 2017. The Reading Brain: Executive Function Hard at Work. Learning Disabilities Association of America. https://ldaamerica.org/the-reading-brain-executive-function-hard-at-work/.

Horrocks, D. 2014. Passive Programs Throw Down! Jbrary. https://jbrary.com/passive-programs/.

Integrated Learning Strategies. 2016. *Corpus Callosum: Your Child's Superhighway for Connecting the Emotional and Logical Sides of the Brain.* http://ilslearningcorner.com/2016-06-corpus-callosum-childs-superhighway-connecting-emotional-logical-sides-brain-better-learning/.

Koester, A. 2014a. "Get STEAM Rolling!" *Children and Libraries* 12 (3): 22–25.

Koester, A. 2014b. Pop-Up Guerilla Storytime! Storytime Underground. https://storytimeunderground.wordpress.com/2014/02/02/pop-up-guerrilla-storytime-at-opening-minds-2014-a-conference-for-early-childhood-educators/.

National Institute for Literacy. 2007. Adapted from *What Content-Area Teachers Should Know About Adolescent Literacy.* www.nifl.gov/nifl/publications/adolescent_literacy07.pdf.

Nouwens, S., M. A. Groen, and L. Verhoeven. 2017. "How Working Memory Relates to Children's Reading Comprehension: The Importance of Domain-Specificity in Storage and Processing." *Reading and Writing* 30 (1): 105–20. http://doi.org/10.1007/s11145-016-9665-5.

Paris, S. G. 2005. "Reinterpreting the Development of Reading Skills." *Reading Research Quarterly* 40 (2): 184–202.

Siegel, D. J., and T. P. Bryson. 2011. *The Whole-Brain Child: 12 Revolutionary Strategies to Nurture Your Child's Developing Mind.* New York: Delacorte Press.

CHAPTER 15

Middle Childhood Is Not Middle of the Road

Developing Exemplary Services and Practices for Six- to Ten-Year–Olds at the Chicago Public Library

Elizabeth McChesney

INTRODUCTION

Since 1873, the Chicago Public Library (CPL) has encouraged lifelong learning by welcoming all people and offering equal access to information, entertainment, and knowledge through innovative services and programs, as well as cutting-edge technology. Through our eighty library locations, including the new state-of-the-art Children's Library-Thomas Hughes Children's Library, CPL provides free access to a rich collection of materials, both physical and digital, and presents the highest-quality author discussions, exhibits, and programs for children, teens, and adults. CPL hosts ten million visitors annually and in 2016 circulated over nine million items. Currently one million people hold active library cards. CPL has received the Social Innovator Award from Chicago Innovation Awards; won a National Medal for Library Services from the Institute for Museum and Library Services; was named the first-ever winner of the National Summer Learning Association's Founder's Award in recognition of its Summer Learning Challenge; and was ranked number one in the United States, and third in the world by an international study of major urban libraries conducted by the Heinrich Heine University Dusseldorf in Germany.

WHAT IS MIDDLE CHILDHOOD?

Welcoming the middle childhood-aged patron into our libraries is pure joy. Children this age are mastering new skills and becoming more independent. They enjoy the company of peers and will reinforce their learning with friends. They tend to be eager learners who are keen to try out their developing literacy skills in public library programs. In school, they are mastering new and complex skills from reading fluency to math, art, and science, and burgeoning technologies are empowering them with the internet at their fingertips. They have a funny bone that is sure to delight almost everyone around them. This is the golden age for joke books, riddles, and Mad Libs.

Middle childhood is often defined by the ages and stages of children from six to ten years old. During this time, a child experiences many changes physically, developmentally, and emotionally. In this age group, a child becomes "elementary school-aged," and traditional public library services support a child at this age level both in school and out-of-school time. But what is really happening to a growing child during this time span?

Child development theorist Jean Piaget called this the *preoperational stage*. Within this stage there are two subsets: by six years old, children are likely to be in the "intuitive age" where they become more logical and perceptive. By age seven, and through the rest of this age span, Piaget theorizes that children enter into the *concrete operational stage*, marked by more adherence to rules, more logical thinking, and a new ability to classify and think critically (Mooney 2013).

Erik Erikson's psychosocial theory of child development holds that a child around this age is in the *Industry vs. Inferiority* phase. This phase has hallmarks of developing a healthy ego and sense of self. According to Erikson's theory, it is in this age group that children can develop a strong sense of pride. This is often times accomplished through social interactions with friends and may also come from positive re-enforcement from the adults in a child's life. Youth this age need strong feedback from adults. Children develop confidence through the "wins" they have in a day. Competency is also built at this age, and when we celebrate it in the child, it helps develop their self-esteem and agency (Mooney 2013).

ABOUT OUR PROGRAMS

The Chicago Public Library supports developing children in this age span and their parents and caregivers through our programs, services, and spaces. We see libraries as learning environments, unique places for children to foster creativity and learning. And we know that twenty-first-century children need new learning experiences that will help them be successful in school and life.

In the Chicago Public Library system, we have an evolving strategy that focuses on five key areas and we have aligned all our children's programming to these areas:

- Access for all
- Nurturing learning
- Support economic advancement
- Strengthen communities
- Serve patrons effectively

This strategy is informed by Institute of Museum and Library Services (IMLS) alignment of twenty-first-century skills with libraries and museum priorities. These include:

- Learning and Innovation Skills
- Information, Media, and Technology Skills
- 21st Century Themes
- Life and Career Skills (Institute of Museum and Library Services 2009, 3)

IMLS also considers that the lines of how and when we learn are blurred between formal education and informal education and learning experiences, introducing the idea that children need self-directed, goal-oriented learning experiences that put the child at the center of their learning. Chicago Public Library-Children's Services synthesized all this and developed a plan to accelerate twenty-first-century learning skills. These skills include: communication, collaboration, creativity, and critical thinking. We chose to focus on this new learning strategy through the lens of STEM/STEAM-based learning opportunities. Our emphasis on STEAM learning helped us align our services to our five impact areas and serve the middle childhood-aged child's evolving needs.

Our design principals (think of these as ground rules) for how children's spaces are developed revolves around library-attainable goals: to create relevant, time flexible, child-centered and attuned spaces that encourage creativity through play and STEM/STEAM learning (see figure 15.1). When children have a successful experience at the library, it helps them build a sense of pride, mastery, and achievement. Research shows that when parents or caregivers are supporting children, the outcomes for children are even better; therefore, it is important that our spaces welcome and encourage parents and grownups in the child's life as well. Passive programming, open-ended experiential learning opportunities, and increased access to collaborative spaces for children and parents now drive our space and programming.

FIGURE 15.1 Children at the CPL-Albany Park Branch interact in the newly designed, flexible space.

SUPPORTING SCHOOL NEEDS

During middle childhood, school-aged children begin to use the library for their new school needs. We must now find new ways to continue our relationship with them in the library. One way is supporting them with homework help.

At CPL we have provided formalized homework help to children in our libraries for many years. In 2012, we doubled down on our offerings by placing an accredited teacher in every library to offer free assistance for children. The Teacher in the Library, privately funded through the Chicago Public Library Foundation, is a program that employs teachers who are paid a stipend. The teachers, or TIL's, provide on-the-spot guidance and assistance after school from approximately 3:00 pm to 6:00 pm. They rove from table to table helping children negotiate the transition from the school day to after-school time, suggesting strategies for assignments, or initiating conversations with students about what is stumping them in their homework. They may pair up children who have similar assignments, play group math games, or have an older student help a younger student with homework. One of the most important goals of our program is to help children learn good homework skills. We call this "homework help": no appointments are taken, and no assessments are administered.

All children are welcome to participate. Parents and other caregivers often ask questions of the teachers as well. In 2016, 93,000 sessions were offered across the city with an average 46 percent of sessions for math, 35 percent reading, 7 percent social studies, and 5 percent other assignments. A very welcome, but unintended, consequence of this program is that the Teachers in the Library are available to support parents and caregivers, so they can navigate the school system and find services for their children, which range from free immunizations to vision tests. We further aid families with homework by offering an online homework assistance site that offers a real-time, digital connection to grade-level homework assistance via the computer. This allows us to deepen our patrons' access to homework help services. A high percentage of families surveyed say the program helps them accomplish their homework and understand the content more deeply.

LIBRARY CARD CAMPAIGNS

Equity and access are the battle cry of providing services to families. To ensure that school-aged children are equipped with a library card, the Chicago Public Library offers an annual library card campaign in partnership with the Chicago Public School System and the Archdiocesan schools. This links to the ConnectED initiative spearheaded by the Obama Administration. Our annual campaign is focused on ensuring that every kindergartener and first grader has a library card. Applications are distributed to schools and are gathered and processed. The cards, accompanied by stickers that say, "Hip, Hip, Hooray, I Got My Library Card Today!", go to the classrooms. Classes are encouraged to take walking visits to the library to help teach children the importance of the library card as an essential "school tool." Approximately 40,000 library cards are issued each year through the campaign, allowing children access to books and online materials, both of which are critical to school success.

DIGITAL NATIVES AND MEDIA MENTORS

Today's youth are digital natives. Born into a fast-paced technological world, they have facility with technology at a very early age. In fact, according to a Wright Group McGraw-Hill Report (n.d.), "A complete picture of reading comprehension in the 21st Century includes the skills, strategies, dispositions, and practices required to comprehend and use a wide range of print, non-print and digital texts for multiple purposes and with multiple audiences."

Librarians are actively working toward becoming media mentors, a role we have always informally played in our public libraries. No longer are we the experts solely on books—now we are the connectors of youth to the digital world. We are the trusted experts of information, so this role is fitting. At the Chicago Public Library, we offer assistance to children in information literacy and informational fact-finding through visits from schools, informal visits, and the gamification of fact finding. Our Knowledge Ninja project offers kids practice in online fact-finding through gamified subject searches. These searches range in topic from the science of fire hoses to traveling to Mars. The games lead children through a series of prompts that allows them to build their digital literacy while gaining information about fun topics. They are accessible online and are often used when classes come to visit the library.

We also support children as they move toward independent reading. Being a skilled or independent reader means that children are interacting with the text: asking questions, making predictions, and using what they know to look for context clues are all reading comprehension strategies. It is commonly believed that reading at grade level by the end of third grade is the biggest predictor of high school graduation and career success. Many states have networks that support the Campaign for Grade Level Reading. At the Chicago Public Library, we have focused our efforts in this area around "Reading on Time by Age 9" to address this need and support our young readers, and as with many elements of our services, we accomplish this through the lens of STEM/STEAM learning. New Reader Book Clubs are offered annually that support newly independent readers as they feel the joy of experiencing reading and exploring book topics together. Noting that there is substantial overlap in the two processes, we commonly employ the Engineering Design Process in tandem with the reading comprehension process to get at key outcomes including STEM-related learning and key twenty-first-century skills, such as literacy, communication, collaboration, creativity, and critical thinking.

To do this in an informal setting (that can also be used in a formal setting) we create challenge cards based on children's literature (see figure 15.2). Noting that children's books are nearly always formed around a key problem that the characters must resolve, we ask children open-ended questions to find solutions to the problem. We then provide them materials through which they can prototype a solution, collaborate on problem-solving, test the solution, and reflect on their learning. The cards are accompanied by maker kits called Curiosity Kits, which allow children to use open-ended resources to iterate, design, and ultimately create solutions. In this way, we are encouraging the maker movement in the middle childhood-aged child.

Our public service campaign, "Take 20, Read Plenty" is aimed at heightening awareness in adults about the importance of language and reading on the developing brain. We urge adults to take twenty minutes every day to read aloud or listen to a child in kindergarten to third grade read aloud to strengthen literacy skills and build vocabulary in the child. Pledge sheets, stickers, and celebrations augment this campaign to increase skills.

OUT-OF-SCHOOL TIME

There is a great deal of research about what happens to youth in the critical out-of-school time hours. We now know that children who participate in out-of-school time (OST) activities have improved school attendance, higher engagement in learning, improved test score and grades, as well as better social and developmental outcomes (National Institute on Out-of-School Time 2009). To this end, public libraries invest in children through a variety of rich program models that include book clubs, drop in art programs, and other traditional after-school and weekend activities.

Family Science Nights and Science Clubs

Many of CPL's out-of-school time programs happen under the umbrella of the grant, ScienceConnections. The motto of this grant-funded project that provides STEAM programming is "hands-on, minds-on learning." Under this grant, the Chicago Public Library supports hundreds of programs annually throughout the city that include family science nights, in which families engage with museum educators and librarians to learn about a science concept and explore it through hands-on discovery. Robotics clubs, preschool science,

The Great Chicago Fire of 1871

On the night of October 8, 1871, in a small barn
on DeKoven Street, a fire started. Two days later,
300 people were dead, 100,000 were homeless
and 3.3 square miles of Chicago were in ruins.

Books to Investigate
The Great Fire by Jim Murphy: This award-winning book is thought to be the definitive
guide to the Chicago Fire.

Fighting Fire! By Michael L. Cooper: A survey of ten deadly blazes that changed the way
we fight fires today, including the Chicago Fire.

The Great Chicago Fire by L.L. Owens: An in-depth look at the events leading up to the
fire and its aftermath.

Firestorm! By Joan Hiatt Harlow: Experience the Chicago Fire through the eyes of two
12-year-old boys in this well researched, fictionalized account.

Articles to Read
The *Chicago Tribune* from October 11, 1871: The *Tribune*'s front page accounts from just
days after the fire was extinguished.

Time Trip: A look at the key facts about the fire.

Great Chicago Fire: *Disasters, Accidents and Crises in American History* article on the fire
and its impact.

Retrospect: October 8, 1871: The Great Chicago Fire: Did the weather or Mrs. O'Leary's
cow start the fire?

Websites to Explore
The Great Chicago Fire and The Web of Memory: Chicago History Museum's site includes
maps, photographs and illustrations, eyewitness accounts, and much more.

Progress of the Chicago Fire of 1871: Follow the fire as it travels across the city.

The Chicago Fire of 1871 and the "Great Rebuilding": National Geographic explores the fire
and examines how the city was rebuilt.

Great Chicago Fire 1871: What role did the weather play in the Great Chicago Fire?

Keywords to Search
great fire, Chicago history, disasters, fires, fire fighting

Call Number Range
F548.42 and F548.33

Think About It

1. How did the weather effect the spread of the Chicago Fire?

2. What would you have done to prevent the Chicago Fire?

CHICAGO PUBLIC LIBRARY CHALLENGE CARD

In the story "The Three Billy Goats Gruff," the three hungry goats must make it over a bridge to get to the green, grassy hill where they can graze. There is a mean troll who lives under the bridge and will eat up anyone who crosses. **Design something to help the goats get safely to the other hill.**

FIGURE 15.2 Knowledge Ninja handout and challenge cards.

floor-based activities that explore scientific concepts, Building Brick Clubs, and science fair programming that supports the annual school district's science fair are also routinely offered. Professional development for staff is included and hands-on programing kits that the librarians can check out are available for everything from coding to making.

A successful model of STEAM programming is designed around a specific concept on the floor (or on a table) in the Children's Room, adjacent to the print collection of books that support this theme (see figure 15.3). In this model, science educators develop a project around a topic, explore it through hands-on discovery, and then have access to the print collections and technology-based library resources, such as database collections and annotated website bibliographies. In experimenting with this program model, we have found that children are more likely to check out a book about the topic being explored than they are in our more traditional programs.

Our science kits are used to further the exploration of a topic. These circulating backpacks with take-home science activities are also offered in branches. Funded through the Institute of Electrical and Electronics Engineers, these kits explore a science topic through books and STEAM discovery. Some of our many kit themes include:

FIGURE 15.3 Children explore STEAM concepts adjacent to the print collections.

- Addition and Subtraction
- Electricity and Circuits
- Gravity, Forces, and Motion
- Multiplication and Division

- Simple Machines
- Robotics

Rahm's Readers Summer Learning Challenge

The largest out-of-school time program that most libraries offer, and indeed the largest of any program offering for CPL, is the summer program for children. In 2012, the Children's Services staff of CPL set out to incorporate twenty-first-century learning into the summer program, broadening the lens on learning in the summertime and encircling the many ways in which libraries embrace summer learning. We learned about the summer slide and the achievement gap from the National Summer Learning Association and the research it has made available. We worked to align our program to key components called out for success. Our Rahm's Readers Summer Learning Challenge has become a national model for sustainable library learning programs. The motto of our program is "All Learning Counts." And, indeed, we know there is much learning that happens in our library.

In 2012, the Chicago Public Library formed a partnership with Chicago's Museum of Science and Industry to create a new solution for summer learning. Our partnership includes a rigorous schedule for professional development and training, access to materials and trained science education experts, time to play and learn together, and easy-to-implement informal science learning tools and programs. Beyond the support to staff, the Museum also provides us with eight Summer Brain Games or STEAM activities and supports teens who conduct programs with younger children. Together we harnessed the power of our two organizations to provide the best outcomes for Chicago youth.

Using STEM/STEAM tools means that we have shifted the content of our programs from rules-bound programming to a more open-ended discovery processes. This new approach to library summer programming is a shift to more self-directed learning. For example: In a traditional library program, after reading Rapunzel, youth may make a princess with long hair. In our new model, participants are given materials to build a tower or design an escape for Rapunzel. By activating problem-solving skills, we are encouraging the six- to ten-year-old to read for meaning, solve problems, and interact with text.

In our program children are challenged to:

- **Read** 20 minutes a day toward a goal of 500 minutes.
- **Discover** through hands-on STEAM inquiry, such as the MSI Summer Brain Games or through a visit to the Museum.
- **Create** through art or maker activities.

By broadening our program to encompass the learning that happens in libraries, aligning it to research about summer learning and summer learning loss, allowing children to explore their interests, and broadening the learning criteria for completion, we have more than doubled our numbers of participants in the middle childhood age group. Research from the University of Chicago-Chapin Hall shows that children who participate in the program demonstrate 15 percent higher reading scores and 20 percent higher math scores than those of their peers who did not participate.

The partnership between Chicago Public Library and Museum of Science and Industry has been lauded as a national model for leveraging the power of two organizations to create a sustainable, child-attuned model. In 2015 we won the National Summer Learning

Association's first ever Founder's Award for Excellence. Through ongoing cross-directional trainings, museum staff now include books in their programming, and CPL children's librarians regularly implement STEM and STEAM practices into their programming, allowing us to maximize our reach to Chicago's youth.

In conclusion, children in middle childhood have complex needs from the public library. We must support school learning, and also help them grow skills, test ideas, and reflect on learning. In Chicago, this has meant overlaying key twenty-first-century learning skills with traditional programming. This realignment of services helps us have maximum impact in middle childhood. Truly, developing these services in a rapidly changing learning landscape means exciting new public library supports for children in middle childhood.

REFERENCES

Institute of Museum and Library Services. 2009. *Museums, Libraries, and 21st Century Skills* (IMLS-2009-NAI-01). Washington, DC.

Mooney, C. G. 2013. *Theories of Childhood: An Introduction to Dewey, Montessori, Erikson, Piaget, and Vygotsky* (2nd ed.). St. Paul, MN: Red Leaf Press.

National Institute on Out-of-School Time. 2009. "Making the Case: A 2009 Fact Sheet on Children and Youth in Out-of-School Time." Wellesley Centers for Women at Wellesley College. https://www.niost.org/pdf/factsheet2009.pdf.

Wright Group LEAD21. n.d. "Reading, the Digital Classroom, and LEAD21." New York: McGraw Hill Education. http://www.frontier.wnyric.org/cms/lib/NY19000265/centricity/domain/20/research-base-reading-digital-classroom.pdf.

CHAPTER 16

A Collaborative Approach to Equitable STEM Programming at San Francisco Public Library

Cristina Mitra

INTRODUCTION

San Francisco Public Library (SFPL) is a large urban public library system "dedicated to free and equal access to information, knowledge, independent learning, and the joys of reading for our diverse community" (SFPL n.d.). With the Main Library, twenty-seven branches, and four mobile outreach vehicles, we aim to reach and respond to the needs of our diverse population in every nook and neighborhood of our city inside and outside of our library walls. Our staff embodies our core values of service, access, community, diversity, and professionalism and we truly stand by our mantra: "All are Welcome." We are fortunate to have at least one full-time children's librarian, serving children and youth from birth to age twelve, at every branch, at the Main Children's Center, and in Mobile Outreach Services. There is also a central Youth Services Team that works together to create programmatic goals (including budget guidelines), partnership opportunities, program and publicity resources, and professional development to support all the children's, teen, and youth services librarians. Our goal is to offer all youth in San Francisco opportunities to learn, explore, innovate, and succeed at the library.

PROGRAMS FOR MIDDLE CHILDHOOD

The following programs are our most commonly offered school-age programs. Each program has an accompanying kit of materials for shared use among librarians. These kits are stored at our Main Library and we work with our internal delivery services unit to coordinate the movement of these kits. The Youth Services Team also maintains a sign-out spreadsheet for the kits that includes time buffers to prevent overlap between programs at different libraries, manages the development and maintenance of these kits by replenishing supplies, reimagines the program design, and phases in or out new kits based on staff and patron feedback. I regularly connect with librarians about their programs to find out how their program went, how useful the materials in the kit were, and how to improve upon them.

While most of our school-age programs take place at one of our library locations, some librarians choose to check out a kit to demonstrate at a school outreach visit. A completed

LEGO WeDo robotic alligator that can snap its jaws on command will quickly get the attention of a boisterous class of third-graders. Some of our programs take place on one of our mobile outreach vehicles, the Techmobile, which is "a fully-equipped computer lab on wheels designed to help bring technology fluency to all San Francisco residents through digital literacy trainings" (Techmobile n.d.). School-age library programs take place in and around libraries and throughout San Francisco.

Alka-Seltzer Rockets

This is a simple science program for children ages seven and up. Kids create rockets that really fly using simple inexpensive ingredients: film canisters, water, and Alka-Seltzer tablets. The magic lies in trying out different ratios of water to tablets to produce the chemical reactions that make the film canisters go pop! The program kits contain all the materials, including safety goggles and instructions. A safety talk at the beginning is key; pulling in an engaged adult or teen volunteer is a good idea to help you pass out the goggles. The success of this program is having an open attitude of "Whatever happens, happens!" A log and tape are available for kids to test and track their progress.

Button Making

This is an easy craft program for ages six through teens. All you need for this program is a button-maker machine, the appropriate materials (mylar film, shells, and pin backs), and art supplies. For younger kids, it helps to pre-cut the button art with a punch cutter. They particularly love making the buttons themselves and pulling the lever down while the librarian encourages them. For older kids, it's great to have magazines available to cut images from or art supplies so kids can create their own designs. It is impressive how this simple activity captures the imaginations of patrons of all ages. Adults inevitably ask if they can also make a button—or two! Although the button machines can be pricey, the popularity of these programs makes the investment well worth it.

iPad Stop Motion Animation

This flexible and easy program for ages eight to twelve uses iPads, a stop motion animation app, a book stand, figurines (LEGO people), and backdrops. Every librarian who does this program has commented on how quickly the children pick up on the technology. It can be helpful to introduce older kids to the creative storyboard process to plan out their stories, but this is optional—it depends on the attention span of the participants. Make sure to offer a variety of figurines and backdrops that inspire imaginations and allow plenty of time for this program (1.5 hours at least) for children to really explore. Finish it off with a film screening with popcorn of everyone's creations for a fantastic finale.

LEGO WeDo Robotics

This is an accessible building and coding program for ages seven to ten. This is not a low-cost program because it requires specific LEGO WeDo sets and laptops loaded with the LEGO

WeDo software. We limit these programs to ten participants and children work in pairs. We always have a model for children to follow. There will be some children who only make the model and others who are interested in making a custom build. It's important as facilitators to show both verbal and nonverbal support to promote children's confidence. Using the WeDo software, kids can make their builds move and make different sounds. It's a great introduction to coding using programming sequencing.

KEVA Contraptions

A building program that is accessible to children ages five through teenagers, this program is all about participants exercising their creativity. It's surprising what the kids make with these simple wooden planks: towers, ball traps, ramps, and more! Unlike LEGO, KEVA planks don't stick to one another so setting up this program on an even surface is important. Librarians should provide one or two examples to spark ideas and bring in other materials, like Hot Wheels cars, to inspire a race. Leave ample time, at least ninety minutes, for children and their families to drop in, stay awhile, and build together.

Marble Machine Tinkering

This creative ball-run contraption for ages six and up was developed by the Exploratorium. This program consists of pegboard panels, posts, and a range of familiar materials (PVC pipes, cone cups, and of course, marbles) that children (and often their accompanying adults) tinker with to create a functioning ball-run. There are infinite possibilities with this challenging, yet super fun program. It's an excellent program for librarians to exercise growth-mindset attitudes.

Rock the Bike

A nutritious food program for ages six and up, Rock the Bike uses a pedal-powered blender. With simple inexpensive ingredients, such as frozen fruit, water, and juice, kids can create their own delicious smoothies. Some of our librarians have also made hummus in the Rock the Bike. This is one of our most popular programs—it has a big "wow factor," because many people haven't seen anything like it before. Small Dixie-sized cups are optimal for giving samples to as many kids as possible. Just like the button machine, the Rock the Bike may be costly for some library systems, but we've found the popularity of this program makes it well worth it.

Scribble Bots

A tinkering program for ages six and up that was also developed by the Exploratorium, this program is a great opportunity for children to learn about motors and power. Built with everyday materials, such as berry baskets, yogurt containers, markers, masking tape, a battery, and a hobby motor, this contraption skitters around on paper and makes interesting designs. This is another program that will benefit from a long program time so kids can truly explore the aspect of the program they love best: making the bot or watching it skitter.

PROGRAM GOALS AND GUIDING PRINCIPLES

STEM programs form the foundation for school-age programming at SFPL. Because SFPL serves so many students from the San Francisco Unified School District (SFUSD)—by far the largest provider of education to San Franciscan youth, serving 57,000 students—we care deeply about creating learning environments at the library that compliment students' experiences in the classroom (SFUSD n.d.). The SFUSD started implementing the Common Core State Standards (CCSS) in 2012 and by 2015 fully adopted the standards (personal communication, April 28, 2017). Knowing that a greater focus on STEM is central to the CCSS, we have prioritized STEM content as a primary program goal for school-age programming. By aligning ourselves with the SFUSD curriculum, we're not only providing a connected learning experience for students, but we're also paving a path for easier partnerships with the SFUSD. For example, when I was a children's librarian, I received more positive responses from teachers to my invitations to come to the library for a LEGO Robotics workshop than a general class visit.

Through this process, we have learned that focusing on STEM is also a win-win situation for us as well as our patrons. Through anecdotes, smiles, and repeat visits, our young patrons show us their delight in participating in our STEM programs. The fun factor is palpable. Their parents' glee and enthusiasm tell us how grateful they are to find *free* STEM opportunities in their own backyard. As for us librarians, we understand that STEM and literacy have a direct connection: the research shows that strong math skills predict long-term success in school in both math and literacy (Rood 2016). We know that LEGO experiences build literacy skills like storytelling, which informs programs like iPad Stop Motion Animation (Osvath 2017). Ultimately, we recognize the special role that the public library can play in young people's learning as an informal learning environment that can "positively influence science learning in school, attitudes toward science, and pursuit of science-related occupations" (National Resources Council n.d.). By speaking "STEM," we find that we're speaking a common language with students, their families, and the school districts that teach them.

The growth toward STEM also carries a more serious agenda in addition to the smiles and glee that the programs produce. Although San Francisco is a geographically small city—measuring just 7 square miles—it holds within it a disparate population. Genuinely "a tale of two cities," about half of San Franciscan adults are highly literate and the other half struggles with low literacy—47 percent read below eighth-grade level (National Assessment of Adult Literacy 2003). With a focus on equity, one of the other reasons we have developed STEM programs is to address this disparity: our goal is to make STEM accessible for *all* children. For example, as a children's librarian at a branch in a low-income neighborhood, I saw that my families generally did not have access to more costly toys like LEGO or something as novel as the Rock the Bike. By providing STEM programs (such as LEGO) at every branch within SFPL, we are increasing the accessibility of free high-quality enrichment experiences across the city's divide.

If STEM is the foundation of our school-age programs, the concept of the growth mindset is the way in which librarians facilitate these programs. We deeply value the research by Carol Dweck, professor of psychology at Stanford University. According to Dweck, children who have "a growth mindset (a belief that intelligence can be developed) outperform those who have a fixed mindset (a belief that intelligence is fixed) (Dweck 2015)." When a young one reaches a presumed end goal, such as creating a LEGO WeDo build, it's our task to then say, as Dweck advises, "Let's talk about what you've tried, and what you can try next," to foster a growth mindset (Dweck 2015). In facilitating our library programs, we strive to support a child's ability to continuously learn. The Center for Childhood Creativity's CREATE Framework builds off the growth mindset and "illustrates key elements of learning environments that support the development of creativity for children ages 2–10" (Resources for Promoting Childhood Creativity n.d.). The acronym can be broken down into the following concepts, which our librarians promote in their programs:

- **Child directed:** Children initiate and feel ownership of their learning.
- **Risk-friendly:** Children are willing to try new challenges and show resilience.
- **Emotionally attuned:** Children feel joy and interest through verbal and nonverbal support.
- **Active:** Physical activity helps children's memory.
- **Time flexible:** Children make new connections and experience a state of flow when allowed to fully immerse in an activity.
- **Exploratory:** Open-ended questions support new possible solutions for children.

Together, the ideas of growth mindset and CREATE form the guiding principles for school-age programming at SFPL.

PROGRAMMING SUPPORT

In spite of the proliferation of literature, conference programs, and blogs about the importance of STEM library programs for children, we have found that many of our children's librarians are daunted by STEM content—but they are curious and open to learning more. By providing the all-in-one STEM programming kits with easy instructions and all the necessary materials, our staff feels increasingly more comfortable leading these programs. Another way that I support skill development and confidence is by hosting a monthly STEM "petting zoo," where more-experienced staff scaffold and encourage less-experienced staff in a quick fifteen-minute demonstration of one of the kits. I provide pop-up trainings as needed on the kits and coordinate more formal professional development with STEM partners from local museums, such as the Tech Museum of Innovation from San José, California. Our programming kits are designed to foster twenty-first-century skills, such as collaboration and teamwork, problem-solving, and creativity and imagination.

PRACTICAL NOTES

There are many practical aspects of program development and delivery to consider. The following questions are practical notes that we have taken into consideration for every one of our STEM school-age programs. We have found that the overall success of a program lies in creating a positive experience for the young patrons and for you, the facilitator. Here are some key issues for reflection:

- **Is it easy to deliver the program?** Is there an intensive set-up or clean-up? Do you have the ability to spend two hours preparing materials? Do you have your manager's support to take off-desk time to prepare the space for your program? Are there staff who can help you clean up after a messy program or will you have to do that on your own? If it would be better for you to have another adult or a teen volunteer to help you with the program, have you recruited the necessary adult or teen volunteers ahead of time?

- **Is it simple and straightforward for the patrons?** Seasoned library programmers understand that some of the most successful programs are the simplest. These are programs that allow children to dive in and spend an open-ended amount of time joyfully exploring and imagining new ideas—that is, getting into a state of flow. Will the program work well with varied ages, families, and group sizes? Also consider learning abilities: is it an accessible and inclusive activity for a diverse group of participants?

- **Does it translate well to a library setting?** A cool craft that you found on Pinterest or a spectacular science experiment on a museum blog may look fun, but can it work at the library? Do the participants need prior knowledge to thrive in the program? Are the materials easy to secure? Is it a better program for a 1:1 ratio between adults and children or in a controlled classroom environment? Given that most library programs are drop-in and do not have a guaranteed audience, does it work if participants arrive at different times or will that disrupt the flow?

- **Is it sustainable?** At SFPL, we try to focus on programs that are easily replicable because we want to be able to tell our patrons, "*yes!*" when they ask us if we will offer it again. If a program takes too much of a toll on staff resources (time, costs, space, etc.), it may be hard to duplicate. Does the program require expensive materials? Does your library have the financial resources to replenish supplies when they run out or are damaged?

While every answer does not necessarily have to be "yes," take time to consider these factors and make the appropriate adjustment to set yourself up for success. For example, if you have decided that a program would be beneficial if the number of participants were limited, set up an easy sign-up process for your patrons. Make the process clear on your publicity materials: your flyers, digital signage, eNewsletter, website, and social media. Inform your staff so that if you're not available, they know where and how to take sign-up information from patrons. Call people who signed up a couple of days before to remind them about the program. Be ready on the day of the program to be flexible because you may have some no-shows, but also have kids eager to join in who just heard about the program that day. Flexibility is truly the name of the game in library programming!

PROGRAM DESIGN AND DEVELOPMENT

We rely on both informal and professional sources to inform program design and development. Listening to our patrons is crucial: they literally tell us specific programs they would like to see at the library (coding!). They will eagerly share the latest trending craft craze (slime!). Then we work quickly to develop kits to support programs. By staying close to trends, we also attract non-library users to programs. And by reading professional journals and blogs, attending conferences, and participating in association committees both locally and through ALSC, we learn quickly about library best practices and programming trends.

Strong equal partnerships are an additional source for new programming opportunities. One such highlight is SFPL's partnership with The Contemporary Jewish Museum (The CJM). Each year I have a partnership-planning meeting with the museum's education staff where they reveal the upcoming exhibits and we discuss the opportunities and alignment for school-age programming given our respective themes and goals. Together, we work to develop a library program that will visit many libraries. One of these, Art on the Go, is a beloved program led by a museum arts educator. This past year, CJM was able to fold a STEM component into the program, which was an added bonus. Through Art on the Go, library patrons learn about CJM while engaging in a high-quality activity. The CJM generously offers these programs to SFPL for free.

ASSESSMENT: SUCCESSES AND CHALLENGES

We pride ourselves in the high quality of our programs, and also understand that we are in an iterative cycle of improvement. Our staff share pictures and anecdotal success stories (and lessons learned) about their programs (both librarian-led and with an outside presenter) via an internal email LISTSERV sent to all SFPL children's librarians in the system—it's a lively and supportive, virtual professional environment. At our monthly system-wide children's services meeting, we provide in-person opportunities for staff to participate in reflective practice by sharing their programming highlights, challenges, and questions in a supportive setting related to a particular program, a new presenter, a different take on a standard program, and so on. We gather feedback via surveys from both our patrons and staff. Our partners are also an important part of our feedback loop; we follow-up on our initiatives to see what went well in the partnership and areas for improvement.

Statistics are another important way that we assess the success of our programs. Our statistics tell us that the number of school-age programs at SFPL is almost equal to the number of early childhood programs. In fact, there is just about a 50-50 split between early and middle childhood programs at SFPL. This is astounding given that, in the past, programming for ages birth to five (read: storytimes) always outweighed school-age programming. This is clearly changing. In FY 2015-2016, out of the 10,000 children's programs that we provided, 5,501 were early childhood programs and 5,401 were for middle childhood. The data tells us that our patrons are appreciating STEM at their libraries—and our librarians are responding with more programs.

The encouraging increase in school-age programming also presents some challenges. In the practical sense, the storage, delivery, and sustainability of programming kits is an ongoing matter. We have a finite space to store these kits so it's important to assess biannually if there are kits that we should phase out, or if we have the ability to create kits that can "live" at each branch rather than being stored at our central location. Sustainability is another issue: Are the supplies in the kits easily accessible? Even if they were in the past, are they still? The final and most important challenge is staff capacity. This refers mainly to time. Does our staff have the time to participate in professional development as they juggle the other demands of their workload? Do they have the time to learn a new program? Regardless of how easy it may be to deliver, there may still be a learning curve. Finally, for programs that really require a long time for open-ended play, such as KEVA Contraptions or iPad Stop Animation, is the librarian able to prioritize this time away from the desk? These are ongoing issues that inform and shape program development and delivery.

The future is exciting for school-age programming at SFPL and newly developed programs are on the horizon. I look forward to introducing two new kits (DIY slime and lip balm) in direct response to our young patrons' requests. It's a fluid research and development process between my role on the Youth Services team and the frontline children's librarians; already many of our librarians have tested out different slime recipes, facilitated programs, and shared feedback. In the summer of 2018, we tried out a new program model called STEMpede that is based on our very successful early childhood program, the Big San Francisco Play Date. In STEMpede, our librarians will transform their program rooms and children's spaces into multi-experience, stimulating, and exploratory STEM spaces for school-age children to make, tinker, and create. Think of it as a pop-up museum experience in a library setting. Our hope is that this will delight and interest school-age audiences so they will further explore and try something new they haven't yet discovered and to cement the library's place in the community as a place for supported, engaged, and creative learning for school-age audiences.

REFERENCES

Dweck, C. 2015. "Carol Dweck Revisits the Growth Mindset." *Education Week,* September 22. www.edweek
.org/ew/articles/2015/09/23/carol-dweck-revisits-the-growth-mindset.html.

National Research Council. Stem in Libraries. Resources for Library Leadership. n.d. www.starnetlibraries
.org/stem-in-libraries/why-stem/.

National Assessment of Adult Literacy. 2003. https://catalog.data.gov/dataset/2003-national-assessment
-of-adult-literacy.

Osvath, C. 2017. "LEGO-Infused Literacy," *Literacy Daily* (blog), April 20. https://www.literacyworldwide
.org/blog/literacy-daily/2017/04/20/lego-infused-literacy.

Resources for Promoting Childhood Creativity through Libraries. n.d. http://elf2.library.ca.gov/pdf/
LibraryResourceDocument.pdf.

Rood, E. 2016. "Reimagining School Readiness." https://centerforchildhoodcreativity.org/wp-content/
uploads/sites/2/2016/03/SchoolReadinessPositionPaper_Issuu.pdf.

San Francisco Public Library. n. d. Mission Statement. https://sfpl.org/?pg=2000002201.

San Francisco Unified School District. n.d. Overview. www.sfusd.edu/en/about-sfusd/overview.html.

Techmobile, n.d. https://sfpl.org/?pg=2000795701.

CHAPTER 17

Middle Childhood Matters at Toronto Public Library

Diane Banks and Peggy Thomas

INTRODUCTION

Toronto Public Library (TPL) serves Canada's largest city of about 2.7 million people (City of Toronto 2017). TPL has become one of the world's busiest library systems, with more than 1.3 million members and 18 million visits to our branches (Toronto Public Library 2015). Over the years, TPL has grown to one hundred branches, including two multistory research branches, seventeen large district branches, and eighty-one smaller community and neighborhood branches.

TPL, like many libraries, has been offering programs to children and families for decades that are fun, promote literacy and learning, and highlight library collections and services. Many of these programs and services in recent years have come to focus on children in early childhood and their parents as a result of widespread research.

While working on various city committees, we became aware of the importance of participation in high-quality, out-of-school activities for the healthy growth and development of six- to twelve-year-olds. This prompted TPL to scan and evaluate our own programs for this age group. What we found was a lack of consistency in quality, quantity, and geographic representation throughout the city. Worse, we were not supporting children and parents as effectively as we had when they were in early childhood, leaving a gap in the transition from early childhood to middle childhood and beyond. This realization spurred our own research review and evaluation of programming and services for children in middle childhood, culminating in the development of the Middle Childhood Framework in 2014, our foundational document for providing service to this age group.

Since then, we've trained staff to develop and deliver programs and services, including After School Clubs, Summer Camps, and Grade Four Outreach, that highlight the unique values of the public library and support the healthy growth and development of six- to twelve-year-olds as they transition from early childhood to adolescence and beyond.

MIDDLE CHILDHOOD

As children grow, they transition between distinct periods of development. The first period, early childhood, includes children from birth to age five. The second, middle childhood, refers to children aged six to twelve, and it's commonly understood that there are two distinctly separate groups within this period: six to eight and nine to twelve. The third period is adolescence, referring to teens aged thirteen to eighteen.

It's important to remember that these periods are not static, because all children are unique and develop at their own pace. Often, even though children are included in a developmental period because of their biological age, they exhibit skills and behavior that would be associated more closely with an earlier or later developmental period.

When thinking about the types of programs and services that your library offers for children and youth, consider if they meet the needs of children from all developmental periods. Do they help children transition from their earliest years into adolescence and beyond?

Most libraries deliver some form of early literacy or storytime program for children six and younger and their parents and caregivers. Many of these programs are informed by and respond to the wealth of research about the rapid brain development of young children and the importance of developing early literacy skills to support reading and writing success when children enter school. Alternatively, to serve teens, many libraries offer programs and services to respond to the education and employment challenges facing them; this has spurred research, programs, and funding for youth.

In between these two high-profile, well-researched periods of development, middle childhood has traditionally been forgotten. Historically, middle childhood was perceived as a time of plateau, where children capitalized on the gains they had made in early childhood and before the teen years. However, there are many developmental and environmental factors that influence the growth, learning, and social development of children in this age group (Larner, Zippiroli, and Behrman 1999). First, this period is usually marked by their entry into formal education, which is why children in middle childhood are often referred to as "school-age." Second, participation in recreation, arts, club activities, and playing or "hanging around" with their friends begin to play an increasingly important role in their lives. Finally, this period marks the time when children become more independent from their families, start relying more on peer relationships, and establish their own identities.

New research shows that it is important to create conditions that continue to enable children to reach their full potential beyond the early years (City of Toronto 2012), and TPL has responded by developing the Middle Childhood Framework to ensure that the long-standing programs and services that we offer to children allows them to thrive as they develop, building lifelong readers, learners, and library supporters as they move from early childhood, to middle childhood, to adolescence, and into adulthood.

TORONTO PUBLIC LIBRARY (TPL)'S MIDDLE CHILDHOOD FRAMEWORK

In 2014, TPL released the Middle Childhood Framework (www.torontopubliclibrary.ca/kidsspace/Offline_Activities/documents/Middle_Childhood_Framework.pdf), which represented a new direction for TPL services to school-age children ages six to twelve and provides a blueprint for supporting school-age children's healthy growth and development. The framework responds to important new research, which demonstrates how quality out-of-school-time programs can have a positive impact on children aged six to twelve. The Framework aligns with the City of Toronto's Middle Childhood Strategy (2012). It also highlights the library's unique value proposition, including extended hours (weekends, evenings, and holidays); responsive, inclusive, and non-judgmental approach; support of intellectual freedom and choice; wealth of resources; and access to opportunity.

The Middle Childhood Framework positions TPL as a place and space that supports creativity, encourages discovery, and celebrates the joy of reading while promoting self-directed learning for children ages six to twelve through fun and play. The framework has helped reshape all aspects of service to children in this age group, meaning that staff also required updated training to ensure that the services TPL offers reflect this vision. A major component of this training has included developing, delivering, and evaluating programs (e.g., After School Clubs, Summer Camps, and Grade Four Outreach) with an emphasis on quality and access.

AFTER SCHOOL CLUBS

From participating in the city's Middle Childhood Strategy and Implementation committees, it became clear that there was a need for programs for children who had either outgrown daycare (usually between ten to twelve years old) or whose parents could not find suitable childcare. Parents are looking for safe, engaging, and readily available spaces for their children to go, and although TPL offered after-school programming regularly in branches, there was little consistency in terms of availability during the week and throughout the city. As a result, TPL identified a solution for children and families at the library in the form of After School Clubs.

After School Clubs at TPL are free, fun weekly programs for children aged six to twelve that operate every week, on the same day and time each week, throughout the school year (between September and June) in every district. By offering the program consistently, it's easier for customers to plan ahead, and it builds capacity in the program. Additionally, by offering a Club in every district, TPL can ensure that customers across the city have access to the program. Most branches offer After School Clubs between one and three days per week.

To help staff ensure that the programs they conduct are of high quality, training has been offered to help define the purpose and goals of after school clubs at TPL. This training includes classroom management practices, developing an expanded understanding of child development, infusing and generating creativity in programs, and applying self-evaluation techniques. Club programs are usually drop-in, last about an hour, focus on a theme for four to six weeks (e.g., magic or coding), and consist of preplanned, structured activities that include learning goals and outcomes. Flexibility is built in, so children have the opportunity to create, discover, and learn based on their own interests and at their own pace. Staff understand that the best after-school programs allow children to be actively involved, include activities that they are able to complete, have achievable goals, encourage creativity and the development of new skills and interests, provide children with a positive space to interact with others, and help them build their sense of self. To accomplish these goals, staff develop detailed program plans for each session, including the goals and objectives of the program, and structure the programs to ensure that children are engaged and having fun, the programming environment is both physically and socio-emotionally safe for all participants, and they gather feedback from children and parents who attend to shape future programs.

Among the things that staff consider when structuring After School Club programs is how to incorporate a variety of activities while balancing times that are structured (team challenges for example) and unstructured (where children are free to choose their own activities and partners). Staff emphasize open-ended activities (e.g., build the highest structure using only the materials on your table) instead of those with fixed outcomes. This maximizes the learning opportunities for children and provides opportunities for engagement in activities that support specific, individual needs.

A typical After School Club program plan would include an introduction, where staff would introduce themselves, ask children to introduce themselves, explain the program schedule, and discuss rules and expectations of participants. This would be followed by a short ice-breaker to help form relationships amongst the children, particularly those who had not attended previously. Next, staff typically conduct a series of activities, starting with a short, fun activity to help the children burn energy, followed by a skill-building activity, then an active or complex challenge, and wrap up with a cool-down activity or free time. To conclude the program, children help clean up and participate in a show-and-tell session where they can debrief on their experience and offer feedback before they leave.

To date, staff have conducted club programs on all kinds of themes, including:

- Gaming (using board, computer, and video games)
- Science (engineering and building programs using K'Nex and LEGO)
- Technology (using Snap Circuits, robotics, circuitry, and coding)
- Making
- Arts (drama, magic, photography, knitting, and puppetry)

One of the most creative and engaging programs that staff developed is Escape It!, a program based on the escape room craze where participants must use wit, sleuthing skills, and teamwork to find clues, solve puzzles, and "unlock" the door to escape. Each week, the escape room is designed around a different book series, which included Percy Jackson and the Olympians, 39 Clues, Harry Potter, and Lord of the Rings. Children cracked codes written in invisible ink, origami puzzles, and secret code math.

In 2016, thirty-seven branches offered After School Clubs, conducting over 1,600 programs with over 23,000 participants. Staff have commented that these programs give children of various ages and backgrounds the opportunity to play together and collaborate and have attracted new families to the library. Most importantly, they allow children to thrive: a mother reported that her son, who has autism, was more confident after attending the magic club and demonstrated some of the magic tricks he learned in front of his classmates at school.

SUMMER CAMPS

Another programming initiative developing out of the Middle Childhood Framework, Summer Camps, are free, half-day programs that operate on a daily basis for a week. These camps are located at branches in specific areas of the city whose residents generally cannot afford a summer camp for their children. These are open to all regardless of ability to pay. These camps offer access to a high-quality experience that supports literacy and learning through fun, interest-driven themes.

Six summer camps were originally piloted in 2015 with robotics, coding, and magic-themed camps. The robotics and coding camps were age-segregated with six- to eight-year-olds attending the morning camps and nine- to twelve-year-olds attending in the afternoon; however, magic camps were open to all children between the ages of six and twelve. In the robotics camp, children built projects that they could take home, and in the magic camp, children took home a magic kit that allowed them to perform tricks and amaze their friends and family.

Campers signed up in May and June and the camps were held in the last two weeks of August. But although many parents were eager to register their children in these programs in the late spring, reminder calls in the summer revealed that some participants had changed their plans. Robust waiting lists helped to fill the gaps and ensure that attendance was stable.

Another unexpected outcome was that, in some communities, children from economically disadvantaged backgrounds were not attending the programs as was originally intended. It was not clear until after the pilot that parents were unable to afford public transportation to the programs (children twelve and under can travel on public transportation for free in Toronto) with their children, which prevented them from registering.

These lessons were applied during the summer of 2016, when the programs moved from the pilot phase to full implementation. Staff targeted the communities where children needed the support, promoted registration, and covered public transportation fees for families for whom these costs would be barriers to participating. As a result, there was a substantial increase in participation from these areas.

In 2016, the number and types of camps offered was expanded. In addition to the camps that were already established, visual and performance art, video-game development, and emerging technologies were added. In most cases, individuals who had expertise in the subject area and in presenting high-quality, age-appropriate programs to children were hired to deliver the camps. These experts were assisted by an assigned staff member who was also part of the camp. The only camps that were delivered by library staff were the emerging technology camps. These were staffed by digital design technicians using equipment from Pop-Up Learning Labs, which are traveling technology labs that travel from branch to branch (see figure 17.1).[1] In these camps, children had the opportunity to learn how to design 3-D items and print them, create circuits, and explore Arduinos.

We have coordinated these camps in several different ways—through partnerships with local universities and museum education departments; through the direct hire of individuals (such as a magician); and through negotiation with organizations that provide services to libraries and schools (for the robotics camps).

The camps have been able to serve between fourteen and twenty-four children each. The limits to enrollment are generally equipment-driven, but also depend on the amount of staff assistance required to work with the participants. In total, 314 children attended the twenty camps in 2016. On the last day of camp, children were asked to evaluate their experiences. Concerning the magic camp, one boy remarked, "I loved it for four primary reasons: (1) the instructor; (2) it didn't take too long; (3) it was close to home; (4) the tricks I learned." Another camper, a twelve-year-old girl, commented that the emerging technology camp was a lot of fun and that she was able to experience many new things based on science and technology. The participants' evaluations were overwhelmingly positive, and it was clear that they enjoyed and had a positive camp experience.

GRADE FOUR OUTREACH

Grade Four Outreach is a key outreach initiative associated with the Middle Childhood Framework that aims to promote the joy of reading and the library as an integral support

FIGURE 17.1 Pop-Up Learning Labs allow kids to learn digital literacy skills by experimenting with new and emerging technology like 3-D printing.

for children and families as children grow into independent learners. This outreach targets children in fourth grade—typically between the ages of eight to ten—as this period marks the time when children transition from learning to read to reading to learn and can take advantage of the library's services to support their own self-directed reading and learning goals. The goal of the initiative is to generate a sense of excitement about visiting the library and to encourage children who visit irregularly or not at all. Library staff receive training and access to resources that enable them to deliver high-quality, engaging, and interactive outreach visits that appeal to the interests of students in fourth grade.

Since it was implemented in 2014, the theme of the campaign has been "Operation Super Sleuth," which encourages students to use their detective skills to solve library-related mysteries. When library staff visit fourth grade students, either at their school or in the library, they distribute a print package that includes reading tips and library information for parents and library challenges for students. The library challenges or "missions" encourage students to visit their local branch to complete quests and earn prizes. Although fourth grade students are the target group, staff also give out packages to third- and fifth-grade students in split classes.

Each mission is goal oriented: Mission 1 teaches students about the catalog and classification with the reward of becoming library card holders. Mission 2 provides an opportunity for library staff and students to get to know one another through fun activities like creating code names. Mission 3 is a riddle or puzzle that encourages students to use their problem-solving skills. Once students complete all three missions, they earn the title "Super Sleuth" and receive prizes. Each mission card features the cover of an age-appropriate book.

During a typical school year, staff see over 25,000 fourth-grade students as a result of this outreach initiative. New library card registrations for this age group have increased annually by 15 to 18 percent and staff are encouraged when children come in with their parents immediately after their classroom visits to get library cards. The return of students who received a package during a class visit to the library is between 25 to 30 percent, and roughly 93 percent of participating students complete all three missions and become Super Sleuths. Students are motivated to follow through with the missions, and many parents have remarked how they themselves would have loved to participate in such a program when they were kids.

While some staff note that many of the students participating in the missions are regular users, the campaign has also attracted new customers. Staff feel that the campaign is successful in helping students achieve an understanding of the library catalog, which builds relationships between students and staff in the branch, establishing the library as a fun place that students would want to visit again. They've noted that some students now come to the library regularly and are able to use the computer independently to conduct research for their own projects. Additionally, students are more comfortable engaging with library staff and more children are attending after-school programs as a result of the outreach. Overall, Grade Four Outreach has worked well to promote programs like After School Clubs and Summer Camps and all the other services that are offered at the library for children aged six to twelve.

CONCLUSION

As we move forward into the future we have many plans for these programs and others, including:

- A new camp on creative writing for children ages eight to twelve, run by a well-known author or illustrator, where each participant will leave the camp with a story written in rough form with planned illustrations
- Creating new themes for our Grade Four Outreach so that we can keep the campaign fresh and relevant for staff and students alike

Because of the success of these programs, we want them to continue to evolve and grow so that they are relevant, engaging, and exciting for children ages six to twelve, including those who are new to the programs and those who have been involved in them in the past. Ultimately, as the implementation of the objectives of the Middle Childhood Framework continue to move forward, TPL is being recognized as a leader in supporting the development of happy, confident, and successful children, providing solid foundations to support these children and their families as they grow and reach their full potential.

NOTE

1. Digital Design Technicians are responsible for providing digital conversion, design, and editorial services to customers, and also conduct user education programs.

REFERENCES

City of Toronto. 2012. Toronto Middle Childhood Strategy. www.toronto.ca/legdocs/mmis/2012/cd/bgrd/backgroundfile-50756.pdf.

___. 2017. Backgrounder: 2016 Census: Age and Sex; Type of Dwelling. http://www1.toronto.ca/City%20
   0f%20Toronto/Social%20Development,%20Finance%20&%20Administration/Shared%20
   Content/Demographics/PDFs/Census2016/2016%20Census%20Backgrounder%20Age%20Sex%20
   Dwelling%20Type%202017%2005%2003.pdf.

Larner, M. B., L. Zippiroli, and R. E. Behrman. 1999. "When School Is Out: Analysis and
   Recommendations." *The Future of Children* 9, (2): 4–20.

Toronto Public Library. 2015. Key Facts. www.torontopubliclibrary.ca/media/key-facts/.

CHAPTER 18

The Dream Team:
The Library as a Partner in Literacy and Learning for Children Ages Six to Twelve

Related Research

John Marino

INTRODUCTION

By the time children reach school age, their relationship with the public library changes. Their learning and literacy experiences shift to the school environment. They, and their parents, will have different expectations for the role of the public library in their lives. This is both a challenge and an opportunity, as library programming for children at this age can address their needs in traditional ways and also open their eyes to new and exciting trends in learning and literacy.

Let me start by stating the magic word in programming for children ages six to twelve: *partnership*. These programs are not designed and implemented *for* children, but *with* children, their parents, and their teachers. Digital-age children are accustomed to taking active roles in their learning and literacy experiences. And parents and teachers are typically eager for after-school and weekend programming that is designed to enhance these experiences. In the following ways, the librarian can collaborate and partner with children, parents, and teachers:

- Inviting input from children on the types of programs they are interested in and the format they prefer
- Seeking feedback from parents on the types of programs that will be valuable and exciting enough to navigate transportation to the library after school and on weekends
- Consulting with local schoolteachers to identify program content that will transfer to successful learning experiences in school
- Designing programs with these stakeholders to generate maximum creativity and innovation

- Facilitating program activities that encourage children to be actively engaged in their own learning
- Requesting feedback from all stakeholders in the evaluation stage to continuously improve the program

This chapter presents research that serves to guide development, implementation, and evaluation of library programs for children ages six to twelve. In the search for relevant research and information about existing initiatives, patterns emerged that identified five principles: Creativity, Connectivity, Collaboration, Cognition, and Community and Change. The descriptions of selected studies and initiatives include a brief summary of each and a review of implications for programming. This bibliography, though not exhaustive, is representative of the consensus on current best practices in the field regarding programming for children at this age.

RESEARCH-DERIVED PRINCIPLE 1: CREATIVITY

Curiosity, inquiry, connected learning, participatory design, problem-solving, child-centered, storytelling, gaming, and makerspaces

Overview

The first guiding principle in the development and implementation of library programs for children ages six to twelve is creativity. At this stage digital-age children are motivated by a natural curiosity about the world, and they are enthusiastic about hands-on learning and opportunities to express themselves. They are easily engaged by stories, games, and solving problems. They may initially welcome guidance and support but will quickly progress toward independent exploration and learning. Participatory design, in which children help plan, implement, manage, and evaluate, is the path to success. Library programs should engage and encourage creativity to follow this principle.

In this section, research and initiatives that support the principle of creativity are presented. The focus of this chapter is on research that guides library programming for children ages six to twelve. However, this research is not extensive. The following studies instead offer evidence for incorporating the principle of creativity in this process.

Annotated Bibliography

Bowler, L. "The Self-Regulation of Curiosity and Interest During the Information Search Process of Adolescent Students." *Journal of the American Society for Information Science and Technology* 61, no. 7 (2010): 1332–44.

This empirical study explores the roles of curiosity and personal interest in the information-seeking process of adolescents. The researcher found that curiosity can be a positive force in motivating information seeking, but negative one for completing tasks. Students in the study who mediated these degrees of curiosity successfully understood the role that curiosity plays in the research process through metacognition.

Takeaway: Design programs that encourage curiosity but incorporate targets so that students develop self-regulation skills.

Copeland, C. A., and M. H. Martin. "Camp Read-a-Rama® and Fully-Engaged Literacy Learning: Implications for LIS Education." *Journal of Education for Library and Information Science* 57, no. 2 (2016): 112–30.

This longitudinal empirical study investigated the effects of a summer day camp where children ages four to eleven participated in activities focused on children's literature. Researchers found that the camp experience positively impacted children's attitudes toward, and interactions with, books.

Takeaway: Incorporate the strategies of Camp Read-a-Rama® in library programs to promote literacy, involve parents and guardians in the program evaluation process, and offer professional development opportunities to library staff in literacy skills instruction.

Crow, S. R. "Exploring the Experiences of Upper Elementary School Children Who Are Intrinsically Motivated to Seek Information." *School Library Media Research* 14 (2011).

This empirical study investigated the factors that influence motivation for information seeking. One hundred children in the fifth grade completed interviews and drawings related to a series of tasks. The researcher found that providing children with choices and control stimulates motivation, as does providing feedback that focuses on more effective strategies for achieving a goal rather than competition or rewards.

Takeaway: Incorporate creativity and play into learning activities, provide a wide variety of material formats, and encourage parents to foster the curiosity and interests of their children.

Eisenberg, M., D. Johnson, and B. Berkowitz. "Information, Communications, and Technology (ICT) Skills Curriculum Based on the Big6 Skills Approach to Information Problem-Solving." *Library Media Connection* 28, no. 6 (2010): 24–27.

There are numerous publications describing the rationale and application of The Big6 information problem-solving process. This concept article provides an outline for a library program that promotes the development of related information, communication, and technology skills.

Takeaway: Problem-solving activities engage the curiosity and interest of children ages six to twelve; library programs can leverage this engagement and incorporate opportunities for skill development.

Hung, C.-M., G.-J. Hwang, and I. Huang. "A Project-Based Digital Storytelling Approach for Improving Students' Learning Motivation, Problem-Solving Competence and Learning Achievement." *Educational Technology and Society* 15, no. 4 (2012): 368–79.

This empirical study investigated the impact of project-based learning and digital presentation tools on the achievement of learning goals by fifth-grade students in a school setting. Researchers found that students were highly motivated by the project-based approach and the integration of the digital presentation tool. This approach also enhanced problem-solving skills and learning achievement.

Takeaway: Spark curiosity and motivation by incorporating problem-solving activities and digital tools into library programs.

Justice, L. M., S. B. Piasta, J. L. Capps, S. R. Levitt, and Columbus Metropolitan Library. "Library-Based Summer Reading Clubs: Who Participates and Why?" *Library Quarterly* 83, no. 4 (2013): 321–40.

This empirical study investigated characteristics of the children participating in a summer reading program. Surveys were completed by more than 700 caregivers of children and youth participating in a summer reading program at a metropolitan library in Columbus, Ohio. Researchers found that participants tended to be female, were already capable readers who were motivated to read, were not motivated by prizes and other extrinsic rewards, and came from homes in which parents had high aspirations for their children.

Takeaway: Summer reading clubs and other literature programs must target those children who may not be already inclined to participate in creative and strategic ways.

Kuhlthau. C. "Guided Inquiry: School Libraries in the 21st Century." *School Libraries Worldwide* 16, no. 1 (2010).

The Information Search Process (ISP) describes the thoughts, feelings, and actions that take place during the inquiry process. Numerous publications describe the rationale and application of the ISP. This concept article presents the application of the ISP to guided inquiry, in which several types of learning are accomplished, including information literacy, learning how to learn, curriculum content, and social skills.

Takeaway: Library programs that guide children through the inquiry process can make a positive impact on the development of lifelong learning skills.

Meyers, E. M., K. E. Fisher, and E. Marcoux. "Making Sense of an Information World: The Everyday-Life Information Behavior of Preteens." *Library Quarterly* 79, no. 3 (2009): 301–41.

This empirical study investigated the everyday life information behavior of tweens, children ages nine to thirteen. Researchers found that children of this age develop information literacy skills in informal social settings as well as in school; their information behavior is nuanced by social and affective factors; and trust is increasingly important in their information determinations.

Takeaway: The development of library programs targeting tweens must accommodate the developmental stage of their information practices.

Prato, S. "Beyond the Computer Age: A Best Practices Intro for Implementing Library Coding Programs." *Children and Libraries* 15, no. 1 (2017): 19–21.

This concept article describes a variety of resources for use in computer science and coding programs. The author aptly describes the spirit of programming in the Fayetteville, New York, Free Library: "Libraries hold a unique position in our communities as informal learning platforms, and so we are perfectly positioned to bring our communities together around these topics" (19).

Takeaway: A makerspace community may be built around any number of topics; the resources currently available make computer science and coding appealing programs for children.

Roman, S., and C. D. Fiore. "Do Public Library Summer Reading Programs Close the Achievement Gap?" *Children and Libraries* 8 (2010): 27–31.

This empirical study replicated a study from 1978 touting the positive effects of public library summer reading programs. Findings do confirm that these programs maintain or increase reading skills in those students who participate, that more girls than boys participate in these programs, and that the public library continues to serve students of every socioeconomic status.

Takeaway: This study provides a call to action, including the investment of more resources into summer reading programs and in collections serving students from needy neighborhoods, collaboration between public librarians and school personnel, and relationships with grandparents and other adult caregivers in the lives of children within the service community.

Valdivia, C., and M. Subramaniam. "Connected Learning in the Public Library: An Evaluative Framework for Developing Virtual Learning Spaces for Youth." *Public Library Quarterly* 33, no. 2 (2014): 163–85.

This concept article describes the concepts of connected learning and participatory culture and provides a framework for the evaluation of informal learning opportunities in virtual spaces through the public library. With a focus on middle and high school-age children, these learning labs promote the development of new media literacies through the provision of digital and social media tools.

Takeaway: This framework serves as an effective guide in the development and evaluation of informal virtual learning spaces for children and youth.

Willett, R. "Making, Makers, and Makerspaces: A Discourse Analysis of Professional Journal Articles and Blog Posts about Makerspaces in Public Libraries." *Library Quarterly* 86, no. 3 (2016): 313–29.

In this empirical study, the researcher analyzed articles and blog posts related to makerspaces in public libraries. Findings highlight the alignment of the makerspace movement as informal community learning with the mission of the public library in providing access to resources that meet community needs.

Takeaway: This study offers a conceptual overview of creating a makerspace program and encourages community analysis in the planning and implementation of a makerspace designed to meet community interests or needs.

Wu, K. C., and H. Chen. "How Curiosity and Uncertainty Shape Children's Information Seeking Behaviors." *Library Hi Tech* 34, no. 3 (2016): 549–64.

In this empirical study, children ages to eleven were asked to complete a series of tasks to determine if their information-seeking strategies were correlated to positive or negative motivation in a virtual world environment. Researchers found that curiosity and uncertainty play distinct roles in the strategies that children apply to information-seeking tasks: curious information seekers employ a route, or exhaustive, approach, whereas uncertain information seekers employ a survey, or general, approach.

Takeaway: Children need guidance in determining the most appropriate source of information and efficient search strategy to fit their needs.

RESEARCH-DERIVED PRINCIPLE 2: CONNECTIVITY

Social networks, digital citizenship, online safety, cyberbullying, and digital tools

Overview

The available research on children ages six to twelve of relevance to library programming suggests another principle: *connectivity*. These children are growing up in a digital age and are familiar with a variety of digital tools. They recognize that these tools connect them to a variety of information sources that require an array of skills to navigate successfully. Moreover, they find themselves connecting easily to others online. This interconnectedness of information sources and social networks offers exciting opportunities, such as new friendships and new ways to communicate, but also pitfalls, such as harassment and unethical behavior.

This section presents research and initiatives related to these topics. Together they inform the principle of connectivity in library programs for children of this age.

Annotated Bibliography

Davis, K., and C. James. "Tweens' Conceptions of Privacy Online: Implications for Educators." *Learning, Media and Technology* 38, no. 1 (2013): 4–25.

> This empirical study investigated the concerns of tweens toward online privacy. Researchers interviewed a group of tweens ages ten to fourteen and found that tweens care about their privacy online and employ strategies to protect their privacy; however, these strategies are not always effective, nor are they employed consistently.
>
> **Takeaway:** Children need guidance in understanding online privacy and in employing effective strategies to protect themselves online. Libraries are well-positioned to address this need.

Davis, K., and L. Koepke. "Risk and Protective Factors Associated with Cyberbullying: Are Relationships or Rules More Protective?" *Learning, Media and Technology* 41, no. 4 (2016): 521–45.

> This empirical study investigated adolescent experiences with cyberbullying. More than two thousand students ages eleven to nineteen were surveyed; researchers found that emphasizing support systems and positive relationships at home and at school was a more effective strategy in decreasing cyberbullying experiences than restrictions or limitations in the use of social media and online programs.
>
> **Takeaway:** Although focused on the effects of cyberbullying on adolescents, these findings are relevant to cyberbullying and online safety programs aimed at younger children, who access games and social media that put them at risk.

Gross, M., E. Dresang, and L. Holt. 2004. "Children's In-Library Use of Computers in an Urban Public Library." *Library and Information Science Research* 26 (3): 311–37.

> This empirical study from 2004 was among the first to shine a light on the way children used computers in the public library. Following a method designed for Project CATE (Children's Access to Technology Evaluation), data from observations, interviews, and computer use were collected from participants in upper elementary and middle school grades in the St. Louis area. Findings indicate that library use in economically disadvantaged neighborhoods is different in ways that traditional methods cannot identify, that library usage patterns are different from branch to branch, and that the public library is critical in bridging the digital divide.
>
> **Takeaway:** The needs for technology programming for children will vary from community to community; an accurate community analysis is especially critical in economically disadvantaged neighborhoods. This study provides an innovative method for such an analysis.

Hill, V. "Digital Citizenship through Game Design in Minecraft." *New Library World* 116, no. 7/8 (2015): 369–82.

> This empirical study investigated the development of information literacy and digital citizenship skills with a group of fifth-grade students in an after-school Minecraft gaming club. The researcher observed students consuming and contributing online content ("presuming"), demonstrating an understanding of digital literacy, and working collaboratively.
>
> **Takeaway:** Gaming library programs spark the curiosity and interest of children, and may serve as vehicles for the development of information literacy and digital citizenship.

Hou, W. A. Komlodi, W. Lutters, K. Hercegfi, J. J. Preece, and A. J. Druin. "Supporting Children's Online Identity in International Communities." *Behaviour and Information Technology* 34, no. 4 (2015): 375–91.

This empirical study investigated the online behaviors of twenty-seven children ages seven to ten from three countries, focusing on how they represent themselves and interact with other children in a different country online. Researchers found that children at this age tend to reveal their true identities, share personal information about interests, ignore cultural differences, and develop positive attitudes about children in foreign countries.

Takeaway: Digital citizenship and online safety are issues of more concern with younger children, but the opportunities for connectivity with others online can promote tolerance and understanding.

RESEARCH-DERIVED PRINCIPLE 3: COLLABORATION

Partnerships with school, parents, community; linked to literacy and learning goals

Overview

Children ages six to twelve are focused and engaged in their school community; the public library may play a different role in their lives during the school year. However, as student-centered design strategies nudge school library programs away from a teacher-directed model and public library programs adopt instructional strategies, the similarities between the two become apparent. In this way, the research-derived design principles are applicable to library program development in both contexts. The principle of collaboration guides the establishment of a partnership that includes parents, who will determine the role that public libraries play in the lives of their children at this age. This principle also guides links to learning goals as identified by district, state, or national standards. Finally, this principle guides navigation through conceptions of information, digital, and numerous other literacies.

Annotated Bibliography

Chu, K. "Inquiry Project-Based Learning with a Partnership of Three Types of Teachers and the School Librarian." *Journal of the American Society for Information Science and Technology* 60, no. 8 (2009): 1671–86.

This empirical study investigated the effect on learning of a project-based strategy, and the collaboration among teachers and librarian. Survey and interview data were collected from children in the fourth grade, the instructional team, and parents. The researchers found that these factors contributed to increased student achievement and interest in the learning activity.

Takeaway: Collaborative partnerships between teachers and librarians are effective in the design of engaging library programs that support the achievement of learning goals for children.

Mackey, T. P., and T. E. Jacobson. "Reframing Information Literacy as a Metaliteracy." *College and Research Libraries* 72, no. 1 (2011): 62–78.

This concept article addresses the confusion surrounding definitions of information literacy and the advent of new literacies related to digital environments. The authors propose expanding the concept of information literacy to include these literacies, with an emphasis on participatory digital environments and metacognition.

Takeaway: Metaliteracy may serve as a guiding framework in the design and development of library programs for children that promote skill development in numerous areas.

Dresang, E., M. Gross, and L. Holt. "Project CATE Using Outcome to Assess School-Age Children's Use of Technology in Urban Public Libraries: A Collaborative Research Process." *Library and Information Science Research* 25, no. 1 (2003): 19–42.

This concept article presents an outcome-based evaluation model to assess children's in-library use of technology. The Project CATE (Children's Access to Technology Evaluation) model was designed to focus on the results of children's use of technology in the urban public library, and to accommodate the rapid change in use in a digital world.

Takeaway: Project CATE provides a model that is flexible, adaptable, and focused on the outcomes of how to effectively assess the needs and use of technology by children in the public library.

Koh, K., and J. Abbas. "Competencies for Information Professionals in Learning Labs and Makerspaces." *Journal of Education for Library and Information Science Online* 56, 20. 2 (2015): 114–29.

This empirical study recognizes that learning labs and makerspaces are finding a home in public libraries. To identify what librarians need to be successful facilitators, in-depth interviews with professionals working in learning labs or makerspaces in both museum and library settings were conducted. Findings reveal the top competencies and skills, as well as their relevance for professional training and development.

Takeaway: With the advent of learning labs and makerspaces in libraries comes the need to identify those competencies, skills, and training that librarians must have to be successful in these environments.

Subramaniam, M., J. Ahn, K. R. Fleischmann, and A. Druin. "Reimagining the Role of School Libraries in STEM Education: Creating Hybrid Spaces for Exploration." *Library Quarterly* 82, no. 2 (2012): 161–82.

This concept article offers a comprehensive overview of the goals of STEM (science, technology, engineering, and mathematics) education and how the library program can play a critical role. The authors describe how a library-based program can promote participation in STEM learning activities for all student groups, and how the librarian is well situated to support this program through reading advocacy, instructional leadership, and collaboration with the instructional team.

Takeaway: Public library programs can play a crucial role in the development of STEM skills through collaborative partnerships with teachers and other school-based staff.

RESEARCH-DERIVED PRINCIPLE 4: COGNITION

Mental models, growth mindset, self-control, and metacognition

Overview

Children ages six to twelve transition from learning to read to reading to learn, and this principle guides library programming in addressing the cognition of these children. Research and initiatives in this section are drawn from multiple fields and illuminate numerous topics related to cognition: mental models, self-control, growth mindset, and metacognition.

Annotated Bibliography

Duckworth, A., C. Peterson, M. Matthews, D. Kelly, and C. S. Carver. "Grit: Perseverance and Passion for Long-Term Goals." *Journal of Personality and Social Psychology,* 92, no. 6 (2007): 1087-01.

This high-profile empirical study investigated noncognitive factors in the achievement of difficult goals. The researchers found that grit, defined as passion and perseverance of long-term goals, accounted for individual differences in a variety of professional domains and events, such as the National Spelling Bee.
Takeaway: Library programs, such as gaming and makerspace activities, may be designed to encourage and highlight children's perseverance, a predictor of success in later life.

Duckworth, A., and J. Gross. "Self-Control and Grit: Related but Separable Determinants of Success." *Current Directions in Psychological Science,* 23, no. 5 (2014): 319.

This review covers the research on learning and achievement related to grit and self-control and serves as a useful companion to the study on grit. The authors describe self-control and grit as separate but related determinants of success.
Takeaway: Librarians familiar with the concepts of self-control and perseverance can foster these determinants of success through the design and effective facilitation of library programs.

Wolf, S., T. Brush, and J. Saye. "The Big Six Information Skills as Metacognitive Scaffold: A Case Study." *School Library Media Research* 6 (January 2003).

This empirical study investigated the potential for a model of information problem-solving, The Big6, to support student achievement of learning goals through the development of metacognitive skills. This study represents one of the few currently available that highlights the value of metacognition, or thinking about one's own thinking processes, during the information problem-solving process.
Takeaway: Incorporating an information problem-solving process like The Big6 into library programs for children promotes metacognitive skills necessary for successful information problem-solving.

Yeager, D. S., and C. S. Dweck. "Mindsets That Promote Resilience: When Students Believe That Personal Characteristics Can Be Developed." *Educational Psychologist* 47, no. 4 (2012): 302-14.

This review reviews the research on children's mindsets. It describes the concept of implicit theories and how students' implicit theories relate to their resilience in the face of academic and social challenges.

Takeaway: Since learning lab and makerspace programs provide both intellectual and social opportunities for growth, librarians who understand the positive impact of a growth mindset may incorporate this concept into program activities.

RESEARCH-DERIVED PRINCIPLE 5: COMMUNITY AND CHANGE

Access, diversity, the future of libraries, and theories

Overview

As public institutions, evidence of libraries embracing change and supporting communities may be found across the country. There has been much speculation about the role of libraries in the face of digital-age changes, such as online services and resources, ebooks, technology tools, lack of funding, and the like. One thing is certain: change is messy and complex, and libraries will be in our communities to support us in making sense of it all, together.

The research and initiatives in this section address issues of access, diversity, and the future of libraries. Also included are writings related to concepts that are useful in the development of library programs for children ages six to twelve.

Annotated Bibliography

Adkins, D., and B. Bushman. "A Special Needs Approach: A Study of How Libraries Can Start Programs for Children with Disabilities." *Children and Libraries* 13, no. 3 (2015): 28–33.

This empirical study investigated the range of services and programming targeting families with disabled children in public libraries. The researchers used survey and interview methods to collect data from contacts in thirty-nine large library systems and found that these services and programs were often initiated by the request of a patron and implemented on a trial-and-error basis. Moreover, library staff reported a lack of training in working with disabled children.
Takeaway: Community analysis is a necessary tool in identifying the needs of the community—in this case, the needs of children with disabilities and their families.

Crow, S. R., and L. Kastello. "The Dispositions of Elementary School Children of Individualistic and Collectivist Cultures Who Are Intrinsically Motivated to Seek Information." *School Library Research* (2016): 191-23.

The researchers in this empirical study investigated cultural differences in information-seeking behavior. They focused on factors that motivated children in the United States to seek information and compared them with factors that motivated children in Uganda, characterizing the predominant cultural differences as individualistic and collectivist, respectively. They found that an affinity for play and creativity was a factor for both groups, but that they differed in the factors of competency and competitiveness, with children in the Ugandan group demonstrating greater resiliency when things did not go as they intended.
Takeaway: Many cultures will be represented in a library community; librarians must take a proactive approach in determining how cultural characteristics will affect needs and program accordingly.

Dresang, E., K. Koh, and M. Mardis. "Radical Change Theory, Youth Information Behavior, and School Libraries." *Library Trends* 58, no. 1 (2009): 26-50.

> This concept article describes Radical Change theory, which applies the principles of interactivity, connectivity, and access to describe the changing information behavior of children and youth in the digital age. The theory explains how the changing nature of information resources in turn changes the way children and youth seek, use, and modify these resources. **Takeaway:** Several theories and models are useful in understanding and designing programs for children ages six to twelve in the library, including The Big6 and the Information Search process. Radical Change theory is directly applicable in understanding the changing information behaviors of these children and anticipating their programming needs.

CONCLUSION

In the *New Librarianship Field Guide,* David Lankes notes, "the public library is the only civic organization tasked to provide direct service to citizens of all ages, all socioeconomic groups, and all vocations" (2016, 145). In envisioning the future of libraries, he presents the mission as "community reference," with "the community as the collection." Library programming for children ages six to twelve, guided by the research-derived principles of creativity, connectivity, collaboration, cognition, and community and change, positions our libraries to fulfill this mission.

REFERENCE

Lankes, R. D. 2016. *The New Librarianship Field Guide.* Cambridge, MA: MIT Press.

RECOMMENDED RESOURCES

Bilal, D., and J. Beheshti. 2014. *New Directions in Children's and Adolescents' Information Behavior Research* 10. New York; Bingley, England: Emerald.

Eisenberg, M., J. Murray, and C. Bartow. 2016. *The Big6 Curriculum: Comprehensive Information and Communication Technology (ICT) Literacy for All Students.* Santa Barbara, CA: Libraries Unlimited.

Graves, C., A. Graves, and D. Rendina. 2017. *Challenge-Based Learning in the School Library Makerspace.* Santa Barbara, CA: Libraries Unlimited.

Harada, V., and S. Coatney. 2014. *Inquiry and the Common Core: Librarians and Teachers Designing Teaching for Learning.* Santa Barbara, CA: Libraries Unlimited.

Kuhlthau, C., L. Maniotes, and A. Caspari. 2007. *Guided Inquiry: Learning in the 21st Century.* Westport, CT: Libraries Unlimited.

Lankes, R. D. 2016. *The New Librarianship Field Guide.* Cambridge, MA: MIT Press.

Mackey, T., and T. Jacobson. 2014. *Metaliteracy: Reinventing Information Literacy to Empower Learners.* Chicago: ALA Neal-Schuman.

Wall, C., and L. M. Pawloski. 2014. *The Maker Cookbook: Recipes for Children's and 'Tween Library Programs.* Santa Barbara, California: Libraries Unlimited.

CHAPTER 19

Why Teens Need the Library and the Library Needs Teens

Sarah A. Evans

INTRODUCTION

What is your first thought when a group of teenagers enters your library? Do you think, "Uh-oh!" or "Oh, great!"? Depending on the day, a librarian may think either or both at the same time. Contemporarily (Chelton 2002) and historically (Walter 2003), teens may have been labeled as "problem patrons" because their habits may clash with adult models of library behavior. However, libraries must maintain positive connections with teens as they make the transition to adulthood. In turn, teens benefit from experiences with materials made possible by libraries. To make this happen, librarians must focus on *relationships* with their youth patrons. In this chapter, we explore adolescent development, the reciprocity of adolescents and libraries in the United States, and the key needs of teens that our libraries can address.

THE DEVELOPING TEEN

To develop an understanding of teens, librarians must be aware of adolescent development. Although new findings in adolescent psychology continue as society changes (for example, Jensen and Arnett 2012), several factors affecting teenagers have been known for well over a century (Arnett 2006). Consider how the following facts impact the youth entering the library:

- A teen's limbs grow faster in early puberty than other organs.
- Puberty spurs accelerated growth in critical connections between parts of the brain that continue through early adulthood.
- Advances in reasoning ability create emotional sensitivity.
- Teens regularly seek sensation-producing experiences in person or vicariously through media.
- Peer relationships consume increasing amounts of attention and energy.

Additional insight into youth development comes from cognitive neuroscience and the learning sciences. With new technologies, we can see the complexity of what happens in the brain during adolescence. Grey matter and cortical thickness decrease while white matter increases, bringing greater intra-cortical connectivity. Though jokes about "grey matter" abound, new lessons about white matter indicate how adolescents can experience increased brain potential for linguistic fluency, including tolerance for a range of genres. In the period of adolescence, young people increase their ability to share information rapidly and efficiently, often handling difficult meaning-making tasks, a skill critical to reading comprehension and retention of information. In essence, brain development during this period accelerates efficient communication between the fronto-cortical circuits and the frontal cortex and other cortical and subcortical regions (Blakemore 2012; Luciana 2010). When connectivity among cortical regions link more efficiently because of increased fibers, adolescents gain more potential for drawing meaning from both written and oral texts.

Much popular talk about adolescent learners involves terms such as *grit, executive function,* and *growth mindset* (Duckworth and Gross 2014). All these concepts necessarily simplify highly complex processes that characterize adolescent brain development. Simply put, all relate to "executive function," a useful umbrella notion. Neuroscientists tell us that within the frontal lobe occurs the critical development of fiber connections behind decision-making, looking ahead to grasp cause and effect, controls for impetuousness, and competency in managing incoming information that often leads to the need to switch course or recalibrate behaviors (Selemon 2013). Emotional associations also figure in all these critical functions, ensuring that decisions and actions carry with them responses such as elation, sorrow, regret, sympathy, and caring (Damasio 2003).

Note that the central findings on learning and development presented in previous chapters also apply to the life of an adolescent. But the changes described above shift the ways in which development occurs. For example, teens continue to need scaffolding from more knowledgeable others (Vygotsky 1978; Wood, Bruner, and Ross 1976), but instead of parents and family members, adolescents turn to peers and non-related adults to fill this role. Libraries are perfect for this kind of interaction. Through their programs, librarians can provide opportunities for teens to learn from their peers while also serving as guides for the program, helping to support their learning. Youth librarians today understand deeply that within such work, reading across types and modes of texts enable young people to be of greatest assistance in the world. There remains, therefore, the long-standing value or "magic" potential of reading. Texts—visual, verbal, and otherwise—have the capacity to transport, engage emotionally, solve problems, fill gaps in knowledge, and help shape identity for teens.

IDENTITY

One of the significant developments for teens is the stabilization of their identities. Psychologist Erik Erickson particularly focused on adolescence as the main time period for individual identity formation (Moje and Luke 2009). Penuel and Wertsch (1995) blended Erickson's work with Vygotsky's idea of cultural tools to demonstrate that, to understand the work of adolescent identity formation, the researcher must account for sociocultural processes. Youth identities are flexible yet become stabilized through social and cultural experiences. Based on these processes, many contemporary researchers examine how, through their interactions, people are "cast in or called to" positions that can become part of their identities.

Dorothy Holland and Kevin Leander (2004) described the process of identity forming over time. They identified "positionings" as crucial to the process, defining them as "pivotal moments in which social and psychological phenomena come to interanimate and interpret one another" (127), which "involves socially producing particular individuals and groups as culturally imagined types such that others and, even the person herself, at least temporarily, treat her as though she were such a person" (130). Through experiences, thoughts, and repeated positioning moments occurs a "thickening" of identity (Holland and Lave 2001; Wortham 2004, 2006). Holland and Leander use the metaphor of "lamination" to describe the identity created through mediated activity, pointing to how each layer in the lamination process may maintain visible characteristics. Our past identities don't leave us but become part of an evolving "social/psychological" entity.

Positioning has been used in education research to explain how teacher-student interactions shape the identity of learners and their future opportunities. In applying this theory to the work of librarians, we can recognize the distinct differences in adult-youth interactions afforded by a different context. Here, teens are positioned as capable individuals with valuable ideas while librarians offer them the freedom and the support to go in any direction desired. Such a relationship opens learning opportunities on both sides that might be unavailable in other settings.

HOW LEARNING FOLLOWS TEENS ACROSS SETTINGS

In their daily lives teens exist across many settings, such as school, home, library, and digital spaces. In these settings they are engaging with a wide variety of people, resources, and information. As they move through each setting they are learning different things, but how does their learning within each setting transfer to other settings or impact their learning as a whole? Researchers have explored this topic and developed various metaphors that account for the different aspects of how teens learn across settings.

Ito and colleagues' ethnographic research into youth media engagement across settings uncovered three levels of participation. Also known as HOMAGO, each represents an increased level of involvement:

- **Hanging out** and using media for social reasons
- **Messing around** with media to develop skills based on interests
- **Geeking out** by developing expert digital skills in an area of specialization
  (Ito et al. 2010)

Ito and other researchers, with a sociocultural lens and commitment to equity, built upon this research to create the "connected learning" framework for education research and design (Ito et al. 2013). This framework aims to address gaps between in- and out-of-school learning, particularly broadening participation for non-dominant youth in rich extended learning spaces. Connected learning contexts feature interest-powered learning, peer-supported experiences, and an academically oriented outlook. Connected learning experiences should be openly networked beyond the immediate venue, production and creation centered, and offer a shared purpose within cross-cultural and cross-generational groups.

Philip Bell et al. (2012) developed the theory of "cultural learning pathways" to account for the ways in which extended learning occurs, based on eight years of ethnographic study on learners across settings. Cultural learning pathways are defined as "connected chains of personally consequential activity and sense-making—that are temporally extended, spatially variable, and culturally diverse with respect to value systems and social practices" (Bell et al. 2012, 270). Within this framework, learning is defined "as constellations of multimodal, discursive actions made in the midst of situational circumstances" (Bell et al. 2012, 275). The cultural learning pathways model brings together the sociocultural-historical theory on identity, literacy practices, texts, and learning previously described in this paper. Identities are both part of the events of learning, during which positioning occurs, and part of the outcomes. Literacy practices also shape both the actions and the sociomaterial practices that a learner experiences. Texts belong to the sociomaterial arrangements that learners encounter in places and contribute to the scopes of possibility.

Focused on how students learn technology, Brigid Barron (2006) created the "learning ecology framework" to describe how interested students continue to develop technological fluency across life spaces. She defines a learning ecology "as a set of contexts found in physical or virtual space that provide opportunities for learning. Each context is comprised of a unique configuration of activities, material resources, relationships, and the interactions that emerge from them" (Barron 2006, 195). The framework rests on three conjectures:

1. Within any life space, a variety of ideational resources can spark and sustain interest in learning.
2. People not only choose but also develop and create learning opportunities for themselves once they are interested in doing so, assuming they have the time, freedom, and resources to learn.
3. Interest-driven learning activities are boundary-crossing and self-sustaining (Barron 2006, 200–01).

While Barron's framework focuses on technological fluency, it also offers librarians a broader way to think about the spaces, programs, and services they provide to inspire and sustain teen learning across informal learning environments.

Within each of these metaphors that account for learning across settings, we can glimpse the role of the library in the development of youth. When a teen is developing a skill, the library functions as a connected learning space by affording access to resources such as information and experienced practitioners. Libraries, with their vast sets of materials and opportunities for interaction, serve as a place for "personally consequential activity and sense-making" (Bell et al. 2012) along cultural learning pathways as well as a potential context in the learning ecologies of adolescents.

HOW ADOLESCENTS LEARN TOGETHER

Since the late 1980s, a substantial body of work on adolescent learning has come from the decade-long Spencer Foundation sponsorship of Milbrey McLaughlin (public policy analyst) and Shirley Brice Heath (linguistic anthropologist) on non-school-related activities of disenfranchised youth in rural, mid-sized, and urban settings. These scholars set out to identify features of access in these communities that might help explain how some youth living in the most difficult of circumstances (and often with rapid growth in gang and drug violence) made it into mainstream adulthood. Their findings made clear that community organizations ranging from libraries to Boys and Girls Clubs and religious groups are critical to youth. In these settings, young people voluntarily came together and engaged in learning (Heath 2012), working together to organize projects and practice a variety of skills related to organizational structure, planning, and communication (Heath 1991, 1996, 2012; Heath and Langman, 1994; Heath and McLaughlin 1994; Irby, Langman, and McLaughlin 1994).

These community organizations refuse to categorize young people according to rank in school class or achievement. Rather, the role of voluntary learning for young people is to provide equal opportunities in such settings to learn to play and take part in extended conversations with adults who share their interests. Essential to these settings is the presence of someone who is seen by the youth as a professional who demands that participants collaborate toward a collective outcome. Youth need the opportunity to read, learn, and think to act with professionalism and to know and be able to explain their current context, its purpose, and its philosophy (Heath 2014). Such learning pushes youth to a level of professionalism many have previously thought unrelated to who they are or could be. In turn, this learning inspires adolescents to reach beyond the immediate to seek deeper knowledge via such resources as information, tools, and people. A library can offer all three, and is a prime location for adolescents to follow the call of their interests and to learn voluntarily.

EXAMPLES OF THE RECIPROCAL RELATIONSHIP
BETWEEN TEENS AND LIBRARIES

The following are examples of programs and services for teens that make the most of the needs of adolescents and the resources of the library. Again, the key to making this work is the relationship. A successful teen services librarian explained that she measures her impact by relationships. "I feel so much work that we do is relational," she said, "and we really have to be good advocates for teens, because they are going to tell you things that they want or need, and you need to be able to figure out the way to do all of that and follow up or we lose our credibility" (Evans 2017).

In many libraries, regular teen volunteers have been utilized in a variety of tasks, such as giving library tours, creating informational bulletin boards, reading with younger buddies, or organizing materials for children's programs (Gallo 2010). Many of these activities require teens to work for or with the community at large. For example, when public libraries became a major source of free computer and internet access in United States, librarians found themselves barraged with patrons who needed technical assistance and training. In some places, teenagers were, and still are, being utilized as on-hand technology assistants or even instructors, leveraging their interest and expertise with technology. Consider the Teen Technology Team at the Turner Free Library in Randolph, Massachusetts (Thompson 2013). The town's new high school football coach was looking for a way their team could contribute to the community. The library staff welcomed the boys as regular volunteers to help patrons with technology challenges, both by appointment and as a drop-in service. The librarian involved reported that the program has not only been empowering for teens and patrons but has started to change stereotypes about teenagers, and that "town communication has begun to cross previously uncrossed boundaries of language, age, and race" (Thompson 2013, 17).

There are other ways to employ teens in the library that are empowering for both the adolescent and the library. Virginia A. Walter (2009) conducted a normative case study on a unique employment program in Philadelphia. The Free Library of Philadelphia was one of nine libraries to receive grants from the Wallace Foundation for the Public Libraries as

Partners in Youth Development Project (PLPYD). The grant required libraries to implement programs that "engaged individual teens in developmentally supportive ways while enhancing services for all teens in the community" (Walter 2009, 67). The project was guided by six developmental outcomes synthesized from research and action agendas and considered "necessary for a successful transition from childhood to adulthood:

- Youth contribute to their community.
- Youth feel safe in their environment.
- Youth have meaningful relationships with adults and peers.
- Youth achieve educational success.
- Youth have marketable skills.
- Youth develop personal and social skills. (Walter, 2009, 67)

In Philadelphia, the library used grant funds to hire teen leadership assistants (TLAs) to work with the established LEAP program, an after-school educational and cultural program for elementary students located in branches across the city. TLAs mentored younger children, developed formal educational and cultural activities with adult guidance, and planned a Youth Empowerment Summit, all of which worked to help the teens develop positive attitudes toward the library's role in the community. In focus group conversations with TLAs, Walter found that the teens gave evidence of all six desired developmental outcomes having taken place as a result of their library employment (Walter 2009).

Shannon Crawford Barniskis, a LIS researcher, asked fourteen teens to be participant researchers in a study to examine "How does art programming in public libraries affect civic engagement in teens?" The study employed a grounded theory approach (Barniskis 2012a, 2012b). Teens reflected on their experiences during and after a series of six arts programs hosted at a public library by giving feedback via surveys, focus groups, and individual interviews. Themes that emerged from the data included the teens' desire to connect and create community without being pushed or made powerless by adults. Although learning and engagement were evident, the author points out that the librarian's motivation is not to educate teens but to learn *with* them without imposing a particular pedagogy. Joint and ensemble learning that join adolescents and adults together in production, performance, and research bring lasting effects to both parties. Libraries, through their ubiquity across communities, provide the ideal place for adolescents to learn with adults as they work to fulfill their curiosity.

IT'S THE LAST CALL

In library after library, youth librarians have seriously considered aspects of youth development and thereby increased opportunities for cross-modal means of learning by adolescents in libraries. Although engaging teens can at times require effort, flexibility, and trial and error, the payoff for the dedication of teen librarians can be exceedingly strong and long-lasting. The key to success, not surprisingly, lies in the relationships that are built and the positive memories that are carried beyond the library into other aspects of the lives of adolescents and young adults. Developing real relationships that are honest, respectful, and motivated by a true desire to learn from and with young people provides rich rewards for librarians and their young clients, who are in turn highly likely to become strong advocates for public libraries as they move into adulthood.

They say it takes a village. That does not end when you're a teenager. They're . . . great big giant children who are really close to being grownups. It's last call at the information bar and so when they graduate from high school, they will not come back to [a] library for a long, long time, till they have children themselves probably. This . . . is an opportunity to engage them, to show them the benefit but also to [show them] that this is a place that they can get access to stuff that they don't even know exists yet and part of that is being that welcoming environment because if we are not open and welcoming to these teenagers, if they feel like they don't belong here, they will not come back even with their kids . . . (Interview with a children's librarian, Evans 2017)

REFERENCES

Arnett, J. J. 2006. "G. Stanley Hall's 'Adolescence': Brilliance and Nonsense." *History of Psychology,* 9 (3): 186–97.

Barniskis, S. C. 2012a. "Graffiti, Poetry, Dance: How Public Library Art Programs Affect Teens Part 1: Introduction and Literature Review." *The Journal of Research on Libraries and Young Adults,* 2 (3). www.yalsa.ala.org/jrlya/2012/09/graffiti-poetry-dance-how-public-library-art-programs-affect -teens-part-1-introduction-literature-review/.

_____. 2012b. "Graffiti, Poetry, Dance: How Public Library Art Programs Affect Teens Part 2: The Research Study and Its Practical Implications." *The Journal of Research on Libraries and Young Adults,* 2 (3). www.yalsa.ala.org/jrlya/2012/09/graffiti-poetry-dance-how-public-library-art-programs-affect-teens -part-2-the-research-study-and-its-practical-implications/.

Barron, B. 2006. "Interest and Self-Sustained Learning as Catalysts of Development: A Learning Ecology Perspective." *Human Development* 49 (4). https://doi.org/10.1159/000094368.

Bell, P., C. Tzou, L. Bricker, and A. D. Baines. 2012. "Learning in Diversities of Structures of Social Practice: Accounting for How, Why and Where People Learn Science." *Human Development* 55 (5–6): 269–84. https://doi.org/10.1159/000345315.

Blakemore, S. J. 2012. "Imaging Brain Development: The Adolescent Brain." *Neuroimage,* 61 (2): 297–408. https://doi.org/10.1016/j.neuroimage.2011.11.080.

Chelton, M. K. 2002. "The 'Problem Patron' Public Libraries Created." *The Reference Librarian* 36 (75-76): 23–32. https://doi.org/10.1300/J120v36n75_04.

Damasio, A. 2003. *Looking for Spinoza: Joy, Sorrow, and the Feeling Brain.* New York: Harcourt.

Duckworth, A. L. and J. J. Gross. 2014. "Self-Control and Grit: Related but Separable Determinants of Success." *Current Directions in Psychological Science,* 23 (5): 319–25. https://doi.org/10.1177/ 0963721414541462.

Evans, S. A. 2017. "Sparking and Sustaining Adolescent Learning: Embodied Values, Contextualized Literacies, and Developing Identities at the Public Library." PhD dissertation, University of Washington.

Gallo, E. M. 2010. "A Year in Volunteering at the Library." *Young Adult Library Services* 8 (2): 17–19.

Heath, S. B. 1991. "It's About Winning! The Language of Knowledge in Baseball. In *Perspectives on Socially Shared Cognition,* edited by L. B. Resnick, J. M. Levine, and S. D. Teasley, 1st ed. 101–24. Washington, DC: American Psychological Association.

_____. "Work, Class, and Categories: Dilemmas of Identity." In *Composition in the Twenty-First Century: Crisis and Change,* edited by L. Z. Bloom, D. A. Daiker, and E. M. White, 226–42. Carbondale, IL: Southern Illinois University Press, 1996.

_____. 2012. "Informal Learning," In *Encyclopedia of Diversity in Education,* edited by J. Banks. New York: SAGE, 2012.

_____. "The Foundational Bases of Learning with the Arts." *The Educational Forum* 78, no. 4, (2014): 358–362. https://doi.org/10.1080/00131725.2014.944078.

Heath, S. B., and J. Langman. 1994. "Shared Thinking and the Register of Coaching." In *Sociolinguistic Perspectives on Register,* edited by D. Biber and E. Finegan, 82–105. Oxford: Oxford University Press.

Heath, S. B., and M. W. McLaughlin.1994. "Learning for Anything Everyday." *Journal of Curriculum Studies,* 26 (5): 471–89. https://doi.org/10.1080/0022027940260501.

Holland, D. C., and J. Lave. 2001. *History in Person: Enduring Struggles, Contentious Practice, Intimate Identities.* Santa Fe, N.M.; Oxford: School of American Research Press; James Currey.

Holland, D. C., and K. Leander. 2004. "Ethnographic Studies of Positioning and Subjectivity: An Introduction. *Ethos* 32 (2): 127–39. http://dx.doi.org/10.1525/eth.2004.32.2.127.

Irby, M. A., J. Langman, and M. W. McLaughlin. 1994. *Urban Sanctuaries: Neighborhood Organizations in the Lives and Futures of Inner-City Youth* (1st ed.). San Francisco: Jossey-Bass Publishers.

Ito, M., S. Baumer, M. Bittanti, d. boyd, R. Cody, B. Herr Stephenson, H. A. Horst, P. G. Lange, D. Mahendran, K. Z. Martínez, C. J. Pascoe, D. Perkel, L. Robinson, C. Sims, and L. Tripp. 2010. *Hanging Out, Messing Around, and Geeking Out: Kids Living and Learning with New Media.* Cambridge, MA: MIT Press.

Ito, M., K. Gutierrez, S. Livingstone, B. Penuel, J. Rhodes, K. Salen, J. Schor, J. Sefton-Green, and S. C. Watkins. 2013. *Connected Learning: An Agenda for Research and Design.* Irvine, CA: Digital Media and Learning Research Hub.

Jensen, L. A., and J. J. Arnett. 2012. "Going Global: New Pathways for Adolescents and Emerging Adults in a Changing World." *Journal of Social Issues,* 68 (3): 473–92. http://doi.org/10.1111/j.1540-4560.2012 .01759.x.

Luciana, M., ed. 2010. "Adolescent Brain Development: Current Themes and Future Directions." *Brain and Cognition* 72 (1).

Moje, E. B., and A. Luke. 2009. "Literacy and Identity: Examining the Metaphors in History and Contemporary Research." *Reading Research Quarterly* 44 (4): 415–37. http://doi.org/10.1598/ RRQ.44.4.7.

Penuel, W. R., and J. V. Wertsch. 1995. "Vygotsky and Identity Formation: A Sociocultural Approach." *Educational Psychologist* 30 (2): 83. https://doi.org/10.1207/s15326985ep3002_5.

Selemon, L. D. 2013. "A Role for Synaptic Plasticity in the Adolescent Development of Executive Function." *Translational Psychiatry* 3, e238. http://doi.org/10.1038/tp. 2013.7.

Thompson, M. 2013. "High School Football Team Boosts Technology Achievement at a Public Library." *Young Adult Library Services* 11 (4): 16–18.

Vygotsky, L. 1978. "Interaction between Learning and Development." In *Mind in Society,* edited by M. Cole, V. John-Steiner, S. Scribner, and E. Souberman, 79–91. Cambridge, MA: Harvard.

Walter, V. A. 2003. "Public Library Service to Children and Teens: A Research Agenda." *Library Trends* 51 (4): 571.

Walter, V. A. 2009. "Sowing the Seeds of Praxis: Incorporating Youth Development Principles in a Library Teen Employment Program." *Library Trends* 58 (1): 63–81. https://doi.org/10.1353/lib.0.0071.

Wood, D. J., J. S. Bruner, and G. Ross. 1976. "The Role of Tutoring in Problem Solving." *Journal of Child Psychiatry and Psychology* 17 (2): 89–100. http://doi.org/10.1111/j.1469-7610.1976.tb00381.x.

Wortham, S. 2004. "The Interdependence of Social Identification and Learning." *American Educational Research Journal* 41 (3): 715–50. https://doi.org/10.3102/00028312041003715.

Wortham, S. 2006. "Learning Identity: The Joint Emergence of Social Identification and Academic Learning." Cambridge; New York: Cambridge University Press.

Young Adult Library Services Association. 2012. *National Teen Space Guidelines.*

RECOMMENDED RESOURCES

Csikszentimihaly, M. 1997. *Finding Flow: The Psychology of Engagement with Everyday Life*. New York: Basic Books.

Fischman, W., B. Solomon, D. Greenspan, and H. Gardner. 2004. *Making Good: How Young People Cope with Moral Dilemmas at Work*. Cambridge, MA: Harvard University Press.

Ito, M., K. Gutierrez, S. Livingstone, B. Penuel, J. Rhodes, K. Salen, J. Schor, J. Sefton-Green, and S. C. Watkins. 2013. *Connected Learning: An Agenda for Research and Design*. Irvine, CA: Digital Media and Learning Research Hub. https://dmlhub.net/publications/connected-learning-agenda-for-research -and-design/.

Jensen, F., with A. E. Nutt. 2015. The *Teenage Brain: A Neuroscientist's Survival Guide to Raising Adolescents and Young Adults*. New York: Harper.

Pennac, D. 2006. *The Rights of the Reader*. London: Walker Books.

Simpson, A. R. 2008. *MIT Young Adult Development Project*. Available at http://hrweb.mit.edu/worklife/ youngadult/index.html.

CHAPTER 20

Empowering Teens to Build Their Own Futures at Carnegie Library of Pittsburgh

Corey Wittig and Kelly Rottmund

INTRODUCTION

Carnegie Library of Pittsburgh (CLP) serves the citizens of Pittsburgh and western Pennsylvania through its seventeen neighborhood locations, the Main Library, and the Library for the Blind and Physically Handicapped. It is the region's most visited asset. With more than 2.9 million visitors and 3.9 million items borrowed each year, CLP is one of the region's largest champions for literacy. CLP's mission is to engage our community in literacy and learning. The library's vision is that, through our work, the people of our region will develop the literacies and connections that support individual achievement and strengthen the power of community. To support this vision, the library provides more than 15,000 programs, classes, and other training opportunities each year. In this way, CLP builds community, facilitates learning opportunities, and provides access to materials and values people. CLP's teen specialists work to fulfill the library's vision for serving teens, which was heavily influenced by YALSA's *The Future of Library Services for and with Teens: A Call to Action* (Braun et al. 2014), the *YOUmedia Network Hallmarks* document (ALA 2016), and the changing Pittsburgh community. CLP has dedicated teen specialists at eighteen locations working to fulfill this vision. Carnegie Library of Pittsburgh offers all teens access to Library programs and services within and beyond the Library's walls. CLP connects teens to mentors, resources and opportunities that reflect their interests, respond to their needs within diverse and changing communities, and *empower them to be builders of their own future.*

PROGRAM OVERVIEW

Teen Time
(Audience: Teens in or going into grades six to twelve)

Our oldest weekly program serves as an entry point for many teens and provides opportunities for staff and teens to develop a rapport. Teen Time is designed around the interests and needs of the teens in each community and can function as:

- A time and place for teens to hang out and talk
- A time and place for teens to hang out and collaboratively decide on activities
- A structured program with a planned hands-on activity that encourages teen interaction
- Tween Scene, a collaboration between children's and teen specialists to meet the needs of youth in grades four through six

Alternative Homecoming
(Audience: Teens in grades nine to twelve)

This annual celebration of reading, art, and civic engagement takes the form of a homecoming dance. Each event is inspired by a YA title—selected by a teen planning committee—that informs the decor, music, and activities. This inclusive event, first held in 2012 and themed after *The Perks of Being a Wallflower,* draws 300+ teens and provides a homecoming experience for teens who may not feel comfortable or welcome at their school's homecoming, whose schools don't have a homecoming, or who are homeschooled or unschooled.

Anime Club
(Audience: Teens in or going into grades six to twelve)

Anime Club builds community around teens' shared love of Japanese culture, including manga and anime. The format is customized to best meet the needs of the community's teens but typically includes a group viewing of anime and a discussion of manga. Teens suggest and sometimes vote on what to watch and on hands-on activities like *suminagashi* (ink marbling) or *shiori ningyo* (Japanese bookmark dolls).

PhenomeCON
(Audience: Teens going into grades six to twelve)

This free, annual pop-culture convention celebrates all fandoms and provides an alternative to costly cons. The library charters buses to transport teens from multiple neighborhood locations to the Main Library, where they can geek out over shared interests, compete in a trivia contest, work on their cosplay, and more.

Teen Gender and Sexuality Alliance (GSA)
(Audience: Teens in or going into grades six to twelve)

The GSA meets monthly or twice a month. The GSA strives to serve as a point of connection to other resources and groups in the city, as well as to teens from around the region. It also works to develop teen leadership by supporting teen-facilitated meetings. These meetings have included mapping out strategies for dealing with family around the holidays and discussing stigmas around mental health.

Life After High School
(Audience: Teens in or going into grades six to twelve)

This concept informs staffs' program planning and everyday interactions with teens. For example, when teens are hanging out in the library, staff will ask who has a part-time job, chat with them about it, and then ask if anyone needs help finding one or putting together a resume. Together we look at teens' neighborhoods in Google Maps to determine which businesses they can easily get to and see if those places are hiring. When planning a hands-on What's Cooking or Teen Time program, staff intentionally talk about how teens can share information about the skills they are learning in resumes or job interviews. We bring in community partners and experts to connect teens to other caring adults who can help them build their personal networks and demonstrate relevant opportunities available beyond the library's walls.

OUR APPROACH

Though they work in library locations of different sizes that have different staffing and resource allotments, teen specialists at Carnegie Library of Pittsburgh all have the same goal: "to empower teens to be builders of their own future." Through their role as caring adults and mentors, the teen specialists work to create a welcoming space where teens can explore their interests at schools, community centers, and other places outside of the library.

To reach teens it is important to get outside of your library's walls to let teens know you're creating a welcoming space for them. CLP teen specialists have done this through our CLP-BAM! (Books & More!) outreach model. Teen specialists visit school lunchrooms where they set up a table to provide library services. There, they sign students up for library cards, check out materials, and offer interactive and often hands-on activities, all of which connect the students with the full library experience. The teen specialists invite the students to visit whichever CLP location is most convenient for them. Staff conduct this outreach on a monthly basis and, in the span of a few hours, are able to connect with the school's entire student population. It's a great feeling when a teen walks into the library and says, "I met you at my school and you invited me to come to the library. Here I am!" Providing services outside of the library walls is an important first step in building relationships with teens and positioning staff as potential mentors. This outreach helps us work with teens who aren't able to visit the library while also providing the complete library experience.

We've experienced a major shift in CLP teen services over the last few years as staff now identify as mentors and educators in an informal environment, emphasizing the free, exploratory nature of our spaces and programs. Traditionally, this has been best communicated during weekly Teen Time programming at all neighborhood locations. Teen Time offers our staff the time and space to identify and plan for opportunities to bridge the growing digital and knowledge divide; leverage teens' motivation to learn; provide support for life after high school; and serve as a connection between teens and community resources, all of which are called for in YALSA's *The Future of Library Services for and with Teens* report (2014).

Teen Time also acts as a way of onboarding teens into the library learning environment. It's a time for interest-driven learning opportunities when teens can mentor one another and share their skills by either helping a peer with the day's activity or planning and leading the activity themselves. Teen specialists are constantly striving to publicize the inclusive spaces that they steward for teens from all of Pittsburgh's ninety neighborhoods. When teens engage with their community within intentionally planned spaces and programs where they often have a say in what goes on, CLP can achieve a number of outcomes: collaboration, building community, literacy, and technology, as shown in the table on page 214.

TEEN OUTCOMES	SHORT-TERM	MID-TERM	LONG-TERM
Collaboration	Teens meet peers in the library.	Teens engage in friendships and meaningful partnerships.	Teens network with peers to accomplish shared goals.
Building Community	Teens participate in library programs.	Teens participate in community programs outside the library's walls.	Teens develop peer communities and take on leadership roles in their local communities.
Literacy	Teens become CLP library card holders.	Teens regularly check out CLP materials.	Teens successfully complete their secondary education.
Technology	Teens gain exposure to technology in the library.	Teens engage in regular use of technology in the library.	Teens become proficient in the use of various types of technology.

Much of our work in recent years to ensure that these outcomes are integrated into our programming and into our spaces has been through The Labs—our creative technology program for teens that focuses on mentorship.

THE LABS @ CLP

Since its launch in 2012, it has become clear that The Labs serves two distinct functions at CLP. First, it is a program and service for teens that aligns with twenty-first-century library services—emphasizing hands-on learning and moving toward a broader definition of literacy with mentorship and teen interest at its core. Second, it is a template for modeling to staff how we provide these services. Though the program often focuses on projects that implement technology toward creative ends, the philosophy of The Labs can be applied broadly, because the tech is not as important as the active role that staff play in the learning process.

So what does the program look like in action? So far, The Labs has been built around two main delivery methods—workshop and open lab. Like Teen Time, The Labs Workshop is an entry point to the kind of experience we want teens to have in the library. Led by a labs mentor, each program is designed to teach teens to make something using equipment and other available tools with the hope that they'll apply this knowledge to future projects. Each workshop is built around the creation of an artifact, like a design for a skateboard deck made using Adobe Photoshop or a baseball cap made with a sewing machine. The medium or method employed isn't important to us and we don't value STEM/STEAM over other forms of creative expression. Our focus is more on the act of making and the sense of agency ("can do" spirit) it encourages, along with the relationship-building that happens between participants and mentors.

We hope that teens who complete projects in a Labs Workshop will have a positive social experience working alongside others and that they'll also be a bit more familiar with equipment, tools, or software available in the library on an ongoing basis. We hope teens will begin to associate the library with these resources as they do with our print collections and friendly Teenspaces.

A Labs Workshop has much in common with a Teen Time that features a hands-on activity. The difference between the two is in the design. In The Labs, we try to be thoughtful about the skill or literacy connected to the activity and be mindful of its connections to other opportunities for youth, whereas a standard Teen Time craft has traditionally been done just for the fun of it and as a social activity (nothing wrong with that!). This small but powerful tweak to program design illustrates the importance of The Labs as a philosophical template for teen specialists and other CLP staff to follow. We take what works from Teen Time and build on it. At two CLP locations, The Labs Workshop and Teen Time are already one and the same. As the program expands, and our services continue to develop, it's likely that these two programs will continue to merge.

The other main mode of The Labs, and a complement to The Labs Workshop, is Open Lab. Open Lab is designed as unstructured time in which teens apply their skills to their own projects. They can also use the time to continue working on the project from that week's Workshop or to earn badges that certify their proficiency with the tools, equipment, and software available in the Teenspace. We think of Open Lab as the context for the hands-on content knowledge teens are picking up both in and out of the library. In this program, the library acts as a resource for teens to use rather than a place they just come to. When this program launched we chose "The Labs" as a name because we wanted teens to think of the library as a place to experiment and create. Five years in, this hope has become a reality at eight Labs Locations (branches where equipment and hands-on programming are regularly available along with a part-time labs mentor, in addition to a full-time teen specialist). Even though Open Lab is scheduled just once a week, it has become the default setting in our Labs Locations after school and on the weekends. Great things can happen when equipment and tools are available in a space and staff are present to support youth engagement with the necessary resources and skills. It's clear that the philosophy "if you build it, they will come" is not enough. Staff must get out from behind the reference desk to engage with youth actively as a way of illustrating the power and purpose of the resources on offer.

The design of The Labs, and particularly the role of labs mentors, is modeled after the Chicago Public Library's YOUmedia program. To take on this work, we needed to hire staff who not only had experience and skill with the various subjects explored in our programming (music, graphic design, photography, fashion, and much more), but who also identified primarily as educators so we could properly engage youth in projects while also training other teen specialists in these new-to-the-library disciplines. Many of our labs mentors have come from other out-of-school-time programs around town. Others have been local musicians, graphic designers, or artists who may have never thought to work at the library were it not for a program like The Labs. As the program has evolved, labs mentors have spent more time training other teen specialists so that skills are on display spread system-wide. We want all teen specialists to identify as youth mentors who demonstrate that they are as comfortable actively engaging youth in learning new skills as they are with readers' advisory.

HOMAGO (HANGING OUT, MESSING AROUND, AND GEEKING OUT)

Though the development of CLP teen services requires a very active role for staff, there is still plenty of room for the library to exist as a relaxing place to curl up with a good book.

Our spaces have taken a cue from the research of Mimi Ito and colleagues, published as *Hanging Out, Messing Around, and Geeking Out* (2009). We want our Teenspaces to include opportunities and space for teens to just relax with friends, but they should also feature opportunities to try new things (à la Teen Time or Labs Workshop) as well as pathways leading toward opportunities to "geek out" or take a deeper dive into their passions. There is value in all these kinds of interactions for youth, but we have the most work to do on fleshing out the geeking-out side of the spectrum. Ten years ago, we were so focused on inviting teens into the library and keeping them there that we offered little beyond comfortable spaces and video games because we feared we would drive them away if things seemed a little too much like school. What we've learned is we don't have to worry about that as long as there is still room for them to simply "hang out," because youth are curious—they want to make meaning and explore identity. By providing opportunities for production-based programming we can really support the development of self. We can never make teens do something they don't want to do—but there is endless opportunity for growth when we encourage them to try something they might learn to love.

The Labs Workshop and Open Lab were at the heart of The Labs services in the early years of programming and still are central pieces, but we have also added the following supplementary programs over the years to help us design for a variety of experiences along the HOMAGO spectrum of youth engagement:

Labs on Location (LOL)

By 2020, all CLP locations will be Labs Locations. Until then, we have instituted Labs on Location (LOL)—by-request programming where a labs mentor lends a hand at another library. The goals of LOL are to offer some form of Labs programming across the system and to provide hands-on training to the teen specialists at these locations. Programming kits that can be shipped to all locations include comic instruction guides designed to help reinforce training so that teen specialists can deliver this programming without a labs mentor present.

The Labs Summer Skills Intensives

Labs Workshops and Open Lab are great, but there is only so much you can accomplish in a once-weekly program. In the summer of 2016, we had the chance to experiment with a deeper dive into our programs. We called these week-long workshops The Labs Summer Skills Intensives and they were a great success. Designing the Intensives allowed us to focus on three key elements of the program that we wanted to improve:

1. **Offering deeper learning opportunities for youth:** Whereas a Labs Workshop is a drop-in, cursory exploration of a project, the Intensive would be a week-long learning opportunity capped at ten participants.
2. **Exploring better partnerships:** Rather than asking community partners to only be guest presenters during workshops, we were interested in co-planning and co-leading programs.
3. **Formalizing leadership opportunities for youth:** Although given the opportunity, youth who take part in programs in the library will often rise to informal leadership roles, we wanted to hire youth as peer mentors who would be paid to assist in the delivery of the program.

What resulted was a series of five week-long programs (one at each of the Labs Locations) focused on the interests of youth in that neighborhood, co-presented by CLP teen specialists and staff from a community organization specializing in the Intensive subject area, with a part-time teen mentor hired as a temporary position to be a leader among the youth involved in the Intensive.

Each program ran from 12:00 p.m. to 4:00 p.m. Monday through Friday for one week. Ten teens were accepted to each Intensive after applying via a Google Form (priority was given to youth who lived in the neighborhood), and all received $100 if they stuck it out to the end. Each one of the five Intensives filled up. Teens created a ton of wonderful work. Two programs explored music recording and songwriting (working with partners at the YMCA Lighthouse Project and 1Hood Media, respectively); another used photojournalism to tackle the effects of infrastructure upgrades in a changing neighborhood (resulting in a blog sharing the work of all teens involved at thelabs.wordpress.com); the fourth explored responsible ways to express yourself via street art; and the fifth dove into Plein Air (outdoor landscape) painting.

Haunted Library

Haunted Library has been happening for years at two of our locations, CLP-Carrick and CLP-East Liberty. It's a great example of community-centered programming. At both locations, teens work alongside teen specialists to design and install a haunted house within the library that is open to the public at no charge during the week of Halloween. These programs are well-loved and attended by their communities and they are a great example of leveraging teen interest into long-term projects with real-life payoff. Well-meaning adults tend to envision lofty projects where teens tackle topics like bullying or social justice—and it's great when those happen—but the Haunted Library is a great example of an authentically "teen" project that gives back to its community while appealing to a wide variety of teens. At both Haunted Library locations, teens spend two to three months planning, designing, installing, and rehearsing for the programs. Labs resources are often utilized to create and install the haunted house. The Labs Workshop is often a time to work on bringing things together.

Teen Media Awards

The Teen Media Awards (TMAs) recognize teens who submit work to the library's Ralph Munn Creative Writing Contest and Labsy Awards. The annual event takes place in August. The Ralph Munn Creative Writing Contest is a spring writing competition for Allegheny County high school students (grades nine through twelve); The Labsy Awards recognize original creations, inventions, and works of art by teens in grades six to twelve and accepts submissions from spring through mid-summer. Although there is a competitive aspect of the TMAs, it is not our focus. Our higher-level goal is for youth to put their work out into the world, so the community can see how creative, passionate, and talented they are and value them.

PROGRAMMING STANDARDS

As we work to standardize program quality across all CLP locations, we continue to develop tools to assist us in this process. For all our core weekly or monthly programs like Teen

Time, Anime Club, and The Labs Workshop, and Open Lab, we provide program guides to the teen specialists that present each program's description, goals, and outcomes, and intended audience. They also provide suggested activities and a planning template staff can use to map out their own programs. The planning template encourages staff to think about how the program will run from start to finish, encourage planning multiple activities to engage teens with different interests, and implement best practices and rules of thumb we want to incorporate.

A committee of CLP teen specialists worked together to create these program frameworks, which now allow teen specialists to provide a consistent experience across locations while still leaving room for their creativity and their teens' interests. For instance, when the teens started watching YouTubers' slime videos, multiple locations switched their Teen Time plans to present slime-making tutorials. At CLP-Allegheny, one teen wasn't happy with the slime recipe staff provided, so she volunteered to find a better one and run the program herself the following week. This teen had previously been very hesitant to participate in programs and talk with staff or other teens.

The planning and development process is much different for new programs (pilots) or large-scale, system-wide programs, like Alternative Homecoming, Battle of the Books, or PhenomeCon. These programs follow a team-development approach with staff from multiple CLP locations working together on design and implementation. For each project, the team develops a timeline that includes individual and group responsibilities, deliverables, and deadlines. This provides a roadmap for the project, which is crucial for large-scale projects being planned by staff who are in different locations. This work is done through a combination of in-person and virtual meetings, independent work, and shared virtual documents. This planning style allows us to gather staff and financial resources to develop and offer programs that draw teens from across the city that are too big for one teen specialist to pull off on their own.

Moving forward, the team development process will include our new Service Design Best Practices. These Service Design Best Practices include, but are not limited to:

- Collecting community and user feedback during the planning and design process
- Determining potential for partnerships and volunteers
- Evaluating sustainability and replicability
- Connecting collections
- Determining if the program or service can be offered or accessed virtually
- Marketing, including print, digital, and word-of-mouth
- Promoting accessibility and equity

PARTNERSHIPS

At CLP we recognize that we don't know everything, and we never will. We aren't, and can't be, experts in everything—and we shouldn't try to be. (What a relief!) The YALSA Futures Report makes clear that library staff should be "embracing our role as facilitator rather than expert" and acting as a connector between teens and other community organizations, services, or individuals. CLP takes this mandate very seriously. Our role is to learn what interests our teens and what they need and then connect them to the best resource to support that need. When we are not experts or best suited to deliver a program, we reach out to those who are. Over the years we have cultivated relationships with many youth-serving organizations and individuals, from the Carnegie Museums to neighborhood-based maker-spaces, and from bike shop owners to seamstresses, who bring their programs or their skills to our spaces.

The manner in which we develop and deliver programs with partners varies based on the needs of the community, teen specialists' knowledge, and the partner's experience and capacity. For instance, when the Mattress Factory Museum of Contemporary Art brings programming to the CLP-Allegheny Teenspace, it does so after an initial planning meeting where the artist educator and teen specialists talk about the teens' interests, where the program will take place, who will introduce teens to the artist educator each week, and other one-time logistics. After that, the museum's artist educator creates the program plan, brings all the supplies, and facilitates the activity.

For The Labs Summer Skills Intensives, the process of developing and running the program is much more collaborative. Teen specialists and the partner draw up a Memorandum of Understanding before co-developing the week's curriculum, assigning specific roles and responsibilities in terms of who will provide specific supplies or lead certain elements of the program, and then co-facilitating the program.

MEASURING SUCCESS

Like other public libraries, we have historically focused on program attendance and positive feedback from teens to measure the success of and assess regular programs like Teen Time. Each teen specialist writes a monthly report that includes program attendance, quotes from teens, and anecdotes that convey the positive impact of the programming.

We are often a bit more rigorous with our large-scale, system-wide programs because they require more staff and financial resources. These events, like Battle of the Books and PhenomeCON, often involve a participant survey, story-gathering, and photo-taking during the event. There is always a post-program meeting where everyone involved in the planning and execution debriefs to identify what worked well; consider what could be improved or eliminated in the future; and review attendance numbers, survey feedback, and any verbal feedback teens provided during or after the event. All this information informs whether the program will continue and what should be included in the next round of planning.

We have known for some time that we need to improve on our ability to measure the learning outcomes of our programs, that is, the measurable change for participating teens. This is one reason that we drafted our vision for serving teens (empowering them to be builders of their own futures) and the outcomes shared earlier in this chapter.

We are still working on our process for measuring these outcomes; we envision that it will involve creating interactive displays in our Teenspaces where teens can self-report on the collaborating and learning they are doing in our programs and spaces. We also believe that our badging process will be integral to measuring these outcomes, as each of our badges has specific learning objectives tied to it. These badges, which are physical badges made with our button makers, can be considered a way of credentialing teens' learning. When teens demonstrate to a teen specialist that they have the necessary knowledge and skill to use, for example, a DSLR camera, the teen earns the badge. Awarding the badge involves giving the teen the physical badge and also noting the teen's name and the name of the badge in our tracking spreadsheet. Over time we'll be able to report on the number of teens earning badges for hard skills like photography, sewing, and audio recording, but will also be able to report on the outcomes of collaboration, community building, technology, and literacy.

HIGHLIGHTS AND CHALLENGES

We're proud of our teen programs because they offer youth a model for how to engage with the library. Programs like the Teen Gender and Sexuality Alliance (GSA), Haunted Library, and Labs Workshops provide opportunities to explore identity through self-expression under the guidance of adult mentors. However, if we focus too intently on programs we run the risk of overlooking the library itself. Within each library there is a Teenspace that exists as a resource for teenagers to access supplies, technology, and print collections, among other things. Although programs are important for making teens comfortable in the space and building relationships between adult mentors and youth, the not-so-secret hope shared by staff members is that one day our teens won't need us to urge them on. They'll simply be able to use the library as a multifaceted resource to accomplish their goals and help them move on to the next place on their journey of self-discovery and growth. Whenever we see a group of teens working together unassisted in the recording booth at CLP-Allegheny, we know we're on the right track. Staff are present in case they are needed, but there is no formal program—just teens using the library in a way that's meaningful to them.

Programs are best when they simply demonstrate services. A workshop on recording music at the library starts teens down the path toward utilizing these tools on their own. It's an important step to encourage them and let them know they can do it, but our sights are always on the next step. Our programs support the growth of every teen's sense of agency; if we're successful, they'll move on sooner or later to creating without our help.

We continue to build our own capacity to design for these opportunities and we get closer to our goals every day. Some key challenges in this work include getting staff enough hands-on training time to understand the rudimentary skills of various projects (sewing, music recording, graphic design, etc.) and to learn how to facilitate learning with these tools. But to achieve this, we need to get every location the equipment and supplies it needs. Much of this work is being done through the expansion of The Labs' programming. What began as a grant-funded program happening in the same space used for more traditional programs and services is now blossoming into what we'd always hoped: a way of seeing a variety of literacies relevant to youth supported within the library. We believe that technology and other hands-on "stuff" shouldn't be confined to a computer lab—it's better when they're right there next to the books because that sends a message that both are of equal value.

The work that's been submitted for the Teen Media Awards is just a sampling of what we've come to expect from our youth. Across the library system we see super-engaged teen volunteers, social justice activists, artists, and makers of all sorts. We believe we'll only see more engaged, inspired youth working together to make things happen if we keep moving forward on this path.

PROGRAM GUIDES

- Teen Time Program Guide (CLP)— http://bit.ly/2RN1UDD
- Anime Club Program Guide (CLP)— http://bit.ly/2zD4KTX
- The Labs Program Guide (CLP)— http://bit.ly/2JW35Op

REFERENCES

American Library Association. 2016. "YOUmedia Learning Labs Network Hallmarks." www.ala.org/pla/
sites/ala.org.pla/files/content/initiatives/iii/YOUmediahallmarks.pdf.

Braun, L. W., M. L. Hartman, S. Hughes-Hassell, and K. Kumasi. 2014. *The Future of Library Services for and
with Teens: A Call to Action.* Institute of Library Services/Young Adult Library Services Association.
www.ala.org/yaforum/sites/ala.org.yaforum/files/content/YALSA_nationalforum_final.pdf.

Ito, M., S. Baumer, M. Bittanti, d. boyd, R. Cody, B. Herr Stephenson, H. A. Horst, P. G. Lange, D.
Mahendran, K. Z. Martínez, C. J. Pascoe, D. Perkel, L. Robinson, C. Sims, and L. Tripp. 2010. *Hanging
Out, Messing Around, and Geeking Out: Kids Living and Learning with New Media.* Cambridge, MA:
MIT Press.

CHAPTER 21

Teens at the Helm

Teen-Driven Programming at the Olympia Timberland Library

Sara White

INTRODUCTION

The Olympia Timberland Library is a busy branch in downtown Olympia, Washington. An average of 14,000 to 16,000 people per day walk through our doors, which means that my job is exciting, action-packed, and never boring. My library is part of the Timberland Regional Library system, which consists of twenty-seven branches throughout five counties in southwest Washington State. Every community in our district is vastly different—we serve a few urban communities, but most of our branches are rural. My branch is situated in a bustling and eclectic city of approximately 50,000 people (and growing). Olympia is the state capital, and we have a diverse population consisting of state employees, college students, families, youth, and adults experiencing homelessness, and more.

As a youth services librarian, I am one of four staff members in my building who serve youth from birth to eighteen years old. Our department is responsible for everything involving youth services in our building. We work at our busy youth services desk and information desk, maintain the collection, plan programming, present storytimes, do outreach in the community, and more. Although I also have the ridiculously fun job of presenting preschool storytime and other programs for kids, I mostly focus on facilitating and implementing teen programming.

PROGRAM OVERVIEW

Teen Summer Reading Volunteers (Audience: eleven- to eighteen-year–olds)

Every summer, we recruit a large group of thirty to forty teens to assist us in running the Summer Reading program. Volunteers staff our Summer Reading desk, sign people up for the program, hand out prizes, and help us run passive programs like scavenger hunts. This volunteer program tends to be mostly made up of middle-schoolers, because it's less involved than our other teen volunteer programs and the age limit is lower.

Teen Library Council (Audience: seventh- to twelfth-graders)

Teen Library Council is a school-year long commitment (October–June) that involves a fairly rigorous application process, similar to applying for a paying job. Often, Teen Library Council members have already shown dedication to the library by volunteering during the Summer Reading program. The group meets monthly, and also takes on extra projects requiring more time than just the monthly meetings.

Teen Tech Tutors (Audience: ninth- to twelfth-graders)

In this intergenerational teaching volunteer opportunity, high school students are paired with adults as technology teachers and guides. Adult students may bring laptops, tablets, phones, and other devices, or ask for help using the library computers. Teens are trained in technology and teaching skills and work one-on-one with their adult students to teach them how to use their devices; troubleshoot issues; and guide them through how to use the internet, library resources, email, and more.

Teen Book Club (Audience: thirteen- to eighteen-year–olds)

Our Teen Book Club meets at the library twice a month. This club is run as a traditional book club—we all read and discuss the same book each month. The books are chosen by book club members, and the Friends of the Library purchase a limited number of books so that teens can take them home on a first-come-first-serve basis. I prepare background information and discussion questions in advance and facilitate the meeting.

Curiosity Society (Audience: seventh- to twelfth-graders)

Curiosity Society is a workshop series that takes place on Saturday afternoons once a month. Each month we invite an expert to impart their wisdom. Teens can come every month and gather a panoply of new knowledge! Some workshop topics include basic letterpress skills, poetry writing, food justice, and illustration.

Teen Coffee House and Open Mic Night (Audience: sixth- to twelfth-graders)

Several times a year, we host this after-hours program where teens are invited to share poetry, music, stories, and anything else they can think of to perform for an audience of their peers. We set up the atrium of the library like a living room, arranging it with floor lamps, Christmas lights, comfy furniture in clusters, and casual board games. We turn the lights low, and provide coffee, tea, hot chocolate, and snacks. Our library system has a sound system we can borrow so teens can perform using a microphone. No adults are allowed at this program; it's a teens-only space.

Onomatopoeia Teen Literary and Arts Magazine (Audience: sixth- to twelfth-graders)

Twice during the school year, the library produces a collection of writing and art by teens who live in our county. Our computer services department created an email address for the literary magazine, so teens can email their entries directly to us. We publicize that we're accepting entries to local schools, and the Teen Library Council also helps get the word out.

The Teen Library Council is also responsible for selecting which entries make it into the magazine and laying out the magazine's design in Microsoft Publisher. We produce *Onomatopoeia* zine-style—meaning we print it out on our color printer and fold and staple it. A copy gets added to our library's zine collection, so the names of the teen authors and artists end up in the library catalog, and people can check out the completed product.

Teen Murder Mysteries (Audience: thirteen- to eighteen-year-olds)

Planning, writing, and implementing an after-hours Murder Mystery is one of the Teen Library Council's biggest projects. They are in charge of conceptualizing the story, creating the clues, playing the suspects, promoting the program, and choosing a movie to watch after the mystery is solved. The entire program takes place after-hours, and the teen participants work in teams to solve the mystery throughout the closed library. Our Friends of the Library group provides food, movie snacks, and prizes.

FanatiCon: (Audience: sixth to twelfth-graders)

FanatiCon is a collaborative program planned and implemented by several library branches in our county during summer reading. We rotate which library hosts (it's held at one of the three large branches in the county, including ours). It is financially supported by the Friends groups of all the libraries in our county. Like most of our successful teen programs, it occurs after-hours, and is a geeky celebration of all things nerdy. You can think of it like a mini Comic-Con just for teens! There are crafts, games, prizes, a cosplay contest, and more. Because it's a joint effort and we have the combined publicity and planning powers of several libraries, this is by far our biggest teen program of the year—in 2017, 155 teens attended.

BUILDING A SUCCESSFUL TEEN PROGRAM

I'll be honest—it has taken a lot of time, energy, effort, and trial-and-error to develop a successful teen program at the Olympia Timberland Library. This probably isn't the case at every library, but I have heard similar sentiments echoed by many of my teen programming colleagues. When I took over in my position in 2010, teen programming was minimal. We had a successful Summer Reading Volunteer program, we had a few school year volunteers, and we offered some one-off programs throughout the year, but that was about it.

There are many reasons why developing successful library programs for teens is tricky, and the number one reason is that teens are busy. They have *so much* going on in their lives, between school and homework and after-school jobs and social lives and activities and sports and theatre and, and, and (you get the idea). It's often hard for teens to fit yet another activity into their schedules. This is why—after a few years of planning programs that I thought teens would be excited about and finding that barely anyone showed up, then struggling and feeling like a failure—I (with the support of my supervisor) decided to change my approach. When I adjusted my teen programming strategy, it was with a two-pronged effort. My new strategies were as follows:

Strategy 1. Let programming take time to build.
Strategy 2. Get teens invested in the library and their own programming.

Teen Book Club

The first program I created that incorporated these two ideas (taking time to build and getting teens invested) was Teen Book Club. It sounds like a simple enough program—we all read the same book, and casually discuss it once a month over snacks—but getting a successful Teen Book Club off the ground was one of my first major challenges as a librarian. I tried several times with limited success (I couldn't get more than three or four people to show up, if any), but then I made some very minor changes that made a huge difference.

The first thing I changed about this program was giving the power of selecting which books we read to the book club members. I am lucky to have an amazing Friends of the Library group that gives us a budget to purchase a limited number of books for our youth book clubs, which affords my teens the freedom to read any book I can find at a bookstore or online for $10 or less. Because of this, I am not limited to books that we have many copies of in our library system, and I can give the book club members total control over what we read. A few times a year, we have a book selection meeting. At this meeting, each book club member can suggest three books they want the club to read, and then the rest of the members vote on those three books. I make sure the book is affordable and decide which book we read in which month.

Giving teens the power to choose has made an immense difference in the success of Teen Book Club. Because all members have ownership over a month, they are invested in reading the book, showing up, and discussing it. It creates an environment of peer respect. The teens want everyone else to read the book *they* selected, so they feel more compelled to read the books their peers selected. The freedom enjoyed by Teen Book Club members has created a sense of camaraderie and fellowship. The teens guide each other (some members have encouraged others to select books written by diverse authors and about diverse experiences, which I support), and I have seen countless friendships form between people who have similar tastes. This freedom also means that my role in Teen Book Club is as a facilitator. I don't dictate what they read; I guide and give suggestions about what to talk about so that the conversation stays on track, I enforce our Book Club rules, and I let the teens speak their minds.

BOOK CLUB RULES

1. At least attempt to read the book. Your peers selected the book, and the Friends of the Library purchased a copy for you, so it is important to respect them by making an effort to read it before the meeting. If for some reason you don't have time to read the book, you should still be involved in the conversation by listening and giving input.

2. Don't talk over each other. We want to hear everyone's thoughts, and it's difficult to do so if everyone is talking at the same time. One voice at a time!

3. It's okay to disagree but do so respectfully. Address another person's opinion instead of the individual. This is a space where all are free to express their own opinions, and disrespect will not be tolerated.

The next change I made was to ensure that Teen Book Club met every month of the year, on the same exact day and at the same exact time. When your schedule is full, it's much easier to keep "the second Tuesday of the month from 6:30 to 7:30 pm" in your head than specific dates. After setting a date and time, the next important thing was to not give up. Attendance is not the only way to measure program success, but you know you're doing something right when your attendance at a program steadily increases over time.

AVERAGE TEEN BOOK CLUB ATTENDANCE: 2013–2017	
2013	5
2014	7
2015	10
2016	13
2017 (as of July)	14

While these numbers don't necessarily seem impressive at first, they illustrate that in programming for teens, patience and persistence are key. Teens join, realize how much fun it is, and then spread the word to their friends. It has taken me four years to build the devoted group of Book Club members I currently have. If I had given up on Teen Book Club at the end of 2013 based on how many people were showing up, I would not have the group of dedicated and passionate teens attending programs and volunteering that I do now. Teen programming builds upon itself—which leads me to the main reason teen programming has become successful at my library over the past three years—Teen Library Council.

Teen Library Council

There are many ways to measure success (including attendance), but for me, success means something deeper than just numbers. It means that the teens who use the library are developing skills that will help them in the world beyond the library and school. It means building meaningful relationships with and among teens who use the library. It means my teen patrons will have something significant to put on their resumes, will learn new ways to interact and work with their peers and their communities, and will learn to be leaders.

When I began at the Olympia Timberland Library in 2010, we had a school-year teen volunteer program in place. There were four or five teen volunteers who signed up for regular volunteer shifts. They came in at the same time every week or month for an hour or two and helped us with whatever we needed. There were multiple problems with this volunteer model, the first of which was that it was causing extra work for staff. It meant that we had to have projects prepared for all the teens who volunteered at the library, and the projects had to be ready to complete at the exact moment the teens' shifts started. Because of this, we were constantly finding ourselves scrambling at the last minute to find some busy-work sort of project for our volunteers to work on.

The second problem with this volunteer model was that our volunteers were not getting meaningful experiences out of the work they were doing. One of the ways I measure the success of my programs for teens is whether they are gaining skills they can put on a resume or use in a cover letter for college or scholarships or to get a job. Although helping with basic collection maintenance tasks and organizing craft supplies was useful for the library, it was not necessarily an enriching experience for our teen volunteers.

This is why, in 2014, we decided to revamp the way we handled teen volunteers. From the beginning, I needed to be clear that this wasn't a casual volunteer opportunity. I wanted the teens to get something significant out of it and for the library to benefit in deeper ways than just having an extra set of hands for projects. I wanted teens to be invested in the library. Out of this philosophy, I created our Teen Library Council. Their purpose would be threefold:

1. to serve as our core group of volunteers throughout the school year, helping with any tasks that may arise;
2. to function as the library's street team, getting the word out to other teens about teen library programs; and
3. to plan, create, and implement programming.

For teens, getting into Teen Library Council is a process much like getting a job. Seventh to twelfth graders are invited to submit applications in August and September, I hold in-person interviews in late September–early October, and those who are selected are required to attend monthly in-person meetings at the library that take place right before Teen Book Club. I make it clear at the interview that I expect Teen Library Council members to be engaged, creative, involved, dedicated, motivated, and reliable.

Since 2014, my Teen Library Council (TLC) has grown from five to fourteen members, and together they have created the robust teen programming we offer at our library. Starting a Teen Literary and Arts Magazine to showcase the creativity of local teens? This idea came directly from a teen at a TLC meeting, and the rest of the group was excited about it, so we made it happen. Hosting regular after-hours Murder Mystery programs for teens? Their idea, and they do 90 percent of the work themselves. Curiosity Society was my idea, but the TLC provides feedback on what types of workshops they'd like to see so that I can seek out members of the community to teach them what *they* want to learn. In 2016 alone, a total of twenty-three Teen Library Council members contributed nearly 400 hours of community service to the library.

At our monthly meetings, the teens brainstorm ideas and decide what programs they'd like to implement. In the case of the Murder Mystery programs, we then set up writing parties for the interested teens to get together and decide on a plot for their mystery, write clues, and assign parts. The Friends of the Library gives them a budget for their programs, and they tell me what they want to spend it on. Because they are so invested in the programs and have worked so hard on them, they are intrinsically interested in their success. They want their friends to come. They want to get the word out to their peers about the awesomeness of the library.

The Teen Library Council members also assist at the programs we put on for younger children. We host a monthly Explore and Create Club for elementary schoolers, often involving STEM skills. At these events, we empower the teens to become technology mentors for younger kids. For example, at one of these programs, we had some of our teens come in and learn how to use Ozobots. They then came up with an activity to teach kids how to use them and facilitated the program themselves. They learned a new skill, and then also learned how to teach that skill to others.

The teens in Teen Library Council are not only creating more robust teen programming at the library for their peers, they are also gaining skills that will help them for the rest of their lives. They are learning how to work in groups and develop relationships with each other and the people in their community, and how to take an idea from inception to implementation. Because the work they are doing is so involved and complex, it also gives me a chance to get to know them and be able to write personal and in-depth letters of recommendation for them to help them get into college, earn scholarships, and obtain jobs. Volunteering at the library is helping them on the path toward becoming excited, engaged, collaborative adults. It is also helping them think of the library as an integral part of their lives, and the lives of those in their community.

The Future of Teen Services in Olympia

Every year, teen programming at my library becomes more robust. Moving forward, one of my major goals is to widen the reach of our programming to reach a more diverse and underserved population. I would like to find a way to attract a more diverse group of teens, especially teens who do not currently use the library, so that all points of view are represented, and our programming reflects the diverse range of interests of all teens in Olympia. To do this, I would like to make myself more of a presence in the lives of teens outside of the library building. I want to find more ways to do outreach to schools, community centers, and organizations that serve teens. The more perspectives we can bring into the library, the better we will be able to serve *all* teens in our community.

Given how much teen services has grown in my library since 2013, I can only hope that the future will bring even higher attendance at teen programs and in teen volunteer opportunities. I foresee having to rethink some of the ways I handle my Teen Library Council and Teen Book Club as interest grows—it is very important to me to remain flexible and adjust services for teens as their needs and interests change. If next year's Teen Library Council isn't interested in writing a murder mystery, we won't write one—we will always design programming that interests and excites them. It's not about me, it's about them, and letting go of being in control of teen programming has been the best thing to happen to teen services at my library since I started working in Olympia. Because of this, I don't know what teen services will look like in my library in another five years, but I am very excited for my teen patrons to help me shape the future and constantly reimagine how I serve my community.

CHAPTER 22

A Vision for an Innovative New Teen Space

Boston Public Library Teen Central

**Jess Snow, Ally Dowds,
and Catherine Halpin**

INTRODUCTION

Teen Central is the designated teen space in the Central Library of the Boston Public Library. The Boston Public Library system includes a central library, twenty-four branches, a map center, a business library, and a website filled with digital content. In 2017, 3.7 million people visited the Boston Public Library system in pursuit of research material, to look for an afternoon's reading, to use the computer or attend a class, and to view the magnificent and unique art and architecture found in many library locations. There were 7.9 million visits to the library's website and 3.7 million books and audiovisual items borrowed or downloaded.

PROGRAMS FOR TEENS

At Teen Central, we provide a wide variety of programs to engage teens on many levels and in many different areas.

Open Mic

Once a month we partner with Books of Hope—a literacy empowerment program with the Mystic Learning Center (MLC) that aims to inspire the next generation of authors and entrepreneurs by engaging urban and at-risk youth through writing and poetry. They facilitate an open mic where teens have an opportunity to share their poetry with their peers in a supportive and engaging environment.

Teen Leadership Council

Teen Leadership Council is a youth-driven council that provides teens in grades six through twelve with the opportunity to develop leadership skills, help build teen services and programs in Teen Central, and connect with the community while volunteering at the library. Teens come together to assist the library in developing and implementing programs, which serve local teens and the community, and create a fun and comfortable atmosphere for teens at the library. Moreover, teens learn about a wide range of library professions and learning opportunities while also gaining valuable work experience.

Teen Gaming Specialists

Two teens are hired and trained in both customer service and the use of several gaming platforms to then develop and implement gaming programs for teens in Teen Central. The program not only focuses on developing programs for teens in Teen Central but also focuses on enabling the teen gaming specialists to build public speaking skills and gain an overview of some possible careers through their own participation in six career-readiness programs throughout the year. They also write blog posts on the programs they develop as well as program reviews and video game reviews.

Career Readiness Programs

One of the program priorities is career readiness, with the goal of exposing teens to a myriad of possible careers as well as strategies to prepare for these careers. To do this, we offer several professional panels during the year. These panels consist of professionals from varying careers who attended college, certification programs, vocational, or technical school. During the panel, the professionals share experiences related to their schooling, careers, etc. and teens have the opportunity to be on other side of the interview table and ask questions to learn more.

Graphic Design

Graphic design programs are regularly offered in the Digital Media Lab. Technology librarians run workshops to introduce the basics of software, such as Adobe Photoshop, by having teens "Photoshop Yourself Famous," combining their picture with that of a favorite celebrity. We've also hired local educators with more advanced training to introduce logo or t-shirt design, usually using Adobe Illustrator, enabling teens to dig a bit a deeper and see how these skills can be applied practically. We've also been fortunate to have professionals offer to volunteer to work with our youth. In one case, a user experience professional ran a sneaker design workshop where teens learned about how designers approach product development by applying styling and colors, incorporating and sourcing different materials, and considering the manufacturing process. Teens then used a template in Adobe Illustrator to customize their own branded footwear. We strive to provide a range of programming options that operate at different levels of interest, skill, and engagement.

3-D Design and Printing

The 3-D printer generates significant interest in our Digital Media Lab. Staff often give demonstrations on the fly and teens are encouraged to explore websites, such as

Thingiverse.com, to discover what can be designed and printed in our lab, and to choose something they want to print. Beyond this informal introduction, it's our goal to have youth become 3-D creators and designers themselves. The technology librarians lead programs in 3-D modeling using introductory CAD software, advertising the sessions as beginner work-shops, and they usually provide a theme. Here are a few examples:

- **Design Your Home.** Teens replicate their own home or design a dream house using 123D Design.

- **Talk to Development.** Teens use Sculptris to create their own original figures, or work from a photo to model a favorite animal or character.

- **Customize Your Phone Case.** Teens use Tinkercad to combine a 3-D file with fonts from Adobe Illustrator to create their own customized phone case to later 3-D print.

All the 3-D design and modeling software used in these workshops are free for download or browser-based.

Teen Tech Mentor Program

Two Teen Technology Mentors work in our Digital Media Lab during the school year for six hours each week. The Teen Central technology librarians work with the mentors to train them in a number of different software programs and assist them in developing workshops they will facilitate for their peers. The teen tech mentors also visit other local technology centers available to youth to learn about additional resources accessible to teens in Boston. Mentors are given the opportunity to take field trips to offices of local companies to expose them to different work environments related to education and technology. Teen tech men-tors also participate in several job-readiness programs, such as resume building, interview skills, and other professional panels. At the end of the Teen Tech program, mentors will have a portfolio of the workshops they have co-developed and facilitated that highlights the skills they have gained as well as an updated resume.

Python Programming for Teens

Python Programming for Teens is a five- to ten-week workshop series taught by Robyn Allen, a software engineer with a passion for teaching. She majored in Aerospace Engineer-ing at MIT and has worked in hybrid automotive design, robotic aircraft, and the energy sector. Python is a powerful language in wide use by professional software engineers but accessible to beginners. During the ninety-minute session, teens learn how to use program-ming in everyday life to build apps for fun, for school, or for summer jobs.

Girls Who Code

Girls Who Code is a free, nationwide summer and afterschool club for sixth- to twelfth-grade girls that explores coding in a fun and friendly way. Teen Central's Girls Who Code club is held on Saturdays for two hours, facilitated by two professional, female software engineers. The group meets weekly to discuss women in coding, collaborate on a commu-nity project, and explore how computer science can solve real-world problems.

Open Lab

Open Lab hours create opportunities for teens to move past that "hanging out" phase and into the "messing around" and ultimately the "geeking out" phases of digital and technological exploration. Although teens must check in with a librarian prior to using it, Open Lab is primarily for teens to utilize the creative software independently, whether for fun, for school projects, or for skill development. On any given Friday, you will find teens in Open Lab creating beats on Garageband, using Wacom tablets and Sketchbook Pro to create original digital designs, or TinkerCAD to construct and 3-D print a replica gaming piece to take home.

Work-Study Program—Wentworth Institute of Technology

In fall of 2017, Teen Central partnered with the Wentworth Institute of Technology (a local engineering college) and hired a work-study student to teach and mentor Boston youth in various tools for STEAM (science, technology, engineering, arts, and math), such as Photoshop, Illustrator, Logo Design, and computer-aided design (CAD). This near-peer learning model provided teens with a teacher who facilitated digital media workshops and a mentor assisting and encouraging curiosity and discovery during Open Lab hours.

Music Creation Workshop Series—Berklee College of Music

This series of workshops, led by a graduate student from Berklee College of Music, included lessons on pop music basics, the business of music, and the exploration of different music genres. Teens utilized Ableton Live 9—music software designed for creating musical ideas and turning them into finished songs—to learn how to sample music variations, fine-tune rhythmic beats, and compose a digital album.

TEEN CENTRAL'S PROGRAMMING FOUNDATIONS

Teen Central is the teen-designated space for teens in grades six through twelve in Central Library of the Boston Public Library. The space, services, and programs were redesigned and re-envisioned in February 2015. The 2,000 square foot space focuses on Ito et al.'s HOMAGO model: *Hanging Out, Messing Around, and Geeking Out* (Ito et al. 2010). It is based on the learning theory of Constructionism: the best learning happens via hands-on experience, as well as providing room for exploration, thinking, and reflection, rather than transmission of knowledge from teacher to student. The space has numerous seating options for teens to make choices for how they want to access comfort (see figure 22.1).

Teens can hang out in the space and are encouraged to do so. There are multiple ways they can access and use the space, from utilizing technology for recreation with any of the thirty available laptops to eating and drinking together to talking and collaborating with friends. These different access points support the different aspects of HOMAGO: "hanging out"(HO) and then moving to "messing around" (MA) with the focus on the gaming space; and then progressing to the "geeking out" (GO) phase in a digital makerspace complete with ten computers, each with more than twenty different types of content-creation software, such as Adobe Photoshop, Illustrator, FL Studio (music creation), Autodesk, and more (see figure 22.2). This space is designed for teens to be introduced to some of this software, experience the programs, and go deeper with what they can accomplish with the software.

The staff makeup in Teen Central includes a teen services team leader (a department head), a youth technology coordinator (75 percent of whose focus is on Teen Central and 25 percent on the Children's Library), a youth technology librarian (75 percent focus on Teen Central and 25 percent on the Children's Library), and two teen librarians.

FIGURE 22.1 Different areas in Teen Central.

For the first three years in the newly re-envisioned space (2015 to 2018), programs were based on findings from a survey conducted to gain input from teens that had used the previous teen space. Questions focused on determining the following:

- Which programs teens participated in
- What they wanted to participate in
- What they felt they needed in terms of future support (career or school)
- How they used the library (to hang out, do homework, meet up with friends gaming, programs, books, etc.)

Based on the survey results, programming for the first three years focuses on two areas: STEAM-based programming and school, college, and career readiness.

What does this look like? STEAM-based programs may focus on introducing teens to various STEAM concepts such as:

- Engineering by using activity kits like Arduinos or Makey Makeys
- Building an app
- Making a 3-D phone case with design software

Career readiness programs may include:

- A panel comprised of professionals in many different types of careers to expose teens to a wide variety of career opportunities
- Resume-writing skills
- Interview skill-building workshops

We try and provide these types of career panels several times a year by working with our own networks as well as utilizing those in the community.

FIGURE 22.2 The "Geeking Out" space in Teen Central.

OUTREACH

In addition to the programs described above, the vision and focus of Teen Central is to provide programs based on direct input from teens, work directly with at least twelve schools (public, alternative, exam school, and regular) and provide direct outreach to underserved populations. Librarians have identified twelve high schools across their service areas where they provide school visits throughout the year and encourage teens to visit Teen Central. In addition to their work with schools, librarians in Teen Central also provide outreach. Outreach is defined as providing library services and programs to underserved and underrepresented populations, such as new and non-readers, teens who may be incarcerated, young parents, teens in foster care, teens in group homes.

Reaching these populations is a priority for Teen Central. Each librarian works directly with an organization that in turn works directly with an underserved and underrepresented population. The reasoning behind this: because not everyone can or does come into the library, how can the library work more closely and successfully with underserved populations? This often means meeting them where they are.

The Boston Public Library has a strong partnership with the Department of Youth Services (a state agency that serves youth in the juvenile justice system). Each month two teen librarians bring ten books to each of the seven units of the DYS system. They booktalk each book to connect with the teens, take book requests, fill those requests, sign teens up for library cards, provide a summer reading program, share program information, and, for the last two years, have offered author visits (Matt de la Peña, Jason Reynolds, Brendan Kiely, Coe Booth, and Patrick Jones have all visited and spoken with teens). There is no expectation that the teens in the Department of Youth Services or any other organization the library works with through outreach should visit the library after this introduction; rather, the focus is on introducing them to the services, programs, and resources they may not know about and could potentially access. It is counterintuitive to go into outreach with the idea that introducing the library will "get them into the library." The American Library Association defines outreach as providing library services and programs outside the walls of the library to underserved and underrepresented populations, such as new and non-readers, LBGT teens, teens of color, poor and homeless teens, and teens who are incarcerated (Ford 2000). As these populations are often marginalized and thus underserved, it is crucial for libraries to recognize these populations and provide services and programs to them wherever they are.

MAKERSPACES

In addition to traditional and outreach library services, Teen Central is home to a digital makerspace—known as The Lab—to expose teens to twenty-first-century skills, including critical thinking, creativity and innovation, communication and collaboration, and the development of digital literacies. The overall design of the space, equipment, and workshop offerings provided in The Lab are influenced by the Connected Learning framework. This framework enables teens to use technology as an avenue for expression and a tool for learning. Access to academically connected resources, a network of mentors, and a peer-supported environment help prepare teens to succeed in school, learn about career paths, and build successful life and job skills. Ultimately, the conscious inclusion of the HOMAGO model within this environment leads to a strong emphasis on self-exploration, self-expression, and the importance of being able to build these experiences into their social networks.

Makerspace Takeaways from Teen Central

So how do you make the best use of a makerspace in your library to support your teens in their consumption and production of media and other forms of creative expression? Here are some takeaways from the programs we've offered in our libraries:

1. **Align your makerspace with your library goals.** At Boston Public Library's Teen Central, a primary goal is to bridge the digital literacy gap evident in urban public schools and youth. Many of our decisions about workshops, equipment, and materials are influenced by this overarching vision.

   Collaborate with your administration, public schools, and community organizations to determine what your teen patrons need. Everyday makerspaces can be low-tech, budget-friendly, and still be extremely engaging. You don't need to win huge grants to stuff your library with various technologies and gadgets you don't know how to use. Instead of turning your teen room into a version of the overflow closet at home, apply the budget you have to meaningful activities that promote your space and the library as a place that is representative of the culture embodied by your patrons and community.

2. **Define your makerspace.** At the Boston Public Library, our makerspace revolves around the comprehensive packaging of creative and technology software in our Innovation Lab—this drives the selection and programming development process. If your focus is technology and software but you have a smaller budget, invest in a few Chromebooks to serve as your makerspace or lab. Access to free computer coding languages and communities is abundant. SCRATCH is a visual programming language developed by the MIT Media Lab that is used to create interactive stories, games, and animations. SCRATCH also can be used in conjunction with Makey Makey invention kits to craft an endless number of STEM-based activities. Hour of Code is another coding initiative where computers are optional.

3. **Create a flexible space.** It is important to have a viable space to host your makerspace and store your materials. If access to a designated teen room is unattainable, here are a couple of alternatives:
   - Create a mobile makerspace—aka "STEAMship." Pool funding with other public libraries in your area to purchase maker materials—arts and crafts, iPads, Chromebooks, invention kits, and the like. Utilizing a schedule, designate days or times your mobile makerspace will be available at local public libraries, allowing your library network to share its technology and innovation resources.
   - Meet outside of the library—Whether you create a teen STEAM group or schedule field trips, create events that meet at local museums, parks,

■ Have Computers **but Not Enough?**

Try pair-programming where teens share computers and code together, which fosters a collaborative learning environment.

No Computers?

Code.org, the founder of Hour of Code and Code Studio, has a variety of resources and class curricula to help facilitate an unplugged lesson utilizing basic household essentials, printed worksheets, and a few curious-minded teens. Celebrate Hour of Code and cap off a great week of lessons by inviting a local volunteer to speak to your teens about the many pathways in computer science.

tech startups, or nonprofits. By involving the community, the public library is encouraging everyone to become invested in teens' access to innovation and technology.

4. **Small budget, big dreams**—Makerspaces cost money, but whether the expenditure is needed to hire local professionals, purchase design software like Adobe Suite, or provide teens with music production software and equipment, there are always cost-effective options.

   ○ Mini Music Studio—Tablets are a Swiss army knife for music creators. If you really want to create access to digital music production but cannot afford studio equipment and software, invest in a few tablets, download free or affordable music apps, and you've got yourself a mini music studio. For as little as $5, apps such as Garageband and VividTracker can be downloaded onto your device. For less than $20, you can download FL Studio, a powerful music-editing application that will provide teens with a complete virtual studio to create their music.

   ○ Don't have an engineering college nearby? Start your own engineering or LEGO club, tapping into the peer-to-peer model. Expand the use of LEGOs beyond childhood building blocks and host workshops where teens build replicas of their neighborhoods and communities or ask them to redesign or reimagine local parks and community centers. Have them build a world of their own that hits many thematic elements of STEAM, such as imagination, creativity, and exploration. Again, ask local volunteers in architecture, real estate, or city planning to meet and speak with teens about their designs. If there is no budget to pay your teen mentors and club leaders, try to partner with local schools to offer community service hours or class project credits.

   ○ Finally, petition local museums, hobbyist groups, artists, and small businesses for volunteers who may offer time, services, or space. View these collaborations as opportunities for teens to learn about graphic design while developing prototypes for a local artist. Tap into the world of computer science and engineering by disassembling and rebuilding old technology equipment for a startup.

Don't overshadow your makerspace by purchasing too much equipment, tools, electronics, kits, you name it! Buy the essentials first. Test them out. What works? What doesn't? Ask yourself the honest question: Does your library really need a 3-D printer or a laser cutter? If not, invest those funds in other STEAM-based projects. Be brave. Go against the current of library trends if it will benefit your teen patrons.

YOU DON'T HAVE TO KNOW IT ALL

Ultimately, we are librarians first, not scientists, mathematicians, musicians, or artists. Our job is not necessarily to have all the answers to STEAM-related questions, but to encourage teens to tinker, explore, and learn together. Reach out to your community, fellow library users, nonprofits, startup tech companies, and schools to find local experts willing to mentor, lead workshops, or coordinate a field trip to their company spaces. You cannot put a price on meaningful collaborations.

Don't feel that you need to be an expert at everything you are planning to share with your youth. Take time to explore the technology and get comfortable, but if teens ask questions to which you don't have answers, don't panic! This is where being an information professional comes in handy—we're great at finding answers! Work through the problem together, and model the resiliency, creativity, communication, and learning behaviors you are trying to encourage.

REFERENCES

Ford, B. J. 2000. "Libraries, Literacy, Outreach and the Digital Divide." 2000 Jean E. Coleman Library Outreach Lecture. www.ala.org/aboutala/offices/olos/olosprograms/jeanecoleman/00ford.

Ito, M., S. Baumer, M. Bittanti, d. boyd, R. Cody, B. Herr Stephenson, H. A. Horst, P. G. Lange, D. Mahendran, K. Z. Martínez, C. J. Pascoe, D. Perkel, L. Robinson, C. Sims, and L. Tripp. 2010. *Hanging Out, Messing Around, and Geeking Out: Kids Living and Learning with New Media*. Cambridge, MA: MIT Press.

CHAPTER 23

Co-Constructing Leadership

The (R)evolution of Discussion-Based Programming

Gabbie Barnes

INTRODUCTION

Hartford Public Library (HPL) is a mid-sized urban library system. Its main branch is centered downtown in Connecticut's 18-square-mile capital city. The library's history spans over 235 years—opening first as the Library Company in 1774 and transforming into the Hartford Library Company in 1799. The company started as a subscription service with a modest 700 books. By 1838 the collection had expanded to include some 3,000 volumes. After joining forces with the Wadsworth Atheneum, Connecticut Historical Society, Watkinson Library, and the Hartford Young Men's Institute, the company hired Caroline Hewins as the head librarian. In 1878, a formal name change to Hartford Library Association set the tone for the future of the institution. The need for free access to resources was apparent in the community and by 1892, with the help of generous donors, the library opened to the public.

Fast-forward to today and Hartford Public Library is a national leader in twenty-first-century urban library services. The downtown branch houses the multi-award winning The American Place (TAP)—a free program designed to welcome immigrants to their new home by providing access to legal services, language courses, citizenship support, and much more. Job seekers can access print and digital resources in the American Job Center—run in partnership with Capital Workforce Partners, a local nonprofit employment service. The library's neighborhood branches serve Hartford's diverse population with thoughtful programming and specialized collections.

Hartford is home to just over 120,000 people. According to the 2015 Census, Hartford's racial makeup is 29.8 percent White, 38.7 percent Black or African-American, 43.4 percent Hispanic or Latinx, 2.8 percent Asian, and 0.6 percent American Indian/Alaskan Native. 46.9 percent of people in Hartford speak one or more languages other than English at home, 15.7 percent of people over 25 have a bachelor's degree or higher, and 33.4 percent lives below the federal poverty line.

CONNECTED LEARNING AND HOMAGO

When I began my career at HPL, it had recently opened its brand-new, teens-only space. YOUmedia Hartford is a digital learning and makerspace for teenagers ages thirteen to nineteen only—no adults, no babies. It's one of thirty Connected Learning Labs across the country that make up the YOUmedia Network. Each lab is modeled on findings from a three-year collaborative ethnographic study done by cultural anthropologist Mimi Ito and colleagues, and funded by the John D. and Catherine T. MacArthur Foundation. The study explored how young people interact with and construct knowledge from new media (Ito et al. 2010). Our lab was built to facilitate a connected learning environment and we construct programming based on the following core principles:

- Interest-powered
- Peer-supported
- Academically oriented
- Production-centered
- Networked
- Shared purpose

Our motto (which the teens know by heart) is borrowed from the findings of Ito et al.'s 2010 report: *Hanging Out, Messing Around, and Geeking Out* (HOMAGO). We see HOMAGO as both a linear and circular trajectory for our youth. Although young people could be geeking out on Photoshop and mastering their DSLR skills, they may have limited experience navigating 3-D modeling for video game development. Depending on where they enter into the conversation—chatting with a mentor about 3-D modeling (i.e., hanging out) or picking up a digital drawing pad and giving it a shot (i.e., messing around)—they can start the HOMAGO process in a brand-new content area and begin on their own learning paths based on where they are. Our HOMAGO setup aims to minimize barriers to entry.

While the research of Ito and her colleagues focused on the role new media plays in learning and socializing, we see HOMAGO play out IRL (in real life). We've designed YOUmedia Hartford's physical space with little pockets of exploration that facilitate one or more of the three spheres of HOMAGO. New teens tend to gravitate toward our "hang out" space equipped with an Xbox One and PlayStation 4. It's an easy way to passively socialize with new people, while surveying the rest of the space for future exploration. Teens can "mess around" in our makerspace and get their hands dirty with new or existing projects. We put many consumable items (things that are used up and must be replaced often) in the makerspace, and we keep the high-quality (and sometimes dangerous) materials (digital cameras, soldering irons, laser beams, etc.) in a cabinet that teens can use, but need to ask for. "Geeking out" is facilitated by high-tech spaces and tools including our fully outfitted recording studio, our DSLR photo/video camera closets, and the three Mac desktops equipped with the full Adobe Creative Suite and other editing software. Teens also "hang out" in these spaces and "mess around" with these tools. With the help of our skilled mentors young people can reach geek-out level in whatever content areas interest them.

YOUMEDIA PROGRAMMING

We have four part-time mentors in YOUmedia, each specialized in a specific content area, who construct and deliver workshops on a regular basis. Our music production mentor runs the studio. They help young people produce, record, mix, master, and distribute their own music. Outside of scheduled studio recording sessions, beginner workshops are offered once per week. Our 3-D design mentor teaches teens the creative mechanics of video game production, from character anatomy to location architecture. Our 2-D graphics mentor helps young people finesse their anime drawing skills and pairs the development of these skills with the often under-appreciated storyline and plot construction that makes anime and manga so much fun to interact with. Our makerspace mentor plans a wide variety of arts and crafts-based workshops ranging from painting to basic robotics.

On a daily basis we offer workshops in one or more content areas for the teens to drop in on: Life Skills, Art and Design, STEM, and Multimedia Production. Like most libraries, YOUmedia Hartford does not require teens to participate in programs to use the space. In fact, we never know ahead of time how many young people might participate in any given workshop but, based on in-program and post-program data collection, we know we're averaging about 5.6 youth per workshop.

As the life skills mentor, I have had to be honest with myself: teens were not going to participate in workshops about resume building, feminism, and mass incarceration when they had the option to play video games, record music, make a craft project, or learn how to draw a manga version of themselves. I wasn't in the business of stopping them from pursuing those interests, instead respecting our core principles of interest-powered learning and the value in social activity.

After failing to engage teens in these workshops during our regular open hours, I revisited my approach. Where most of our programming is designed as one-off workshops that any teen can join at any time, I developed curriculum for two long-term, scaffolded programs, with required participation during our "off" hours:

- **Strong Girls Camp,** a six-week intensive workshop for female-identified youth
- **Woke Teens Forum (#WTF),** a ten-session workshop on the intersection of institutional systems and racial oppression

PROGRAM DESIGN

The inspiration for Strong Girls Camp came after I had attended a workshop at the 2016 PLA conference. Nancy Evans from the Levittown Public Library in New York presented her "Strong Girls School." I loved the idea of starting a group for girls to talk and learn from each other, so I reached out to Nancy, who kindly sent me all the documents she had created for her program. Ultimately, I decided not to use her curriculum and instead developed my own, but I did keep adapting the name, changing *school* to *camp* for a more summer vibe.

To create the curriculum, I started with a list of topics and chose one topic per each session (if you feel that a topic needs more than one session or additional debriefing time, it's okay to build that in).

Strong Girls Camp topics:

- Intersectionality
- Feminism: What Is It and Is It for Me?
- What Is Beauty and Who Decides? Body Positivity and Fat Shaming

- Media Representation and Negative Messaging
- Gender in the Workplace
- Social Media and Depression
- Relationships
- Career Pathways
- Creating a Support Network

From there, I did some light internet research to find as much relevant media as possible, searching YouTube videos, music, photo essays, blog posts, and so forth. My goal was to find resources that were as informative as they were entertaining, because I've sat through some pretty terrible instructional videos over the years and I didn't want the delivery to detract from the message. It was also very important to me that I focus on cultural icons with whom I was familiar, supplemented with cultural icons whom the girls could relate to. Most importantly, I knew my group members would be almost all girls of color, so I made sure every resource was by and about people of color.[1]

After familiarizing myself with the content for each week, I separated the topics between those I knew well and could facilitate discussions around and those that I knew I could leverage community asset expertise. I reached out to some partnership contacts I already had and to one that I didn't know. My request was simple: I told them the days and times the group would be meeting and the topic I was inviting them to talk about, then left it up to them to decide how and what they wanted to present—lecture style, conversation, interactive, and so on.

Presenters included:

- Planned Parenthood of Southern New England (on relationships)
- A teen-presenter from the National Conference of Community and Justice (on intersectionality)
- The education manager from the Connecticut Women's Hall of Fame (on "cultivating confidence")
- A small panel of women from Young Women Rising (on careers)
- A friend of mine who works in the male-dominated audiovisual industry (on women in the workplace)

Additionally, I scheduled a docent-led gallery tour field trip to the Wadsworth Atheneum, convenient because it's just down the street from our library. Strong Girls Camp kicked off in the summer of 2016, when the CSLP (Collaborative Summer Learning Program) theme was "Get in the Game: READ!" and the library had already planned a list of healthy, body-based activities, including yoga. As such, I was able to schedule and incorporate yoga and meditation into each week. Once I started to hear back from presenters about their availability, I had to create a schedule to stay organized. The schedule was useful as a road map, but I knew that a topic would only be set in stone for those meetings when a presenter was scheduled to come.

As I started to develop closer relationships with the teens through our discussions, the conversations became richer, more personal, and much less linear. One idea would morph into the next, and before I knew it, a conversation about the cost of being a woman turned into an advice session on menstruation management (this really happened). That was all okay because I had familiarized myself with the content of each week, so jumping around was not a distraction at all. In fact, it acted as a teaser for upcoming discussions;

I could give them a snippet of information and say, "but we'll be talking about that next time," which created anticipation and managed expectations. In fact, during our discussion about menstruation, I brought up the *Vagina Monologues* and a film called *V-Day: Until the Violence Stops* and the girls asked if we could watch it. Remaining true to the core principle of interest-driven curriculum, the next time we met we watched the film, and it inspired a rich conversation about female circumcision and violence against women in an international context. Reminding myself that my role in the space was as a facilitator and not a teacher or expert helped me relinquish the desire to control the content and narratives being formed naturally in the moment, which allowed space for the transfer of facilitative leadership.

Riding on the coattails of the successful Strong Girls Camp, I developed Woke Teens Forum (#WTF) using the same frameworks, but the structure was slightly different. For Strong Girls Camp, any female-identified teen could drop into any session, as long as they were willing to contribute to the conversation and abide by our discussion guidelines. With Woke Teens Forum, having conversations about race and inequity required a foundation of understanding. Teens participating in this workshop had to come to the first session to participate in successive sessions.

Woke Teens Forum Topics:

- Orientation and Types of Oppression
- Pop Culture and Representation
- Voting and Race
- Education and School-to-Prison Pipeline
- Housing and Race
- Food and Race
- War on Drugs: Weed and Race
- Mass Incarceration
- Healing, Reflecting, Inspiring, Educating: Where Do We Go from Here?

I did not invite guest speakers to these workshops. The space was designed to be raw and emotional and include personal and anecdotal stories of oppression because they help to frame the larger conversation of structural and institutional oppression. Inviting strangers into sensitive conversations can sometimes limit teens' comfort to speak difficult truths. Knowing that the teens I would be working with are youth of color, the perspective from which we approached conversations about race was completely different from how I would have designed it for a more integrated group or a group composed of only White teens. To that end, the workshop sessions (with the exception of the orientation day) included more story sharing than didactic lecturing. Similar to Strong Girls, I built in space for the teens to co-construct our trajectory by listening to their ideas, analyzing their thought patterns, and connecting topics as they came up in conversation, rather than just sticking with the topics that were outlined on my planning documents.

PROGRAM FRAMEWORKS

In designing the curriculum for both intensives, my goal was to build community through informal learning environments that were designed using three frameworks: HOMAGO (discussed above), media-based organizing, and storytelling for social justice.

■ Best Practices

Know Your Audience—Know Yourself Better

Be aware of what level your teens are engaging with your program. Are teens coming to your program because they look like you and they relate to you, or because they see that you have something to offer them in some way? Or is it for some other reason(s)?

How does your identity affect your work? How does it affect how your teens relate to you? How does it impact the content you are or aren't choosing to engage with? How will it impact the conversations you will have and the way you approach them as a facilitator?

Involve Young People in the Process

We all want to feel like we're making a difference or that we're contributing to our communities in some way. Teens are no different.

YALSA's 2012 National Teen Space Guidelines (http://www.ala.org/yalsa/guidelines/teenspaces) state that teens involved in the planning and decision-making process for new space development feel a sense of ownership, which contributes to the overall quality of their library experience. Expanding that to planning and decision-making for library programming, this idea ties in nicely with the media-based organizing principle of collective visioning.

Be Flexible with Your Content

Know what you want to talk about and decide what has to be brought into the space to serve a real learning goal and what can be sacrificed if need be. When co-constructing content with teens using frameworks like HOMAGO and media-based organizing, it's really the teens' own interests and ideas that are going to propel conversations and momentum, so yours need to take a backseat. Adultism is real, ya'll!

Bring in Community Partners with Expertise

I don't know everything, and you might not either, and that's okay! Inviting community partners to be guest speakers opens your teens up to new organizations they may not be familiar with, develops or strengthens your relationship with the partner, and takes some of the burden of content preparation off your shoulders. Win, win, win!

Pop Culture Is Your Friend

Constructivist theory says that we build new knowledge by making connections to our prior knowledge. Essentially, using popular culture helps teens feel like they know something about a topic while simultaneously helping them connect what they don't know about it. Thanks, Piaget!

Be Yourself

This goes hand in hand with the previous bullet point. Teens can spot a fake and know when you're trying too hard or not enough. Don't feel obligated to put in pop culture references that you don't connect with just because you think the teens will like it. Do some research and find content that is new, relevant, and that you enjoy. Don't be afraid to throw in things of your own. If you love it, the teens will too (even if they don't admit it).

Build in Socializing Time

Once relationships start to form, the teens will need at least fifteen minutes of transitional socializing time at the beginning of the workshop. Placing value on their social time shows teens that you care about their whole self, not just the part of them that contributes to your program goals.

Quality over Quantity

Strong Girls Camp had four participants who attended every workshop (with a total enrollment of eight participants) and Woke Teens had two (seven total participants). With low numbers like this we were able to have deep and lengthy conversations without too much concern about time. I prefer smaller groups because they're easier to manage and facilitate. To mitigate this, the attendance cap for both programs is fifteen teens and each group is considered a cohort.

Media-Based Organizing

A framework borrowed from Allied Media Projects, "media-based organizing" is a collaborative process that uses media to address problems and develop solutions. I have listed the nine essential traits of media-based organizing below (you can read more about them on the Allied Media Projects website at https://alliedmedia.org/).

- Root problem analysis
- Holistic solution-building
- Collective vision and purpose-development
- Essential question-asking
- Deep listening
- Facilitative leadership
- Synthesis with integrity
- Power and resource-mapping
- Iteration

Storytelling for Social Justice

Although the content, audience, and structure for Strong Girls and Woke Teens were different, because of the frameworks I chose to operate within, both workshops shared transferable elements. For each program, the first workshop was always a collaborative development workshop, in which I shared my idea and vision and then asked the teens to tell me how they wanted to get from start to finish. Afterwards, I merged their ideas with my outline.

From there, each individual workshop began with a five-minute writing exercise. The prompts were created after each session as a way to tie the previous session to the next. Teens were encouraged during writing time to continue writing even if they had run out of ideas. Instead, they could write questions that had come up for them or just write about their day, but the goal was to keep them writing and engaged with their thoughts and reflecting on their feelings.

Each workshop also used a variety of media to provoke conversation and prompt immediate reflection. For example, after watching or engaging with a new resource, the questions I would ask were, "What are your thoughts and how did that make you feel?" These two questions were never met with silence.

At the end of the whole workshop, I collected anonymous feedback using an online form.

Feedback questions included:

- What did you like most about [insert workshop name]?
- What would you change about [insert workshop name]?
- One a scale of 1 to 10 (1 being "not at all" and 10 being "I already did it!") how likely are you to recommend [insert workshop name] to a friend?
- Are you interested in learning how to become a leader or apprentice for [insert workshop name]?
- Is there anything else that you would like to share or that you think I should know?

LOOKING AHEAD—IDEAS FOR THE FUTURE

The future of Strong Girls Camp and Woke Teens Forum is ever-changing, but the next steps are to create spaces for those teens who are interested in taking on leadership roles to participate in an apprentice capacity, so that they can lead workshops themselves. In fact, one of the young women from Strong Girls Camp reached out to tell me that she wanted to develop and test her own curriculum for a Gender and Sexuality Alliance based on our workshops. She will be running the workshops in YOUmedia this summer with my support.

I also plan to incorporate zine-making into both programs as a way to strengthen the storytelling component. Essentially, we are setting aside time during each workshop to create quick-and-dirty zines about the topic of the day. I'd love to see the teens put their reflective writing into the zines, but I'll need to check with each group to see how they feel about that idea first!

NOTE

1.   Visit bit.ly/gbarnesALA for links to resources and media covered during the workshops.

REFERENCES

Ito, M., S. Baumer, M. Bittanti, d. boyd, R. Cody, B. Herr Stephenson, H. A. Horst, P. G. Lange, D.
        Mahendran, K. Z. Martínez, C. J. Pascoe, D. Perkel, L. Robinson, C. Sims, and L. Tripp. 2010. *Hanging
        Out, Messing Around, and Geeking Out: Kids Living and Learning with New Media*. Cambridge, MA:
        MIT Press.
"Population Estimates, July 1, 2015, (V2015)." *Hartford City Connecticut QuickFacts from the US Census
        Bureau*. Web. 06 Apr. 2017.

CHAPTER 24

Teens and Public Libraries

An Annotated Bibliography of the Research

Denise Agosto

INTRODUCTION

Effective library programming for teens should build on what we know from the research about teens and libraries—their library use patterns and preferences and their library beliefs, perceptions, and attitudes.

This selective annotated bibliography covers research published in English between 1999 and 2017. It includes studies based in the United States and Canada that have either gathered data from teens about their use of libraries or library resources or that have analyzed preexisting data about teens' use of libraries or library resources. Although there are many additional studies that present analyses of YA books and other resources, these are not covered in this review. The focus here is on understanding teens' thoughts and behaviors to be able to design library programs that best meet their wide-ranging needs and interests, beyond just focusing on building good collections.

The studies that follow are organized into three general themes and presented in alphabetical order by authors' last names within each of the three thematic areas. The three areas are: 1) studies of teens' public library perceptions and use; 2) studies of teens' information and reading needs and perceptions, and of the roles of public libraries in meeting those needs; and 3) studies of the design and effects of public library programs and spaces for teens.

TEENS' PUBLIC LIBRARY PERCEPTIONS AND USE

Over the past two decades, several studies have considered teens' frequency of public library use and their perceptions of libraries. Most of the studies have found about two-thirds to three-fourths of US and Canadian teens visit a public library at least once a year. Common themes across studies include teens' limited views of public libraries as paper book providers and negative perceptions of librarians and libraries. Study authors often suggest that improved marketing is needed to change these views and to increase the impact of library services on teen communities.

Abbas, J., M. Kimball, K. Bishop, and G.D'Elia. "Youth, Public Libraries, and the Internet, Part One: Internet Access and Youth's Use of the Public Library." *Public Libraries* 46, no. 4 (2007): 40-45.

In the first of a four-part series, researchers from the State University of New York at Buffalo present the results of a survey of over 4,000 students in grades five through twelve about their use of the internet and of public libraries. About two-thirds of the respondents reported having visited a public library at least once during the school year. However, the respondents indicated that public libraries were not common internet access points, even among students who lacked home internet access. The researchers concluded that widespread internet access had not replaced students' use of libraries. Rather, they accessed the internet from home and other places, continuing to use libraries for book circulation, homework purposes, and other reasons.

Abbas, J., M. Kimball, K. Bishop, and G. D'Elia. "Youth, Public Libraries, and the Internet: Part Four: Why Youth Do Not Use the Public Library." *Public Libraries* 47, no. 1 (2008): 80-86.

In the fourth paper to report the findings of the survey described above, researchers considered why approximately one-third of respondents indicated that they hadn't used their public libraries even once during the school year. To investigate reasons for non-use, survey respondents were provided with a list of common use barriers derived from focus group interviews with middle and high school students. The researchers organized the most commonly selected reasons for non-use into three factors. The first factor included negative opinions about the library, such as worries about physical safety and dislike of unwelcoming library staff. The second factor was a preference for using internet resources over library resources, as well as dislike of returning library materials and a general dislike of reading. The final factor was a preference for using school libraries instead of public libraries. Public librarians can study these common reasons for non-use and craft marketing campaigns to improve students' perceptions of the library, teaching youth that libraries offer more than just books and internet access.

Agosto, D. E. "What's Next in US Public Library Services for Teens? A Peek into a Promising Future." *Public Library Quarterly* 35, no. 4 (2016): 344-50.

Based on an address at the 10th International Symposium on Library Services for Children and Young Adults, the author outlines six current and future trends in US public library services for teens: 1) an emphasis on library services over library resources; 2) a growing focus on digital information services and resources; 3) the importance of the physical library as noncommercial spaces for individual and group use; 4) the expansion of the concept of "literacy" to include not just reading and writing but an understanding of information production and information assessment in a variety of formats; 5) increased teen participation in library service design and delivery; and 6) increased collaboration with community organizations.

Agosto, D. E. "Why Do Teens Use Libraries? Results of a Public Library User Survey." *Public Libraries* 46, no. 3 (2007): 55-62.

This paper discusses an open-ended survey of ninety-seven teen public library users, ages fourteen to seventeen, in two US states. The survey asked users about their reasons for visiting the public library. Their reasons for library use fell into three broad categories. First, the teens turned to libraries as information gateways that could provide them with information resources and information access. Second, they used their libraries as social interaction and entertainment spaces, enabling the building and maintenance of social relationships, as well as leisure and creative pursuits. Third, the teens used libraries as beneficial physical environments, seeking positive atmospheres for refuge from life fears and stresses, for volunteer and work opportunities, and for intellectual fulfillment. Public librarians can use these three library-use reasons as a framework for teen library space and programming design.

Agosto, D. E., R. M. Magee, M. Dickard, and A. Forte. "Teens, Technology, and Libraries: An Uncertain Relationship." *The Library Quarterly* 86, no. 3 (2016): 248–69.

Based on surveys and interviews with twenty-five high school students enrolled in a technology-focused urban US high school, the authors analyze students' library use preferences and attitudes. As a group, the students were infrequent users of their public libraries, reporting much lower use of public libraries than was found in previous studies. These students tended to view libraries as outdated and to be unaware of library services other than paper book circulation. Several of the respondents also identified public library staff as unwelcoming and as disapproving of teens. They were collectively more enthusiastic about information technology, tending to feel that information access via smartphones and other devices had supplanted their need for libraries. The authors suggest that these negative library attitudes necessitate a profession-wide focus on improved image marketing to teenagers and a need for highlighting libraries as places not just for information access but also for positive social and community interaction.

Agosto, D. E., K. L. Paone, and G. S. Ipock. "The Female-Friendly Public Library: Gender Differences in Adolescents' Uses and Perceptions of US Public Libraries." *Library Trends* 56, no. 2 (2007): 387–401.

The authors analyze the results of a survey of one hundred teens in two public libraries in the Eastern US to consider gender-based differences in public library attitudes and use. Girls indicated more frequent public library visits than boys. In addition, the girls held generally higher opinions of libraries, both in terms of meeting their information needs and in terms of making them feel welcome and comfortable. The authors recommend targeted public library programs aimed at making male teens feel more welcome and involved in their public libraries and hiring more male teen volunteers for increased male visibility in libraries.

Cook, S. J., S. Parker, and C. E. Pettijohn. "The Public Library: An Early Teen's Perspective." *Public Libraries* 44, no. 3 (May/June 2005): 157–61.

This study also used a survey to investigate teens' public library perceptions. More than 600 Missouri teens in grades six through nine completed the survey. Respondents indicated that they visited their libraries primarily for homework purposes, to borrow books, and to patronize the library restaurants. Further analysis of the survey results showed teens' positive perceptions of public libraries to decline as they age, with sixth- and seventh-graders providing significantly more positive feedback than eighth- and ninth-graders. In agreement with Agosto, Paone, and Ipock's (2007) findings, this study also showed girls held more positive opinions of public libraries than boys. The researchers suggest that increased marketing highlighting public libraries as places for social interaction would likely lead to increased library use among this age group and to improved overall perceptions of libraries and library services.

Howard, V. "What Do Young Teens Think about the Public Library?" *The Library Quarterly* 81, no. 3 (2011): 321–44.

Working with Eastern Canadian twelve- to fifteen-year-olds, Howard provided yet another examination of teens' public library perceptions. Two hundred and sixty-seven junior high school students completed surveys while at school, followed by nine focus group interviews with a smaller subset of students. Over 80 percent of participants reported having visited a public library during the preceding year, but most students had visited their libraries infrequently during that time period, calling into question the utility of defining "library use" as infrequent as just one visit per year, as is common across studies. The survey findings showed the major barriers to more active public library use to include lack of familiarity with library staff, unappealing physical facilities, unappealing library websites, and limited teen involvement in library service design and delivery. As in several similar studies, a main motivating factor for library use was the ability to socialize with peers, adding to growing evidence that public libraries should devote more attention and funding to promoting libraries as spaces for teen social and community interaction.

Meyers, E. "The Coolness Factor: Ten Libraries Listen to Youth." *American Libraries* 30, no. 10 (1999): 42–45.

In the earliest of the studies reported here, Meyers discusses the results of interviews with teens in ten US urban public libraries, with the goal of understanding how libraries can better appeal to teens' interests. Teens in all ten communities suggested that libraries are "uncool" and mostly attract "nerds." They also expressed negative perceptions of library staff, library spaces, and library collections, while simultaneously expressing the need for homework assistance, community volunteering, and job opportunities. Respondents suggested that teens be enlisted to help improve library service offerings, which would in turn lead to improved library perceptions among the teen population.

Sin, S. J. "Modeling the Impact of Individuals' Characteristics and Library Service Levels on High School Students' Public Library Usage: A National Analysis." *Library and Information Science Research* 34, no. 3 (2012): 228–37.

Working with data from a survey of 13,000 US twelfth-graders, Sin used quantitative analysis methods to show that school information environment, frequency of school library use, race and ethnicity, and home computer availability are all tied to frequency of public library use. Levels of public library service provision were also a factor, with teens living near well-supported libraries using them more frequently than those living further away, even when differences in socioeconomic status and achievement motivation were considered. The author concluded that, "Offering a higher level of information services, especially in disadvantaged areas and through economic hard times, will encourage more frequent use of the quality resources that public libraries provide. These efforts in facilitating information access, particularly for disadvantaged individuals, will help bridge the information gap and benefit society as a whole" (2326).

Vavrek, B. "Teens: Bullish on Public Libraries." *Public Library Quarterly* 23, no. 1 (2004): 3–12.

This survey of 4,000 US households with youth ages twelve to seventeen found that about three-fourths of teen respondents had used a public library within the preceding year, but only about one-sixth of respondents had taken part in a public library program, lecture, or meeting during that same time period. Although this low level of program participation might be partly attributed to public libraries offering fewer programs for teens than for children, the survey also showed that nearly one-fourth of teen respondents considered library staff to be unhelpful, a possible barrier to program participation and a common thread throughout much of the teens and public library use research.

TEENS' INFORMATION AND READING NEEDS AND PERCEPTIONS AND THE ROLES OF PUBLIC LIBRARIES IN MEETING THOSE NEEDS

Other studies have considered the types of information teens need and seek, and how reading plays a part in their daily lives. The selected papers discussed here tie these examinations to public library services. Together, they show the continuing importance of the public library as information and literacy promoter and point to the broad range of information areas that public library teen services should actively support.

Agosto, D. E. and S. Hughes-Hassell. "Toward a Model of the Everyday Life Information Needs of Urban Teenagers, Part 1: Theoretical Model." *Journal of the Association for Information Science and Technology* 57, no. 10 (2006): 1394–1403.

Twenty-seven inner-city teens completed surveys, audio journals, information activity logs, and semi-structured interviews for this study. The authors then developed a theoretical model of urban teens' everyday-life information needs based on analysis of the resulting data. The model encompasses seven areas of youth development that everyday life information supports: the social self, the emotional self, the reflective self, the physical self, the creative self, the cognitive self, and the sexual self. The authors stress that library staff should design library services to support these seven areas of youth development and to support the full range of teens' information needs beyond just schoolwork and leisure reading needs.

Agosto, D. E., and S. Hughes-Hassell. "Toward a Model of the Everyday Life Information Needs of Urban Teenagers, Part 2: Empirical Model." *Journal of the American Society for Information Science and Technology* 57, no. 11 (September 2006): 1418–26.

In the second part of this two-part paper, Agosto and Hughes-Hassell present twenty-eight types of everyday-life information urban teens look for, connecting these types of information to the seven areas of teen development introduced in the previous paper. The most common types of information needed related to daily life routines, such as weather and transportation; planning and organizing social activities; artistic and creative pursuits; schoolwork; personal finances and shopping; and current events. Although the urban teens in the study turned frequently to the internet when looking for information to satisfy their everyday-life needs, they nonetheless expressed an overwhelming preference for seeking information from humans.

Hughes-Hassell, S. 2008. "Urban Teenagers Talk about Leisure Reading." *International Association of School Librarianship. Selected Papers from the 2008 Annual Conference.* International Association of School Librarianship.

This survey of more than 800 fifth- through eleventh-grade students in two US states, one in the Northeast and one in the South, examined urban teens' reading. A small subset of the study participants also kept readings logs for a week and participated in interviews about their reading experiences. Nearly three-fourths of respondents reported reading for pleasure, yet only about a third indicated that they enjoyed reading. Less than half of the students reported getting their leisure reading material from public libraries. The author offers a list of suggestions that teachers, librarians, and other educators can use to increase urban teens' interest in leisure reading, such as making reading discussions a social activity, putting more of the kinds of materials that teens like to read into library collections, and actively promoting summer reading to urban teens.

Koh, K. "Radical Change Theory: Framework for Empowering Digital Youth." *The Journal of Research on Libraries and Young Adults* 5, no. 1 (2015). www.yalsa.ala.org/jrlya/2015/01/radical-change-theory -framework-for-empowering-digital-youth/.

In the first half of this paper, Koh describes Eliza Dresang's theory of Radical Change, which she first introduced in the 1990's to describe changes she had observed in youth litera-ture. Radical Change suggests that the concepts of connectivity, interactivity, and access can explain many of the changes in information formats and environments that occurred during the digital information explosion. In the second half of the paper, Koh describes a study that tested the applicability of the theory to digital environments, using individual and group interviews with teens involved in an online digital design community. She found Radical Change Theory to help to explain teens' learning, creating, and socializing in the online community, and suggested ways that librarians can use the theory to increase the benefits of teen library programs in digital environments.

Rothbauer, P. "Rural Teens on the Role of Reading in Their Lives." *The Journal of Research on Libraries and Young Adults* 1, no. 2 (2011). www.yalsa.ala.org/jrlya/2011/02/rural-teens-on-the-role -of-reading-in-their-lives/.

To consider how rural public libraries can improve reading support for community teens, Rothbauer interviewed twenty-seven rural Canadian students ranging from age fifteen to age nineteen about their reading preferences and habits. When asked to describe the role of reading in their lives, participants described four common roles. First, reading provided them with a sense of personal autonomy and independence. Second, reading served as a source of comfort and habit. Third, reading enabled them to experience and understand other people's lives. Finally, reading was seen as a source of new knowledge and learning. Unlike studies of teens living in more urban areas, these teens did not express strong peer influence on reading preference and habits, which the author interpreted as proof of a largely absent reading culture among the respondents' peer groups. She suggested that rural libraries can help to build stronger reading cultures among rural teens by providing more reading-related programs and more readers' advisory services. Above all, she suggested that libraries can provide visible spaces in rural communities for reading activities and for help-ing young people to develop stronger reading identities.

PUBLIC LIBRARY PROGRAMS AND SPACES FOR TEENS

The last group of studies provides a useful examination of the impact of library programs and space design on the teens they serve. These studies suggest that teen involvement in space and program design and delivery can improve teen library participation and perceptions.

Crawford Barniskis, S. "Graffiti, Poetry, Dance: How Public Library Art Programs Affect Teens, Part 2: The Research Study and Its Practical Implications." *Journal of Research on Libraries and Young Adults* 2, no. 3 (2012). www.yalsa.ala.org/jrlya/2012/09/graffiti-poetry-dance-how-public-library -art-programs-affect-teens-part-2-the-research-study-and-its-practical-implications/.

This paper is one of only a handful of studies that have provided research-based evidence of the benefits library programs provide teens. Crawford focuses on library art programs, using both a focus group and individual interviews to explore how library arts program participation affects teens' civic engagement. The teens in the study took part in a range of arts programs, such as graffiti, digital photography, dance, and poetry sessions. The fourteen study participants felt that the arts programs enabled them to make deep connections with each other and with their communities, leaving them more open to new experiences and to taking active roles in their communities. However, the degree to which the content of the programs led to these changes is unclear; perhaps any type of library programs might have led to similar results. As such, further research into connections between program content and benefits to teen participants is needed.

Kuhlmann, M., D. E. Agosto, J. P. Bell, and A. Bernier. "Learning from Librarians and Teens about YA Library Spaces." *Public Libraries* 53, no. 3 (2014): 24–28.

As part of a larger study of YA library space design, the authors asked teen library users and teen librarians to film video tours of their public library YA spaces. The researchers analyzed the videos to consider what aspects of library physical spaces appeal to teens and to the librarians who work with them. As shown in their video tours, teens and librarians stressed the importance of access to technology, spaces for studying, spaces for leisure reading and "hanging out," and attractive furniture and lighting as key features of good YA library space design. These findings show the importance of thinking about YA library spaces not in terms of the items housed there (e.g., spaces for fiction books, spaces for magazines, etc.), but in terms of the activities that take place there (studying, hanging out, listening to music, etc.), thereby moving the focus of design from supporting library resources to supporting the people that the library serves.

Rhinesmith, C., M. Dettmann, M. Pierson, and R. Spence. "YouthStudio: Designing Public Library YA Spaces with Teens." *Journal of Research on Libraries and Young Adults* 6 (2015). www.yalsa.ala.org/jrlya/2015/11/youthstudio-designing-public-library-ya-spaces-with-teens/.

Building on previous studies of library spaces for teens, Rhinesmith et al. designed a semester-long library program that involved teens from Moore, Oklahoma, in creating a redesign plan for their public library teen space. The program design and evaluation used community informatics techniques and an action research framework to create a model for involving teens in using digital tools for library space design. The study participants stressed comfortable spaces for hanging out, for informal learning, and for community information exchange as vital to good library space design. In addition to building a community-based library redesign plan, the YouthStudio program also led to digital literacy and leadership skills building for program participants and serves as a replicable program model for other libraries interested in involving teens in design projects.

Shaulskiy, S. L., J.L. Capps, L. M. Justice, and L. H. Anderman. "Motivational Attributes of Children and Teenagers Who Participate in Summer Reading Clubs." *Journal of Research on Libraries and Young Adults* 4, no. 1 (2015). www.yalsa.ala.org/jrlya/2014/05/motivational-attributes-of-children-and -teenagers-who-participate-in-summer-reading-clubs/.

Related to the study of reading habits and preferences is the study of five public library summer reading clubs. Shaulskiy et al. surveyed 440 children and teens in five libraries in the Columbus (Ohio) Metropolitan Library system. They found that youth who participated in summer reading clubs typically viewed themselves as strong readers, and that they valued reading highly. Girls and boys rated themselves to be equally strong readers, but girls tended to consider reading to be more important, more interesting, and more useful than boys did. Awards and prizes were not strong motivators for reading club participation; instead, participants tended to value reading itself as the participation end goal. These findings suggest that public library summer reading clubs tend to attract youth who are already motivated readers, with less appeal to reluctant readers, and that libraries should seek methods for encouraging weaker, less motivated readers to participate in summer reading programs.

The studies reviewed here represent a small body of work, leaving much that we still need to learn about how teens use libraries and how we can reshape library services to better fit their use preferences and needs. Fortunately, new research is being published on a continuing basis, leading to an ever-growing understanding of effective library service design. There is no one central publication outlet for this work, but much of it appears in journals, such as *Journal of Research on Libraries and Young Adults* (www.yalsa.ala.org/jrlya/), *Public Libraries* (www.ala.org/pla/resources/publications/publiclibraries), *The Library Quarterly* (www.journals.uchicago.edu/toc/lq/current), and *Library and Information Science Research* (https://www.journals.elsevier.com/library-and-information-science-research). To a lesser extent this research can also be found in single-authored or edited books, such as those published by ALA Editions (www.alaeditions.org/) and Libraries Unlimited (www.abc-clio .com/LibrariesUnlimited.aspx). To keep abreast of new developments, librarians and other adults who work with teens in libraries should monitor these outlets and seek new ways of incorporating what they learn into their services for teens.

CONCLUSION

PUTTING THIS ALL TOGETHER

As this book comes to a close, we hope that you are inspired to create innovative programs that reach and serve the children, youth, and families in your current and future communities. You now know the importance of listening to your community's aspirations and letting them be your guide. You have blueprints and guidelines on how to do outreach; how to forge community partnerships; and how to design meaningful, interest-driven, inclusive programming that bridges formal and informal learning and focuses on production and peer interactions. Librarians know that the development of these programs is ongoing, and you are committed to understanding communities' dynamic needs and designing programs to meet those needs. These programs won't look the same in just a few years, but the core values and objectives will remain the same—to support children, families, and teens in their lifelong pursuit of learning and knowledge building through playful, interest-driven, production-centered programming that changes perspectives, changes form and format, and breaks boundaries.

Looking forward, we see several exciting developments on the horizon for children's and youth programming in public libraries. You may have noticed an increased emphasis on design in various ALA conference programs and publications. What is design, you may ask? Although there is no simple or unique definition of design, you can think of it as a mindset—a way of looking at the world as a collection of opportunities to improve various aspects of life for the people who live in the world. When you employ design thinking, you're constantly looking around you and asking: What ought to be here? What should this look like? By engaging in co-design activities within your communities, you can gain a sense of what should be present in these communities with respect to children's and young adult programming to support families to help their children in their learning trajectories. By reflecting on what your library has done so far and would like to do going forward, you can be more thoughtful and intentional about how you plan and deliver programs. The Design Thinking for Libraries toolkit (http://designthinkingforlibraries.com/), developed by IDEO in conjunction with DOKK1 in Denmark and Chicago Public Library, and funded by the Bill and Melinda Gates Foundation, offers a good introduction to design concepts, techniques, and principles to help guide and inform your work. When you approach children's and youth librarianship from the perspective of design, you will see your work as iterative and reflective, dynamic and ever-changing, and grounded in the research that has come before and in the needs of the communities you serve.

In addition to this new emphasis on design, work is also being done to continue to strengthen the connections between practice and research by YALSA and ALSC, the two prominent ALA divisions in the area of public library services for children and youth. YALSA has emerged as a leader in connecting research and practice with the creation of their research agenda on libraries, learning, and teens. The research agenda highlights five priority areas for research into library services to young adults: The Impact of Libraries as Teen Formal and Informal Learning Environments; Library Staff Training, Skills and Knowledge; Equity of Access; Cultural Competence, Social Justice and Equity; and Community Engagement (www.ala.org/yalsa/guidelines/research/researchagenda). To bring attention to research occurring in these areas and others, YALSA also created the *Journal of Research on Libraries and Young Adults* (www.yalsa.ala.org/jrlya/), which presents research relevant to young adult services in libraries.

From its research agenda, YALSA has published other research documents written over the last few years that have sought to develop a roadmap for teen services. In addition, in conjunction with YALSA, teen librarians have developed new competencies (www.ala.org/yalsa/guidelines/yacompetencies) that are grounded in these various research documents. These competencies focus on helping teens succeed and develop the skills they need for the life ahead of them by covering a variety of aspects of teen services, including cultural competency, learning experiences and environments, teen growth and development, and more. These competencies and the resources that support them offer teen librarians new ways to reach their patrons and be inclusive and thoughtful in the programs they develop for teens.

ALSC is also beginning to move forward in strengthening the connections between research and practice by creating a research agenda task force charged with developing a research agenda that focuses on library services for children. Although ALSC's research agenda is still in development, a survey was done of the ALSC membership to understand their specific desires and need for research. Overall, the survey revealed that there is a great interest and desire for research across a variety of areas related to children's services. At the time of writing, specific findings from the survey had not yet been made public, but we feel sure that they will have a significant impact on ALSC's strategic direction moving forward.

At the same time, ALSC is stepping back from continuing to grow the Every Child Ready to Read® @ your library® product. However, the philosophies behind this toolkit, that parents are their children's first and best teachers and that everyday activities with their young children offer meaningful opportunities for learning, will continue. The Project VIEWS2 research findings, which you read about in the Early Childhood Section, inspired OCLC (formerly known as the Online Computer Library Center) to write a grant to develop the study's intervention content in an online format for librarians in six pilot states around the country. This project, called Supercharged Storytimes (https://www.webjunction.org/explore-topics/supercharged-storytimes.html), emphasized the six early literacy skills covered in the research intervention in a series of online, synchronous webinars that reached thousands of library staff. The success of that project has led to a second grant and the expansion of the content to cover other areas of early learning including STEM and inclusive practices. These online webinars provide librarians with the knowledge and skills they need to enrich and supercharge their programming for young children and their families to impact and enhance school readiness and later school success.

Middle childhood remains a largely untapped area for children's librarianship. While we have included an introduction to sociocultural development, a few library profiles, and an annotated bibliography of research on middle childhood, there continues to be a gap in understanding how to develop meaningful library services for children in the six to twelve age group in libraries. This is a crucial age for learning development and school success. The Middle Childhood Framework, developed by Toronto Public Library and highlighted in this book, offers one strategic and grounded approach to developing and delivering this targeted programming.

As a discipline, we need to continue to find innovative and creative ways to provide interest-driven, radical ideas for programs that excite children, engage them in activities that build their learning, and emphasize play and games as a way to remain anchored in the kind of informal learning that libraries do so well. We look forward to all the ways you will contribute to advancing this part of children's and youth librarianship.

If you have read this while in a MLIS program, we hope that you will return to this book in your future work as a children's or teen librarian. If you are a working librarian and find yourself newly assigned to children's and youth services, we hope this book has provided you with a gold mine of theories, developmental tips, and innovative ideas that will give you the confidence to succeed in your work. Always remember that your work helps demonstrate the essential importance of libraries to the people you serve. This is the end of this book, but it's the beginning of an innovative, service-oriented approach to creating library programming for children and youth. This is your call to action.

REFERENCES

Design Thinking for Libraries Toolkit. http://designthinkingforlibraries.com/.
Journal of Research on Libraries and Young Adults. www.yalsa.ala.org/jrlya/.
OCLC Supercharged Storytimes. https://www.webjunction.org/explore-topics/supercharged
　　-storytimes.html.
Young Adult Library Services Association. National Research Agenda. www.ala.org/yalsa/guidelines/
　　research/researchagenda.
_____. Teen Competencies. www.ala.org/yalsa/guidelines/yacompetencies.

ABOUT THE EDITORS AND CONTRIBUTORS

Kathleen Campana is an assistant professor at the Kent State University Information School, where she teaches in the area of youth services. Her research focuses on understanding the learning that is occurring for children and youth in informal learning environments and how the environment encourages and supports that learning. Prior to joining Kent State, she earned her PhD at the University of Washington Information School.

J. Elizabeth Mills is a PhD candidate and the Beverly Cleary Research Assistant at the University of Washington Information School. She received her MLIS from UW in 2013. She studies how public children's librarians use the design concept of reflection in their storytime planning, delivery, and assessment. She has written many books for children, including *The Spooky Wheels on the Bus,* published by Scholastic, Inc.

Liz and Katie were both researchers on the award-winning Project VIEWS2 study, which sought to measure early literacy outcomes in library storytimes. They are currently studying public library outreach programs with underserved communities in Project LOCAL as well as investigating technology use in libraries with young children and their caregivers on behalf of ALSC. They are co-authors, with Saroj Ghoting, of *Supercharged Storytimes: An Early Literacy Planning and Assessment Guide.*

■■■

Denise Agosto is a professor in the College of Computing and Informatics at Drexel University, where she serves as the director of the Master of Library and Information Science program and as the executive director of the Center for the Study of Libraries, Information and Society. She is the editor of ALA's *Journal of Research on Libraries and Young Adults* and is widely published on the topics of youth, technology, and libraries. In recognition of this work, Agosto has won more than thirty teaching and research awards, fellowships, and grants.

R. Lynn Baker is a former children's librarian and author of *Counting Down to Kindergarten: A Complete Guide to Creating a School Readiness Program for Your Community* and *Creating Literacy-Based Programs for Children: Lesson Plans and Printable Resources for K-5* (both published ALA Editions). She teaches Children's Programming for Northern Kentucky University and leads online trainings for ALA and Library Juice Academy. Baker is a credentialed early care and education trainer and an early literacy consultant, providing workshops for early childhood and library professionals. She holds an undergraduate degree in interdisciplinary early childhood education and a master's in library and information science.

Diane Banks is the manager of children's programs at Toronto Public Library (TPL) and has over twelve years' experience working in children's services. Most recently, she implemented TPL's Middle Childhood Framework, which focuses on revitalizing collections, services, programs, and spaces for children aged six to twelve and their families.

Gabbie Barnes is a Black multiracial-dreamer living, working, surviving, and thriving in the Hartbeat: Hartford, CT. She is an auntie, soul sister, daughter, cat mother, mentor, librarian, consultant, mentee, and cinephile. She offers spiritual advising, tarot readings, and essential oil advice. Barnes received her MLIS during a short, four-year stint exploring life as a Pacific Northwesterner. She has institutional experience in academic, special, and public libraries.

Christine Caputo oversees citywide programming and special projects for children, teens, and families and serves as a member of the Free Library of Philadelphia's leadership team.

Beth Crist is the youth and family services consultant at the Colorado State Library. She is dedicated to providing high-quality library services to underserved audiences outside the library. She partners extensively with a variety of state agencies and nonprofits to provide innovative statewide initiatives. Crist oversaw Supporting Parents in Early Literacy through Libraries, a three-year project funded by IMLS grants, which empowered low-income parents of children aged birth through three with simple ways to effectively incorporate early literacy activities into their daily lives.

Melissa Depper is the storytime supervisor for Arapahoe Libraries, where she works primarily with early childhood programs and services, and leads, trains, and mentors a team of fourteen storytime providers. Depper is a founding member of Colorado Libraries for Early Literacy, an advisory group to the Colorado State Library that supports early literacy training and advocacy efforts; served on the ALSC/PLA Every Child Ready to Read Oversight Committee; and presents nationally on storytime issues and competencies.

Betsy Diamant-Cohen is an author, consultant, trainer, and creator of the research-based Mother Goose on the Loose® early literacy program. She was proud to receive the 2013 ASCLA Leadership and Professional Achievement Award for "revolutionizing the way librarians work with children from birth to age 3." She holds an MLS and a DCD and served on ALSC's Every Child Ready to Read Oversight Committee. She can be contacted via her website: www.mgol.net.

Ally Dowds is the youth technology librarian for Teen Central at the Boston Public Library. She coordinates efforts to bridge the technology gap among urban youth by identifying and collaborating with community partners to design and implement STEAM-based programming. Dowds also serves as a library advisor for ALA's Great Stories Club and currently is piloting the program's latest theme, Empathy: The Cost of Switching Sides, at a public school providing special education to Boston youth.

Sarah A. Evans is an assistant professor in the School of Library and Information Studies at Texas Woman's University. Her research examines the literacies and identities taken up in voluntary learning experiences. Evans holds a bachelor's degree in Drama, a Master of Library and Information Science degree, and a PhD in Learning Sciences from the

University of Washington, as well as an elementary education certificate from Western Washington University.

Saroj Ghoting is a children's librarian and, for the last fifteen years, an early childhood literacy consultant who presents face-to-face workshops and online courses on early literacy and storytimes, including STEM in Storytimes and Supercharging Your Storytimes. She has coauthored several books for ALA Editions including *Supercharged Storytimes* and *Storytimes for Everyone,* based on Every Child Ready to Read®.

Annette Y. Goldsmith is a Los Angeles-based lecturer who teaches online graduate courses in children's and young adult literature and storytelling that draw on her experience as a public librarian in Toronto, Miami, and Tallahassee, Florida, and a synagogue librarian in Los Angeles. Her most recent book, co-authored with Theo Heras and Susan Corapi, is *Reading the World's Stories: An Annotated Bibliography of International Youth Literature* (Rowman and Littlefield 2016).

Melissa Gross is a professor in the School of Information at Florida State University and a past president of the Association for Library and Information Science Education (ALISE). Gross has published extensively in the areas of information-seeking behavior, information literacy, library program and service evaluation, information resources for youth, and teacher-librarian collaboration. Her work has been supported by grants from a variety of agencies and published in top LIS journals.

Claudia Haines is the youth services librarian and media mentor at the Homer Public Library (Alaska). She serves on both local and national committees that support families and literacy. With Cen Campbell, Amy Koester, and Dorothy Stoltz, she is the co-author of the ALSC white paper *Media Mentorship in Libraries Serving Youth* and the book *Becoming a Media Mentor: A Guide for Working with Children and Families* with Cen Campbell (ALA Editions 2016).

Catherine Halpin is the youth technology coordinator for the Boston Public Library. She collaborates in the management of Teen Central's digital media lab, where she develops and implements innovative programming that encourages teens to see themselves as creators while exploring new media in an environment that celebrates youth culture and empowers youth voice. Halpin also helped launch the Teen Tech Mentor program, a paid employment opportunity for teens to act as peer leaders and mentors in The Lab.

Susan Hildreth served as the inaugural Bill & Melinda Gates Foundation-funded distinguished practitioner in residence at the University of Washington Information School. She is a fellow at the Aspen Institute and was appointed by President Obama as the director of the Institute of Museum and Library Services from January 2011 through January 2015. Hildreth served as Seattle's city librarian and state librarian of California. She also was San Francisco's city librarian and held other leadership positions in California public libraries.

Amy Koester is a public librarian at Skokie Public Library in Illinois. Koester co-authored the ALSC white paper *Media Mentorship in Libraries Serving Youth* along with Cen Campbell, Claudia Haines, and Dorothy Stoltz. From 2013 to 2015, she was an editor for Little eLit, a grassroots community of librarians thinking about young children and new media. In addition to media mentorship, Amy's library interests include STEAM, civic engagement, and capturing outcomes.

Dr. John L. Marino, Jr. is an assistant professor in the Information Science Department at the University of North Texas. He has been a school librarian and technology integration coach in K–12 schools. He currently investigates information behavior and learning in context, including the Big6 information problem-solving process, library programs for children and youth, digital learning environments, and the preparation of library professionals for service.

Michelle H. Martin is the Beverly Cleary Endowed Professor for Children and Youth Services in the Information School at the University of Washington. From 2011 to 2016 she held the inaugural Augusta Baker Endowed Chair in Childhood Literacy at the University of South Carolina. She published *Brown Gold: Milestones of African-American Children's Picture Books, 1845–2002* (Routledge 2004) and co-edited *Sexual Pedagogies: Sex Education in Britain, Australia, and America, 1879–2000,* with Claudia Nelson (Palgrave 2003).

Elizabeth McChesney is the director of children's services and family engagement for the Chicago Public Library System (CPL). She is known for having created the move from summer reading to summer learning, earning the first National Summer Learning Association Award for Excellence given to a library. With Bryan W. Wurnar, she co-authored *Summer Matters: Making All Learning Count* (ALA Editions 2017). She has put play spaces and STEM learning into CPL libraries. Among her awards, she is a 2014 *Library Journal* Mover & Shaker.

Cristina Mitra has a passion for Spanish bilingual services. Since 2015 she has been the family engagement coordinator of the youth services team within the San Francisco Public Library's Community Programs and Partnerships division, where she spearheads STEM and cultural programs for youth at the main library and twenty-seven branches. Prior to this she was a children's librarian serving low-income children and families. She is a certified Brazelton Touchpoints trainer within the groundbreaking Touchpoints in Libraries California cohort. An active member of ALSC, she chairs the ALSC School-Age Programs and Service Committee.

Jamie Naidoo is the Pauline Foster-EBSCO Endowed Professor at The University of Alabama School of Library and Information Studies. A former elementary school librarian and public youth librarian, his research interests include library services to diverse populations and diversity in children's print and digital media. He has published numerous books, articles, chapters, and professional publications related to these topics. Naidoo is also actively engaged in the Association for Library Service to Children (ALSC), the United States Board on Books for Young People (USBBY), and the National Association to Promote Library and Information Services to Latinos and the Spanish-Speaking (REFORMA).

Judy T. Nelson was the customer experience manager for youth for Pierce County Library System. She oversaw three branches along with all youth initiatives. She chaired the ALSC/PLA Every Child Ready to Read Oversight Committee and served as an at-large member. She is currently on the Public Library Association's Family Engagement task force. She received the CAYAS Visionary Award for Service to Children and Young Adults from the Washington Library Association for her work in early learning and served as president of YALSA, the young adult division of the American Library Association. She is currently a board member and steering committee for First 5 FUNdamentals' Project Child Success.

Susan Anderson-Newham oversees the Early Learning Program for the Pierce County Library System (Washington). As the early learning supervising librarian, she works closely with parents, childcare providers, and community organizations who focus on early learning. She also trains librarians on early literacy skill development and storytime creation.

Emily Romeijn-Stout is a PhD student at The University of Washington Information School. She holds an MLIS from the University of Washington and has served as a children's services librarian with the Sno-Isle library system. She has participated in early literacy studies at the University of Washington as both a student researcher and a research coordinator. Her current research focuses on how libraries can address the needs of the autism community.

Lori Romero is the coordinator and supervisor of the Arapahoe Libraries' early literacy team, which is dedicated to serving young children and families. Romero holds a master's degree in literacy and has years of experience as an educator, reading specialist, and staff developer. Besides loving her work in support of families, literacy, and children's librarians, Romero presents at local and national conferences including PLA, ALSC, and Young Child's Expo. She served on the first Colorado Libraries for Early Literacy Steering Committee.

Kelly Rottmund is the teen services coordinator at Carnegie Library of Pittsburgh. She received her Master's in Library and Information Science from the University of Pittsburgh. Rottmund feels extremely lucky to spend her days focusing on how the Library and its staff can empower teens to be builders of their own future as she works with forty teen specialists across nineteen locations. Rottmund has been a teen librarian for ten years and has been in her current role for three years. She has been a member of the Amelia Bloomer Project (an ALA booklist committee) and the YALSA's Young Adult Services Symposium Planning Taskforce. She is a prolific letter writer and a lover of jellyfish.

Jess Snow is the teen services team leader of Teen Central at the Boston Public Library. She is passionate about outreach services to the underserved (youth who may be in transition, incarcerated, foster youth) and has written and presented on the subject. Snow is also a member at large on the YALSA Board of Directors for 2017 to 2020.

Sarah Stippich coordinated many projects and activities for young children and families, including the Words at Play Vocabulary Initiative, Sundays on Stage live entertainment series, Summer of Wonder, a program for the youngest participants, and Philadelphia's participation in the statewide One Book, Every Young Child program.

Peggy Thomas worked for twenty-two years as a teacher and teacher-librarian in a Toronto-area elementary school system. She has served as the president of the Ontario School Library Association and has also served as the president of the Ontario Library Association. In 2010, Thomas went back to school for her MLIS. She currently works for Toronto Public Library (TPL) as the manager of Children's Services, helping to redefine services for children at TPL.

Sarah Ward is an independent researcher and evaluator whose background in play, creativity, studio-based learning, and informal learning propelled her into her current research on organizational change and community engagement. She received her PhD and her MEd in Learning Sciences from the University of Washington. She also holds a BA in French and Journalism from the State University of New York at New Paltz.

Mariko Whelan is the early learning coordinator for the Scottsdale Public Library. She holds an MEd and has a background in curriculum development, providing trainings and workshops on a national level. Whelan's role as the early learning coordinator for the library has allowed her to merge her background in developmentally appropriate practices for children and knowledge about early learning and development at a new venue that supports interactive programming to help prepare families with children for school success.

Sara White, who is originally from Seattle, has lived and worked in Olympia, WA, since graduating with her MLIS from the University of Washington in 2010. Before realizing librarianship was her perfect job, she dabbled in theatre, both as an actor and behind the scenes. In addition to working with kids and teens in the library, she has possibly unhealthy obsessions with cheese, horror movies, and overly complicated board games.

Corey Wittig, a school librarian at The Falk Laboratory School in Pittsburgh, PA, has an interest in the ways libraries can support an expansive definition of "literacy" in the lives of children and adults. Corey worked for Carnegie Library of Pittsburgh (CLP) for eleven years, with much of that time spent leading the design and development of The Labs, CLP's teen learning lab and creative technology programming.

INDEX